695
6

The Sociologist as Detective

The Sociologist as Detective

AN INTRODUCTION TO RESEARCH METHODS

SECOND EDITION

Edited with Introduction and Exercises by
William B. Sanders
University of Florida

PRAEGER PUBLISHERS
New York

Published in the United States of America in 1976
by Praeger Publishers
A Division of Holt, Rinehart and Winston
200 Park Avenue, New York, N.Y. 10017

Library of Congress Cataloging in Publication Data

Sanders, William B   comp.
    The sociologist as detective.

        1.   Sociological research—Addresses, essays,
lectures.   2.   Social science research—Addresses,
essays, lectures.   3.   Criminal investigation—Addresses,
essays, lectures.   I.   Title.
HM48.S24   1976   301.07'2   75-36210
ISBN 0-275-24030-4
ISBN 0-275-85560-6 pbk.

Printed in the United States of America

789   006   98765432

To Eli, Billy, and David

Contents

Preface

Originally this book was intended to be a reader-field manual, but it became a little more than that. Not much more, but just a little. It certainly was never intended to be a text by itself, but it was necessary to include a number of things that gave it a text-like appearance in much of the editorial material around the readings. I suppose it can be best characterized as a "soft" introduction to research methods, with a point of view. The "softness" is designed to gently bring students into research without scaring them half to death and letting them get their feet wet in a little research of their own. Once they get in they'll find it isn't as bad as they had feared and will be eager and willing to go in deeper. This is somewhat better than drowning most of them and letting the rest make it by Darwinian exclusion.

In order to do this, it seemed a good idea to find something paralleling sociological research that had everyone's attention. Since I had been doing my own research on police detectives and found many natural parallels between what they were doing and what I was doing in the research, and because detectives have held the public's attention ever since Sherlock Holmes came on the scene in Victorian England, detectives seemed like a natural group to compare with sociologists. The basic idea is that both detectives and sociologists gather information about people and their relationships, and even though it is easy to overdraw the comparison, one can easily see how the two processes are similar. With the inclusion of Marcello Truzzi's chapter on Sherlock

Holmes in the second edition, the connection is drawn tighter than before, but we must keep in mind that even though both sociological research and detective work can be equally exciting and interesting, there are differences.

The point of view I hope to convey is that the research method chosen should be linked to the problem one is attempting to solve and not to what the "fad" in research methods is at any particular time. Furthermore, I want to impress upon the reader that we should not confine ourselves to a single method in doing research. Both quantitative and qualitative methodologies can be used in a single project, and one can employ experimental, survey, ethnographic, and content analysis methods in one piece of research. Every method has its strengths and weaknesses, and while we may prove our hypothesis by one method, it might fail if we looked at it from another methodological point of view. Therefore, if we want to have the strongest possible validity, we should not limit ourselves to a single methodology.

A final point I hope to make is that doing research is not the same as reading about it. The exercises are designed to give the student first-hand experience in the contingencies of actual research. These are the kind of things we are never told in textbooks and are hidden from us in research reports. The victimization survey (Chapter 4) is the result of a class-conducted survey, and in it we reported a number of things that went wrong when we attempted to replicate a relatively simple survey. Both the students and professor learned more about how *not* to conduct survey research in that exercise than could have been filed in a hundred volumes of research texts, but the important thing was that we *did* learn. Moreover, we had a lot of fun doing it.

The research examples chosen for this collection were based on their ability to illustrate a particular method. Many are taken from the areas of deviance, criminology, and criminal justice since these are the areas we would be most likely to find detectives; but the most important criterion was whether or not the chapter could show students what research looks like. We have included more works of this genre in this second edition than in the first, with the hope that the readings will be more interesting and pertinent. The editorial material has been expanded slightly to rectify certain shortcomings in the first edition.

Like all works of this nature, the editor is indebted to others for their aid and assistance. For this second edition I am most grateful to Brian McCarthy, who helped me run down some new examples of research and assisted me in writing Chapter 4. Jim Bergin and Herman Makler of Praeger Publishers were most instrumental in smoothing the way for the book's rebirth. Also, I will always be indebted to Gladys Topkis who led me through the first edition of what was my first book. Detectives Anthony Baker, Chip Marchbanks, Moorman Oliver, Jr., Frank Wright, Fred Holderman, William Harris, James Taylor, Don McCormick, Gil Chayra, Roger Best, William Crook, William Baker, James Regan, "Sully" Skeehan, Ed McCauley, Mike Kirkman, Ed Picino, Fred Ray, Roy Rosales, Larry Gold, and others of the detective bureau where I conducted research are gratefully acknowledged. Jay Moore and Dave Hersman provided introductions to the detectives, and I am thankful for their assistance.

Many suggestions were offered by several people, all of whom I cannot remember, but those who were the most helpful include Donald R. Cressey, Don Zimmerman, D. Lawrence Wieder, Howard Daudistel, and Charles Frazier. Jackie Moore and Peggy Dever typed the manuscript, and they will be cherished forever for that fearful task. Finally, my wife Eli was instrumental in getting everything put together on time, and my sons Billy and David served as a cheering section.

WILLIAM B. SANDERS

1. Introduction

THE METHODS AND EVIDENCE OF DETECTIVES AND SOCIOLOGISTS
—William B. Sanders

IN THE COURSE OF THEIR WORK, both detectives and sociologists must gather and analyze information. For detectives, the object is to identify and locate criminals and to collect evidence to ensure that the identification is correct. Sociologists, on the other hand, develop theories and methods to help them understand social behavior. Although their specific goals differ, both sociologists and detectives formulate theories and develop methods in an attempt to answer two general questions: "Why did it happen?" and "In what circumstances is it likely to happen again?"—that is, to explain and predict. Detectives' theories consider such questions as: "What motives would explain a specific type of crime?" "What do certain crimes have in common?" "Where is a given type of crime likely to occur?" Sociological theories are developed around such questions as: "How is social order possible?" "How is social conflict regulated?" "What forms are displayed in social interaction?"

To test their theories, detectives and sociologists rely on empirical evidence and logical modes of analysis as well as on their imagination. Both employ observation techniques, interviews, experiments, and other empirical methods to test the validity of their theories. Nevertheless, there are differences in their methods of gathering and analyzing information, and each can profit from techniques developed by the other. Sociologists, for example, rarely if ever employ such devices as the polygraph machine (lie detector), and detectives do not use multivariate analysis (charting several causal variables). Detectives have made much more use of physical evidence than have sociologists, who have seldom bothered to analyze the physical features of social phenomena. (The work of Webb and his associates [1966] stands as a notable exception.)*

In investigating a crime, detectives interview victims, witnesses, informants, and suspects. They compare these interviews with physical evidence that they gather in order to piece together a consistent account of what took place and to determine whether the people they interviewed were telling the truth. They may conduct an experiment to see whether a crime could have occurred in the way suggested by the accounts and the physical evidence. Finally, the detectives may discern a pattern from several cases involving crimes of the same sort. (A pattern would include the typical method used to commit the crime, the type of place in which the crime occurred, and the time the crime occurred.) Knowing this pattern, the detectives would then observe ("stake out") certain areas during the times the crime is likely to occur.

Sociologists, on the other hand, generally use only a single method and only a single source of data. Survey researchers will use only the data gathered in interviews, experimental researchers will only conduct an experiment, and participant observers will conduct no surveys or experiments and will report their findings solely in terms of their field notes. Moreover, it is unlikely that any of them will use available physical evidence. However, the sociologist could greatly profit from using multiple methods and measurements in a single study. Each method or source of data has its strengths and weaknesses. Experiments have questionable external validity, attitudes elicited by interviews often have no relation to people's actual behavior, and observational studies lack control. By using more than one method and source of data in a single study,

* Modern detectives use more sophisticated modes of analysis than did Sherlock Holmes, who was able to detect that Dr. Watson had been in Afghanistan after merely shaking hands with him, or Charlie Chan, who could tell whether a person was left- or right-handed by noting how matches had been torn from a matchbook, but they devote the same attention to details and basic reasoning.

as detectives do, sociologists can discover and compensate for the weaknesses of the various methods and will multiply their strengths (Webb *et al.*, 1966:3).

The stereotype of the detective who asks for "just the facts" is inaccurate, for detectives are always working with and testing theory. In any investigation a detective would be at a loss for questions to ask and interviewees without at least a rudimentary theory. For instance, in homicide cases, the first people generally contacted by detectives are friends, relatives, or acquaintances of the victim. Behind such investigative procedures is the theory that most homicides are committed by people who are socially close to the victim. Theory even determines what facts are noted. For example, in "Silver Blaze," a case of a stolen racehorse, Sherlock Holmes's observation of the fact that a dog was *not* barking was directed by the theory that dogs do not bark at people they know. The "fact" that the thief must have been known to the dog was overlooked by Dr. Watson and readers who were not guided by that theory.

Similarly, sociologists develop theories that lead them to ask certain questions and not others, and these questions in turn lead them to notice certain "facts" and not others (Parsons, 1937). For example, Max Weber's theory of the relationship between religious belief systems and economic systems led him to formulate certain questions concerning the economic structures of societies with and without predominantly Protestant beliefs (Weber, 1958). Likewise, Durkheim's theory of anomic suicide led him to examine suicide rates in various countries in terms of each country's dominant religion (Durkheim, 1951). In both of these theories, religion was a fact to be noticed. In Goffman's examination of mental hospitals (1961), on the other hand, the focus of his theory on the social world of patients in a mental hospital as they developed and sustained it led him to ignore the issue of what bearing their religious background had on their being committed. Problems relevant to certain theories are not relevant to others, and certain questions are relevant to certain problems and not to others. The facts that are located in research stem from the researcher's theory.

Central to theories and research are concepts, which Blumer (1969:155) calls "fashioners of perception," in that they direct the researcher to "see" the world in certain terms and configurations. For instance, the concept of "social class" directs the researcher to look at elements that give some people power and deny it to others. The concept of "the situation" directs the observer's attention to the context of encounters between people rather than just to the individuals in interaction. Concepts provide the crucial link between theory and research, in that they tell the researcher what is of theoretical interest and what to look for. If a theory states, for example, that there is a relationship between associations and criminal behavior, the researcher will not look at head shapes, economic position, or family size, but will concentrate on whom criminals associate with.

Detectives' investigations are also guided by certain concepts. The concept of "motive," for example, plays a central role in many investigations. Assuming that people are generally rational, detectives attempt to identify those who would benefit from a crime. This conceptual view leads them to certain people as possible suspects and away from others. For example, in an arson case, detectives try to determine whether the owner of the house or business or anyone else would benefit more from the building's absence than its presence. Without such a guiding concept, there would be no starting point for an investigation and no grounds on which to build a theory or finish an investigation.

EVIDENCE

Just as theories direct researchers to facts and give meaning and relevance to facts, so facts in turn give validity and shape to theories. And since sociology, like detecting, is an empirical enterprise, sociological theories require evidence for them to be considered valid, just as detectives' theories do.

Beginning with a hypothesis, the researcher gathers concrete evidence to either substantiate or disprove it. For example, detectives may hypothesize that the butler was responsible for the murder of the lord of the manor. Before they can arrest him, however, they must locate evidence to show that there is "probable cause" for considering him a suspect. For conviction, they must show that the butler was guilty beyond a reasonable doubt. If the butler's fingerprints are found on the murder weapon, for example, this would stand as cause for arresting him; however, if the murder weapon is found to be something the butler normally handled, such as a poker for tending the fire, other corroborating evidence would have to be located to prove the hypothesis that he was guilty.

Similarly, sociologists must prove their hypotheses. For example, in attempting to discover whether there is a relationship between amount of education and income, the sociologist might hypothesize that the more education an individual has, the greater his income will be. But he gathers evidence to prove or disprove this hypothesis, not by showing that one person with a college degree has a greater income than another person with less education, but by taking the average amount of education of several people and comparing it with their average income. Thus, instead of working with single cases, sociologists typically work with several cases.

An important feature of detective investigations is the practices involved in recognizing evidence as evidence. At a crime scene and in the course of an investigation, there are numerous elements that may or may not be regarded as evidence. Physical artifacts, statements by witnesses, and written documents can all turn out to be evidence, but whether they are so treated depends on the formulated circumstances of the case. For example, in an investigation of a burglary with attempted homicide, detectives searched an area around the crime scene for evidence. Overlooked but quite visible was a plastic bleach bottle that had been partially ripped apart. Later, when a suspect was arrested, a similar piece of plastic was found in his possession.* The old bleach bottle was now seen retrospectively in an entirely new light. If the piece of plastic found on the suspect could be matched to the piece missing from the bottle found on the crime scene, the suspect could be linked to the crime. Thus, from being merely a piece of trash, the bleach bottle was elevated to a piece of evidence.

Because what comes to be seen as evidence depends on the context of the situation and what will be evidence is often unclear until a context has been provided or a hypothesis is more fully developed, detectives keep everything that appears to be potentially useful (Stukey, 1968:21). Intelligence units, for instance, keep all sorts of information in their files. Much of it is never used or even seen as useful at the time it is collected, but if a situation comes up where they need the information, they will have it. In a crude way, much of what is collected by detectives is like using seat belts.

---

* Credit cards, plastic playing cards, and other flat, thin pieces of plastic are commonly used by burglars to slip open door locks.

They do nothing for the driver until he has an accident, but, for the value they have on the occasions when they are needed, they are worth the little inconvenience they cause.

Similarly, sociologists know that concepts may be indicated in different ways, depending on the research situation. Using the concept of social status, the sociologist cannot assume that the status symbols of one group will be the same for another group. For example, having a big, expensive automobile may indicate status among most Americans, but status among environmentalists may be indicated by the lack of such a car. Thus, before specifying big cars as an indicator for social status, the sociologist sensitizes the concept to the research situation. In this way he ensures that what is taken to indicate an instance of a conceptual phenomenon actually does so.

Related to this is the issue of contextual embeddedness of meaning and evidence. That is to say, what something means and whether or not it is seen as evidence depend on the context of the situation. For instance, consider the question "Do you have a match?" If the sociologist is studying pickup strategies in bars (cf. Cavan, 1966), this would be taken as an indicator of an attempt to initiate a conversation. In the context of male-female bar interaction, the question has a certain meaning. However, in another context—say, in a conversation between two old friends or in a gymnasium where boxers train—it has an entirely different sense. In a study of pinball players (Sanders, 1973), the author found that the term "match" generally refers to a free game. Hence, what is defined as evidence for the sociologist as well as for the detective depends on the context of the situation.*

PURPOSES AND PROBLEMS OF RESEARCH

In the very broadest sense, the purpose of sociological research is to test and develop sociological theory. Theory, in turn, explains and predicts social behavior. However, there is a good deal of sociological research that only indirectly tests or develops theory. A researcher may collect data to determine the *frequency and distribution* of various features of social life. For example, a researcher may conduct a survey to find how many students smoke marijuana.

* For a full discussion of the contextual embeddedness of social phenomena, see Wilson (1970) and Garfinkel (1967).

On the other hand, a sociologist may want to conduct a study simply in order to describe the forms of behavior in a given setting, such as bars, airports, laundromats, or department stores. Both of these types of studies, though, are related to theory. In looking at the frequency and distribution of marijuana smokers, the researcher may find that students who live in urban areas are more likely to smoke marijuana than are rural students. Such findings would serve as tests for a theory linking crime with population density. Similarly, by describing typical forms of behavior in various social settings, the researcher may test the theory that social settings determine the type of behavior to be found in a given setting.

Let us turn now to some of the problems in sociological research. Some of these issues are specific to certain kinds of research, and they will be explained in other parts of the book. Here only the general problems common to all research will be considered.

Validity. Simply stated, validity refers to the correspondence between the researcher's collected data and the real world. The extent to which the collected data reflect naturally occurring social behavior and processes determines its validity. For example, if for some reason respondents to a questionnaire elected not to tell the truth, the data collected by the researcher would not reflect the real world and would be considered invalid. (See Chapter 2 for a full discussion of this point.) Internal validity is generally considered in the context of measurement (Campbell, 1963), but here it will be used to entail description as well. If data have internal validity, any significant differences observed in a comparison can be attributed to a predicted cause, and not to measurement or description error. For example, in a study of assembly workers (Roethlisberger and Dickson, 1939), the researchers predicted that the workers would increase production if the lighting were heightened. As the lighting improved, so did production; however, work production also went up when the lights were dimmed. The researchers concluded that the assembly workers increased their efforts as a result of the presence of the researchers. The increased production had nothing to do with the lights. Thus, the prediction that work production increased with lighting proved to be erroneous. Similarly, in descriptive studies, notably participant-observation research (Chapter 8), often what the researcher describes is due to the researcher's presence rather than being a picture of normal behavior that occurs in the researcher's absence. Field experiments (Chapter 7) and unobtrusive measures (Chapter 10) have features that avoid some of the problems of internal validity.

External validity, on the other hand, refers to the generalizability of the findings. If the data cannot be generalized to other, theoretically similar settings, situations, organizations, or populations, then the study lacks external validity. For example, if a researcher were interested in finding out the attitudes of a given community but interviewed only members of the upper class, he would have no way of knowing whether the attitudes he found were truly representative of the entire community. Thus, he could not generalize his findings to the entire community, and the study would lack external validity.

In order to increase external validity, researchers attempt to choose *representative* samples. If they are to have a representative sample of the population under study, every member of that population must have an equal chance of being selected in the sample (Babbie, 1973:78). Sampling techniques, based on random sampling, are employed so that, when the researcher is drawing his sample, there is a minimum bias as to which members are chosen. If the sample is random, it is assumed that all of the various relevant aspects of the universe (e.g. social class, education, etc.) will be proportionately represented; therefore, the findings can be generalized to the entire aggregate of interest and be considered externally valid. The procedure for drawing a random sample and variations of random sampling will be explained in Part II.

Reliability. Another problem encountered in research is that of reliability (Forcese and Richer, 1973). Reliability is the ability of a method to replicate results when it is used by different researchers. For example, a researcher in California conducts an experiment and finds that individuals under a specific set of conditions will conform to group norms even though they do not personally agree with them. The researcher sends his experimental design to a researcher in New York who conducts the same experiment under the same conditions and finds the same results. The experiment is then considered reliable, since different researchers using the same instrument found the same thing. Fixed-choice questionnaires are considered highly reliable, whereas participant-observation studies are considered to have lower reliability.

Ethics. A final problem that should be discussed here involves research on human beings. This problem is in part an interactional one pertaining to such issues as soliciting subjects to participate in experiments, gaining access to an observation setting, and getting people to respond to interviews. This aspect of the problem will be developed in the readings and exercises, since the problem differs depending on the nature of the research topic and method. Here we will deal with ethical problems.

Unlike the detective, the sociologist does not face legal constraints in gathering evidence. The sociologist's data will not be invalidated if he does not warn his subjects that what they say may be used against them, nor do defense lawyers instruct subjects not to speak to sociologists. However, sociologists do have an unwritten code by which they attempt to abide.

Sociological researchers should not invade the privacy of others without their permission. For instance, even if they were legally able to do so, sociologists should not plant bugs in people's homes or locate themselves so that they can secretly observe others in private places. Similarly, sociologists should avoid lying, cheating, and stealing as resources for gathering data. Often it may seem that the only way to get information is by using techniques that are unethical and rationalizing their use in the name of sociology. Not only is such behavior unethical, but if sociologists began to engage regularly in these practices, they would soon lose their position of trust and would find it difficult to persuade informants to reveal information.

While sociologists are not ethically required to announce their research intentions in public places, in some situations it may be difficult to differentiate between private and public settings; some very private business takes place in public. An excellent example is the research by Laud Humphreys (1970) in which Humphreys, in the role of a "watch queen," or voyeur, observed impersonal sex between men in public toilets. On the one hand, Humphreys was not invading a private space, and that criterion alone justified his presence without announcing that he was a sociologist engaging in research. On the other hand, the sexual activity was private, and it was not the type of behavior with which most of the participants would want their names associated; therefore, in this sense the research can be taken as an invasion of privacy. The resolution of where the invasion of privacy begins and where the public domain ends must be in terms of the general standards of the members' understanding of public and private places. Thus, since no one needs special permission to enter a public toilet as one would need for entering a private home, it can be argued that observation of such domains should not be forbidden to the unannounced researcher.

This does not, however, exclude the sociologist from using data from private places that have been discarded and from which inferences can be made as to what takes place in those places. By analyzing what people put in their trash, for example, sociologists have found certain private activities that, although unseen, are easily inferred. Sawyer (1961), for example, estimated drinking habits from the frequency and distribution of liquor bottles found in trash cans. Thus, like detectives, who are barred from invading privacy without permission, either in the form of a search warrant or by the controller of the private space, sociologists need to develop methods for *seeing more than that to which they have access.*

A final ethical consideration lies in the confidentiality of the sociologist's subjects. Much of the information gathered by sociologists may be harmful to those who were observed or questioned. In order to protect their subjects, sociologists do not reveal the names of their subjects, the names of the organizations, or (sometimes) even the location of the study. Confidentiality, besides having ethical implications, has practical ones as well. Much of the information gathered by detectives is based on what their informants tell them. If detectives revealed the names of their informants, soon there would be no informants. Similarly, if sociologists made public the names and places of their studies that uncovered adverse information, soon no one would speak to them.

CHOOSING A METHOD: THE PLAN OF THIS BOOK

For testing their theories, propositions, and hypotheses, sociologists have a vast array of methods from which to choose. The choice of method depends on the type of information the researcher needs to resolve his problem. For example, if the problem is to find what people think about correctional programs in the criminal-justice system, the researcher will want to employ a method that includes interviews or questionnaires. On the other hand, if the researcher wants to know how people handle crisis situations, he will either design an experiment to simulate a crisis and observe what the subjects do or he will go to places that typically involve crises, such as emergency receiving rooms in hospitals, and observe behavior there. In the first case, the researcher is interested in *beliefs*; in the second case, in *action*. To elicit beliefs in research, as in everyday interaction, researchers generally ask questions. To discover how people act in various situations, they use experimental or observation techniques.

The general considerations for any research are: *What information is necessary? What sources of information are available? What methods are there for gathering the information?* Determining the various sources of data necessary for resolving a problem is called *theoretical sampling.* Even though sociologists typically use only a single method, usually information from a variety of sources is necessary and available. For example, if a researcher wants to find out about the public's reaction to crime, he might decide simply to interview people. However, his findings would be more substantial if, in addition to interviewing, he observed whether people, especially old people and women, ventured out alone after dark, the number and quantity of locks people employed, and the number of people who had large dogs. In other words, if the researcher took a proper theoretical sample, more than a single source of data would be tapped.

Perspective. The first section of this book deals with the researcher's perspective. The perspective suggested is that of the detective, who does not believe everything he hears or sees. Broadly speaking, a *perspective* refers to an *angle of observation*, and a "critical perspective" refers here to several angles of observation (Schatzman and Strauss, 1973). Such a perspective not only prevents one from jumping to unwarranted conclusions based on a single source of information but also forces the researcher to look at a problem from several angles. In researching any social phenomenon, the first consideration is the perspective from which the researcher will view the issue.

Surveys. More than any other single method, sociologists have been identified with survey research. Essentially, a survey entails interviewing or observing people in terms of a specified set of dimensions. Various polls, such as the Gallup Poll, in which the researchers may want to find out the population's views toward presidential candidates, the economy, the military, and similar dimensions of society, are the best-known examples of a survey. Surveys are used most efficiently when the researcher's problem pertains to the frequency and distribution of a relatively few aspects of a population (Zelditch, 1962). In the survey by Sanders and McCarthy (Chapter 4), the researchers were interested in the frequency and distribution of crime victims and reporting of crimes to the police; in Wiseman's survey (Chapter 5), social types are surveyed in terms of court dispositions.

Experiments. Experiments are the prototype of the scientific model. They are designed to find if there is a link between two or more variables by controlling the situation so that only the variable to be tested is present in relation to the other variables of interest. The two types of experiments presented in Part III involve introducing an *experimental variable* to determine what change occurs as a result of its presence. Moriarty (Chapter 6) uses stigma as an experimental variable in assessing the subjective experience of deviance. The field experiment by Russo and Sommer (Chapter 7) introduces "sitting too close" as an experimental variable in a unique experiment on personal space.

Ethnographies. Ethnographic research has traditionally been the prime tool of anthropologists, and it actually refers to more than a single method. Ethnographies are basically analytic descriptions of cultures (including subcultures), organizations, or settings. They involve *participant observation,* wherein the researcher spends a great deal of time observing and listening to those of interest. In the study by Sanders and Daudistel (Chapter 8), the authors went on cases with detectives, observing and participating in the detectives' day-to-day activities. *Intensive interviewing* entails long, unstructured talks with subjects and is generally used in all ethnographies in addition to whatever other method is employed.

Cressey (Chapter 9) explains how, using intensive interviews, he developed an explanation of embezzlement. A third method used by ethnographers involves *unobtrusive measures*. This means the observation of various artifacts that have been affected by social behavior, but since the observations themselves do not affect the behavior they are nonreactive. Webb and his associates (Chapter 10) offer numerous ingenious suggestions as to how valuable data can be gathered by noting such artifacts.

Content Analysis. The last section deals with a method that indirectly serves an information-gathering function and is often used in conjunction with other methods. Content analysis is employed to find underlying forms and structures in social communication. By analyzing the content of written or transcribed documents, the researcher hopes to find themes, forms, and structures that will account for the pattern of the communication. For example, Jacobs (Chapter 11) studied suicide notes and the various forms of accounts explaining why people took their own lives. A newer form of content analysis is *conversation analysis*, in which transcriptions of conversations are analyzed in terms of their structure. The final reading (Chapter 12) is an analysis of police interrogation, in which the author shows how the conversational structure is subtly used to get suspects to talk.

Multiple Methods. Several of the readings deal with more than a single method. Deutscher (Chapter 2), in his discussion of the relationship between what people say and what they do, shows that by using only a survey, a researcher may be led to erroneous conclusions. Likewise, Sanders and Daudistel (Chapter 8) use interviews and participant observation as well as content analysis, and Winick (Chapter 11) employs a questionnaire along with content analysis.

Besides being a means by which the researcher can get the necessary information in terms of a theoretical sample, the use of multiple methods serves to "triangulate" the findings (Webb et al., 1966; Denzin, 1970). That is, each method serves to "correct out" erroneous data supplied by the other methods; thus, the findings represent only those data that have been shown to be valid in terms of all the methods used. This puts the researcher in a much stronger position to claim validity for his findings.

ANALYSIS

Once the researcher has collected his data, he must ask, What does all this mean? Do the data prove or disprove the hypothesis? Does the experimental variable really cause a change? What structures, forms, and patterns does this group display, and why? All of these questions depend on analysis of the data, for analysis is the process of extracting information (Simon, 1969:333).

The most common form of analysis is testing hypotheses. A hypothesis is a statement of relationship between two or more variables that may be empirically tested (Goode and Hatt, 1952:74). In its most elementary form, a hypothesis will state a relationship between an *independent variable* and a *dependent variable*. The independent variable, in the context of the hypothesis, is observed in terms of what happens to the dependent variable when the independent variable changes. For example, we might say that, as the density of the population increases, so does the crime rate. The logic of such a statement assumes some effect of population density on amount of crime. We would not assume from such a hypothesis that the crime rate affects the population density, with the crime rate being the independent variable and population density the dependent variable. The independent variable *implies* the dependent variable (Zito, 1975:36). Substituting X for the independent variable (population density) and Y for the dependent variable, we would say that X implies Y. Thus, our hypothesis might be represented as

$$X \longrightarrow Y$$

In order to test our hypothesis that crime increases as does the population density, we look to see whether there is any covariation between crime and population density. If we find that crime increases when the population density increases, then we have tentative confirmation of our hypothesis. We would have to look further to see if something else was linked to the crime rate and sort out other possible variables that may be related to crime or population density. However, the first step in the analysis of hypotheses is to look for such relationships. If there is no relationship between the two variables, then we are left with the *null hypothesis*, which is a statistical negation of relationship.

Quantitative Analysis. Quantitative analysis requires that the researcher have some numerical value assigned to the data that are to be collected. Crime rates, population, and the number of people who brush their teeth with a certain kind of toothpaste are examples of quantitative data. In your readings you will see several tables where data have been represented in numbers, and these data are analyzed quantitatively. The analysis involves the use of statistics, which are used to determine if there is a statistical relationship. Most such statistical analysis tells the researcher what *probability* there is that a relationship is within the realm of chance. The extent to which there is very little chance that a relationship is random attests to the strength of that relationship. On the other hand, the most simple statistics simply represent differences or similarities between groupings of data and serve to describe patterns. Here we will look at some of these simple statistics.

Suppose that you have collected data from urban and rural areas and you want to know whether people living in cities are more likely to be graduated from college than those living in the country. The problem is that you have more data from the city than from the country; therefore, comparing the actual number of college graduates will only reflect the larger sample taken from the city. A simple statistic to make such a comparison is the *percentage*. To find the percentage of college graduates, the number of college graduates is divided by the total sample and then multiplied by 100. For example, if your urban sample contained 500 cases and 200 had been graduated from college, 200 would be divided by 500 to get .40. Multiplying .40 by 100 would give you a percentage of 40. Similarly, if your rural sample contained 200 cases and 80 had been graduated from college, 40 per cent would have been graduated from college. By comparing the percentages, the researcher can now see that there is no difference between college graduation and living in the city or country. Both have 40 per cent college graduates.

The following formula can be used for computing percentages

where N equals the total number in the sample and n equals the number in the category:

$$\frac{n}{N} \times 100 = \text{percentage}$$

A second group of basic statistics involves *means, medians, and modes.* These statistics are used to locate center points and are used for comparisons and in determining amount of change. Using the following data as an example, each will be explained.

Monthly Income

Group 1		Group 2		Group 3	
1.	$1,000	1.	$2,000	1.	$700
2.	900	2.	1,800	2.	700
3.	800	3.	1,000	3.	700
4.	700	4.	100	4.	700
5.	700	5.	100	5.	700
6.	500	6.	100	6.	700
7.	400	7.	100	7.	700
8.	200	8.	100	8.	700
9.	200	9.	100	9.	700
	$5,400		$5,400		$6,300

Each group has nine members, and they have been arranged in descending order according to monthly income. To find the mean income of any of the groups, simply divide the total of all incomes by the number of cases. Group 1 has 9 cases totaling $5,400, and by dividing $5,400 by 9 we find the mean of $600. Group 2 also has a mean of $600, and Group 3 has a mean of $700. Thus, based on mean income, Group 1 and Group 2 are the same.

A *median* is the value of the middle item when the items have been arranged in increasing or decreasing order (Freund, 1960:54). In the three groups presented, Item 5 is the median, since it is midway between the first and last items. Thus groups 1 and 3 have a median income of $700, and Group 2 has a median income of $100. Now, based on the median, groups 1 and 3 are the same.

A final measure of location is the *mode*, and it is based on the category with the highest frequency. In Group 2, $100 is the modal income, since it is more frequent than any other income figure.

That is, more members earn $100 than any other amount. Group 1 has two modes, since there are an equal number of members who earn $700 and $200. Finally, since all of the items in Group 3 are $700, its mode is $700. (Note that the mean, median, and mode in Group 3 are all $700).

Before making comparisons using any one of these statistics, the student is cautioned to first look at the distribution. For example, even though Group 1 and Group 2 have the same mean, the groups are different in that they are differently distributed. Similarly, Group 1 and Group 3 have the same median, but Group 3 has an equal distribution, whereas Group 1 has an unequal distribution. In making comparisons or in looking for changes, the analysis will be much better if more than one statistic is employed.

In ordering data for purposes of measurement, it is important to understand what *scale* the data properly fall into. Some data have qualitative differences only, while other data have quantitative differences, and often researchers confuse one type of scale with another in measuring differences. There are four basic scales for making different types of measurements. The first is the *nominal scale*, which places social objects in mutually exclusive categories (Denzin, 1970:99). Nominal data point to qualitative differences between observed phenomena. For example, burglaries and rapes are two different types of crimes and can be categorized on a nominal scale. Similarly, ethnic backgrounds can be broken down into nominal categories including blacks, whites, Latin, Oriental, Slavic, native American, and any other ethnic category of interest. If nominal data are to be treated with quantitative analysis, the researcher counts the number of instances a given nominal category occurs and compares the different categories. In Chapter 4 Sanders and McCarthy use quantitative analysis with nominal scale data in the form of different types of crimes. A second scale is the *ordinal scale*. Ordinal scale data reflect some kind of rank-order (Babbie, 1973:138). If we were to talk about the seriousness of property crimes ·in terms of the penalties, we could establish an ordinal scale beginning with petty theft on one end of a continuum and end up with armed robbery on the other end, with such crimes as grand larceny and burglary in between. Similarly, we can place social class on an ordinal scale ranking social class from lower to upper class. Sometimes researchers will use numbers on ordinal scales to indicate differences between one end of an ordinal scale and another. For example, we might rank property crimes as follows:

Petty Theft	1
Grand Theft	2
Burglary	3
Robbery	4

We could score the amount of crime in an area creating an index based on the values assigned to the categories. If Town A had seven petty thefts, one grand theft, two burglaries, and three robberies in one week, and Town B had one petty theft, four grand thefts, one burglary, and one robbery, we could compare the different indexes of crime by multiplying the number of a certain crime by its scaled value. Town A would have a score of 27 and Town B would have a score of 16. We could *not* say that Town A had almost twice as much crime as Town B since there is no standard difference between the numbers. That is, the difference between a score of 3 (burglary) and a score of 4 (robbery) is not the same as the difference between a score of 1 (petty theft) and a score of 2 (grand theft). The numbers represent only a rank order and nothing more. One community could have nothing but petty thefts and another nothing but robberies, and if we said that the two towns were the same because one town had 8 petty thefts and the other had 2 robberies scoring a total of "eight" for both communities, it would be misleading. Ordinal scales can be used to make statements about "greater and lesser" degrees of phenomena, but they do not tell us *how much* more or less. A third scale, the *interval scale* will give us measured differences between numbers on the scale in addition to the properties of an ordinal scale (Siegel, 1956:26). The zero point on an interval scale is arbitrary and is not absolute. For instance, the most common type of interval scale is on an ordinary thermometer, whether measured in centigrade or Fahrenheit. The centigrade scale is based on the freezing and boiling points of water, with zero degrees centigrade at the freezing point and 100 degrees at the boiling point. We know that the difference between 20 degrees and

30 degrees is the same as the difference between 70 and 80 degrees. However, the zero point does not mean "no temperature," but instead it is an arbitrary starting point, and if we compare Fahrenheit with centigrade scales we can readily see that the different zero points are merely different arbitrary starting points for measuring temperature. Unfortunately, we have nothing in social science that will give us an accurate interval scale, and even though there are numerous ordinal scales, it is important to remember that the differences between scores are not measured. Finally, there is the *ratio scale*. A ratio scale is the same as an interval scale except that it has a nonarbitrary zero point (Blalock, 1970:39). We could compare the number of arrests, income, and anything else with an absolute zero point on a ratio scale. For instance, if a person has ten arrests, that person has twice as many arrests as a person with five arrests. We would not want to say that a person is "twice as criminal" because he has twice the number of arrests, but since there is an absolute zero point (a person cannot have minus one arrests) we can measure arrests on a ratio scale. Furthermore, we can maintain a constant ratio between measurements. On the interval scale, we cannot say that 70 degrees is "twice as warm" as 35 degrees, but if the population of a city increased from one hundred thousand to two hundred thousand, we can say it has doubled or is "twice as large" as it used to be, since population has an absolute zero point.

These scales are used (and misused) in social science research to measure degrees of differences in variables. Most social science data can be transformed into nominal categories, and some data can be measured on the ratio scale. Where we get into trouble is when we treat ordinal data on an interval or ratio scale. For this reason, it is important to remember when dealing with scales that unless the researcher can show a constant interval between the data in his categories, he is dealing with either nominal or ordinal data.

Qualitative Analysis. Qualitative analysis is much more complex and subtle than quantitative analysis, since we cannot use statistics. However, since most of the phenomena we deal with in social science research are nominal, it is extremely important.

The basic elements of qualitative analysis entail description and breakdown of social patterns and processes and explanation of these processes and patterns from different points of view. Qualitative analysis is especially important in accounting for the social actor's point of view in observed patterns. For example, in Chapter 8 the authors describe the exigencies in detectives' decisions whether or not to investigate a crime. Similarly, in Cressey's (Chapter 9) discussion of how he formulated hypotheses based on his interviews with embezzlers, the process of qualitative analysis is outlined. Researchers use qualitative analysis to test and develop hypotheses, but, rather than using numbers to show relationships, they describe the relationships and present descriptive data to make their point. In the readings and exercises that follow, the various nuances of qualitative analysis will be explained.

REFERENCES

BABBIE, EARL R. 1973. *Survey Research Methods*. Belmont, Calif.: Wadsworth Publishing Co.

BLALOCK, HUBERT M., JR. 1970. *Introduction to Social Research*. Englewood Cliffs, N.J.: Prentice-Hall.

BLUMER, H. 1969. *Symbolic Interactionism: Perspective and Method*. Englewood Cliffs, N.J.: Prentice-Hall.

CAMPBELL, DONALD T. 1963. "From Description to Experimentation: Interpreting Trends as Quasi-Experiments." In *Problems in Measuring Change*, Chester W. Harris (ed.), pp. 212–42. Madison: University of Wisconsin Press.

CAVAN, SHERRI. 1963. "Interaction in Home Territories," *Berkeley Journal of Sociology*, Vol. 8, pp. 17–32.

DENZIN, NORMAN K. 1970. *The Research Act*. Chicago: Aldine.

DOYLE, SIR ARTHUR CONAN. "Silver Blaze." In *The Annotated Sherlock Holmes*. Vol. II. William S. Baring-Gould (ed.), pp. 261–81. New York: Clarkson N. Potter.

DURKHEIM, E. 1951. *Suicide*. New York: Macmillan.

FORCESE, D. P., and S. RICHER. 1973. *Social Research Methods*. Englewood Cliffs, N.J.: Prentice-Hall.

FREUND, J. E. 1960. *Modern Elementary Statistics*. Englewood Cliffs, N.J.: Prentice-Hall.

GARFINKEL, H. 1967. *Studies in Ethnomethodology*. Englewood Cliffs, N.J.: Prentice-Hall.

GOFFMAN, ERVING. 1961. *Asylums*. Garden City, N.Y.: Doubleday.

GOODE, WILLIAM J., and PAUL K. HATT. 1952. *Methods in Social Research*. New York: McGraw-Hill.

HUMPHREYS, L. 1970. *Tearoom Trade: Impersonal Sex in Public Places.* Chicago: Aldine.

PARSONS, T. 1937. *The Structure of Social Action: Volume I.* New York: The Free Press.

ROETHLISBERGER, F. J., and WILLIAM J. DICKSON. 1939. *Management and the Worker.* Cambridge, Mass.: Harvard University Press.

SANDERS, W. B. 1973. "Pinball Occasions." In *People in Places: The Sociology of the Familiar,* Edward Sagarin and Arnold Birenbaum (eds.). New York: Praeger Publishers.

SAWYER, H. G. 1961. "The Meaning of Numbers." Speech before the American Association of Advertising Agencies.

SCHATZMAN, L., and ANSELM STRAUSS. 1973. *Field Research.* Englewood Cliffs, N.J.: Prentice-Hall.

SIEGEL, SIDNEY. 1956. *Nonparametric Statistics for the Behavioral Sciences.* New York: McGraw-Hill.

SIMON, J. L. 1969. *Basic Research Methods in Social Science.* New York: Random House.

STUKEY, G. B. 1968. *Evidence for the Law Enforcement Officer.* New York: McGraw-Hill.

THOMAS, W. I., and D. S. THOMAS. 1928. *The Child in America.* New York: Alfred A. Knopf.

WEBB, EUGENE, D. T. CAMPBELL, R. D. SCHWARTZ, and L. SECHREST. 1966. *Unobtrusive Measures: Nonreactive Research in the Social Sciences.* Chicago: Rand McNally.

WEBER, MAX. 1958. *The Protestant Ethic and the Spirit of Capitalism.* New York: Charles Scribner's Sons.

WILSON, T. 1970. "Conceptions of Interaction and Forms of Sociological Explanation," *American Sociological Review,* Vol. 35, No. 4, pp. 697–709.

ZELDITCH, MORRIS J. 1962. "Some Methodological Problems of Field Studies." *American Journal of Sociology,* Vol. 67 (March) pp. 566–76.

ZITO, GEORGE V. 1975. *Methodology and Meanings.* New York: Praeger Publishers.

I: THE CRITICAL PERSPECTIVE

THE TWO READINGS IN THIS SECTION ARE INTENDED TO SENSITIZE THE student to a critical perspective and to point out that what the researcher will come to see depends on what perspective he takes. On the one hand, Deutscher shows that there is an unknown relationship between what people say and what they do. This is a somewhat cynical point of view in that it suggests that people don't always tell the truth. More importantly, it suggests that a truer picture of social life is gained by using more than a single method or viewing device.

Truzzi fills out this section by showing how Sherlock Holmes approached an investigation. On the one hand, Holmes was a systematic observer, noting everything he could. This scientific observation was a key to Holmes's success, and the great detective modestly refers to his scientific investigation as "systematized common sense." On the other hand, Sherlock Holmes placed a great deal of reliance on imagination. This latter aspect is the real genius of Holmes, for any hack can stand around and make observations, but without imagination mere observations mean little. Watson, the police, and the reader "observed" that the dog did not bark in the Silver Blaze adventure, but it was Holmes's imagination that led him to point out that since the dog did not bark when the race horse was stolen it suggested that the horse thief was probably someone close to the family who was known to the dog. Similarly, in sociology it takes little simply to collect a lot of "facts," and, as C. Wright Mills stressed, a sociological imagination is what makes all the difference (Mills, 1959). By looking beyond the obvious, commonsensical and mundane accounts, imagination leads us first into the unknown and then beyond into the light of discovery.

The combination of observation and imagination is interdependent. Without imagination, observations are limited in two ways. First, one's imagination sets up theoretical guidelines to point out observations. In the world, there are billions and trillions of observations to be made or not made, and, depending on the theoretical guide, certain events will be seen and others ignored, unseen, and invisible. Second, as I pointed out with Holmes's observation about the dog, one needs imagination to make something out of the observations one has made.

But what is imagination without observations? If we used our imaginations without ever making observations, we would live in a never-never land of unsupported conjectures, theories, and hypotheses. Observations are necessary for confirming or denying ideas. Moreover, observations are food for the imagination. They provide input beyond gross speculation and constitute the building blocks for expanding ideas and insights.

Both of these readings are designed to point the way to a critical perspective. By "critical," I do not mean a negative perspective, but a perspective that looks beyond the obvious into the many possible meanings to be found in the world about the world. Perhaps it is best to characterize such a perspective as one where the researcher is skeptical. It is not so much that one dismisses everything as having a meaning other than what is obvious as it is a perspective that requires the researcher to "check it out," to look at it from a different angle, and in general to question thoroughly before acceptance. Deutscher demonstrates the payoffs for making a single check on initial observations, but by making several checks on initial findings one can both come up with very solid validity and make new discoveries.

As I pointed out in the introductory chapter, it is silly to limit oneself to a single method. Sociologists have the depressing habit of ridiculing methods other than their own favorite one and concentrating on using and refining a single method. They are like a carpenter whose favorite tool is a hammer trying to build a house with that single tool. Imagine how strange it would look to attempt to saw a board with a hammer! This is what researchers who insist on using only one methodology are doing. A critical perspective demands that one use more than a single method to increase the validity of his observations. Findings from surveys should be checked with experimental and ethnographic observations. Ethnographies require systematic follow-up by surveys, content analysis, and field experiments. Be skeptical and imaginative, and make a complete investigation before drawing conclusions!

REFERENCE

MILLS, C. WRIGHT. 1959. *The Sociological Imagination.* New York: Grove Press.

2. Words Versus Deeds

WORDS AND DEEDS:
SOCIAL SCIENCE
AND SOCIAL POLICY
—Irwin Deutscher

THE SOCIETY FOR THE STUDY of Social Problems was established by and continues to attract sociologists with a dual commitment. We seek, on the one hand, to achieve a better understanding of the problems society creates for some of the people within it and, on the other, more effective application of socially relevant knowledge to the solution of those problems. Ultimately most of us are concerned with finding ways to alter this world in such a manner that more people may find it a better place in which to live. Our orientation leads us to search for effective alterations of the society rather than effective adjustments of individuals to the society. We tend, therefore, to shun efforts to improve treatment of individuals who reflect symptomatically the malfunctionings of the society—whether they be defined as sick, deviant, pathological, nonconformists, outsiders, or whatever. Since our focus is upon the society rather than the individual, whatever changes we have to recommend, whatever advice and criticism we have to offer, must be directed toward those who make or influence policy in our society.

My point of departure is the basic research, the evaluative studies, and the demonstration projects which are the "scientific" materials from which social scientists generally derive their recom-

From *Social Problems*, Vol. 13, No. 3 (1966), pp. 233–54. Reprinted by permission of the author and The Society for the Study of Social Problems.

mendations to policy makers. Our scientific conclusions, for the most part, are based on analyses of verbal responses to questions put by an interviewer. Those responses may be written or oral and the questions may range from forced choice to open ended, but the fact remains that what we obtain from such methods are state ments of attitude, opinion, norms, values, anticipation, or recall. The policy maker is interested in none of these things; as a man of action, he is interested in overt *behavior*. Although we rarely study such behavior, we do insist that the object of our discipline is to understand and even to predict it. Therefore, to oblige the policy maker, as well as ourselves, the assumption must be made that verbal responses reflect behavioral tendencies.

In his definitive volume on interviewing, Hyman (1954:17-8) makes this assumption explicit: "If one could wait around indefi- nitely," he writes, "the natural environment would ultimately lib- erate behavior relevant to a given inference. However, practical limitations preclude such lengthy procedures. As Vernon puts it (1938): 'Words are actions in miniature. Hence by the use of questions and answers we can obtain information about a vast number of actions in a short space of time, the actual observation and measurement of which would be impracticable.' " This inferen- tial jump from verbal behavior to overt behavior appears to be tenuous under some conditions.

Acting out a relationship is not necessarily the same as talking about a relationship. We have known this for a long time and we have known why for a long time, but we proceed as if we did not know. With the advantage of hindsight, I intend to suggest that we began to make incorrect choices in the early 1930's, and once having begun, managed easily to build error upon error. Although we have frequently proceeded with rigor and precision, we have, nevertheless, been on an erratic course. In restrospect, we may well have had a thirty-year moratorium in social science.

THE LAPIERE EXPERIMENT

Symbolizing the period during which we had the choice to make is a classic experiment designed by Richard LaPiere and reported in 1934. LaPiere's quest for answers to a haunting methodological problem can be traced through a trilogy of his papers, the last of which is "Attitudes vs. Actions." If such quests can be thought of as being initiated at a specific point in time, LaPiere's probably began while he was attending a seminar with Malinowski at the London School in 1927. During the course of that seminar, the term "verbalization" was employed to indicate a distinction between what informants may say and what may be the actual custom of the primitive society. LaPiere (1928) was formulating a comparative survey of race prejudice in France and England. Interested in the concept of "verbalization," he attempted to check his questionnaire findings against actual practices. This he accomplished by questioning hotel proprietors about their policy. The results left LaPiere satisfied at the time that he had found a fair concordance between verbal responses and nonverbal responses and, consequently, that his survey results were sufficiently valid.

Upon his return to the United States, LaPiere undertook a study of an Armenian community (1936), as a result of which he writes, "I began again to doubt the certain value of verbal evidence." Perhaps as a result of this doubt, LaPiere (1934:231) reconsidered the evidence from his French study and realized that "at that time I overlooked the fact that what I was obtaining from the hotel proprietors was still a 'verbalized' reaction to a symbolic situation." He had not compared verbal and nonverbal behavior. What he had done was to compare attitudes with self-reports of behavior. His concern resulted in the carefully designed and controlled experiment which consumed two years in the field and over 10,000 miles of driving and culminated in the publication of "Attitudes vs. Actions."

Traveling with a Chinese couple, twice across country and up and down the West Coast, the investigator recorded the treatment they received in hotels, auto camps, tourist homes, and restaurants. Of the 251 establishments approached in this manner, one auto camp refused to accommodate them. Here then was an estimate of Caucasian-Oriental integroup behavior.

Allowing a time-lapse of six months after being served by an establishment, a questionnaire was sent to each. Half of them were asked only, "Would you accept members of the Chinese race as guests in your establishment?" The other half were asked additional questions about other ethnic groups. Only one "yes" response was received—this from a lady who reminisced about the nice Chinese couple she had put up six months earlier. Here then was an estimate of Caucasian attitudes toward Orientals.

Most important is the juxtapositioning of these two estimates.

We have, then, in 1934, strong empirical evidence, not only that there may be no relationship between what people say and what they do, but that under some conditions there may be a high inverse relationship between the two.

LaPiere's conclusions are primarily theoretical and methodological. With scientific caution he restricts empirical conclusions to the empirical data and warns against careless generalization. He reminds us that the conventional questionnaire is a valuable tool for identifying such phenomena as political or religious *beliefs* (1934:235). But, he continues, "if we would know the extent to which [his belief] restrains his behavior, it is to his behavior that we must look, not to his questionnaire response:

> Sitting at my desk in California I can predict with a high degree of certainty what an "average" businessman in an average Mid-Western city will reply to the question, Would you engage in sexual intercourse with a prostitute in a Paris brothel? Yet no one, least of all the man himself, can predict what he would actually do should he by some misfortune find himself face-to-face with the situation in question [1934:235–36].

In LaPiere's work we find a line of continuity leading toward new theoretical insights into human behavior, new methods for attaining knowledge, and new kinds of evidence which could be used with confidence by policy makers bent on reducing some of the problems of the contemporary world. But that line of continuity has hardly extended beyond the publication of "Attitudes vs. Actions" in March, 1934. . . . For the most part social science proceeded in other directions.

LaPiere contends that no one has ever challenged his argument that what men say and what they do are not always in concordance. "On the other hand," he writes, "it seems to have had no effect at all on the sociological faith in the value of data gathered via opinion, attitude, and other kinds of questionnaires. The 'Attitude vs. Action' paper was," he continues, "cited for years by almost everyone who wrote on attitudes or opinions as a sort of caution not to take their data too seriously; whereupon each author promptly ignored the caution and proceeded to assume that his data was indicative of what people would actually do in real-life circumstances."

LaPiere was certainly not alone; there were other voices crying in the wilderness. In the late thirties some of the best young minds in American sociology were clearly concerned with the problem. Reading a paper at the 1938 meetings of the American Sociological Society, Robert K. Merton was critical of his own recently acquired survey data on attitudes toward Negroes. He wondered if it wasn't possible that Northerners treat Negroes less favorably than they talk about them and that Southerners talk about Negroes less favorably than they treat them. He asks, "May we assume the amount and direction of spread between opinion and action to be relatively constant for members of different groups? To my knowledge," Merton (1940:21–22) continues, "no systematic research on this problem has been carried out."

At about the same time, C. Wright Mills (1940) argued, "Perhaps the central methodological problem of the social sciences springs from recognition that often there is a disparity between lingual and social-motor types of behavior." Mills suggested that we need to know "*how much* and *in what direction* disparities between talk and action will probably go."

Herbert Blumer has been the most consistent spokesman for the point of view suggested by LaPiere's data. For the past thirty-five years in at least a half-dozen articles, Blumer has argued the logic of this position, in terms of theory (1954, 1940, 1931), in terms of method (1956), and in terms of substantive fields such as Industrial Relations (1947) and Public Opinion Polling (1948). In his presidential address to the American Sociological Society in 1956, Blumer suggests that, not only do we know nothing about behavior or the relation between attitudes and behavior, but we don't know much about attitudes either: "The thousands of 'variable' studies of attitudes, for instance, have not contributed to our knowledge of the abstract nature of an attitude; in a similar way the studies of 'social cohesion,' 'social integration,' 'authority,' or 'group morale' have done nothing so far as I can detect, to clarify or augment generic knowledge of these categories." Yet, in the closing lines of his address, after thirty-five years of persistence, Blumer acknowledges defeat with the wistful hope that people at least know what they are doing. He concludes, "In view, however, of the current tendency of variable analysis to become the norm and model for sociological analysis, I believe it important to recognize its shortcomings and its limitations."

Why have both the empirical evidence and the theoretical

rationale been ignored? There is adequate reason to suspect that behavior toward words about social or cultural objects (i.e., responses to questions) may not provide an adequate basis for imputing behavior toward the objects themselves (i.e., responses to the people or situations to which the words refer). Three decades ago LaPiere's explanation was couched in terms of economy and reliability: "The questionnaire," he observed, "is cheap, easy, and mechanical. The study of human behavior is time consuming, intellectually fatiguing, and depends for its success upon the ability of the investigator. The former method gives quantitative results, the latter mainly qualitative. Quantitative measurements are quantitatively accurate; qualitative evaluations are always subject to the errors of human judgment. Yet," he concludes, "it would seem far more worthwhile to make a shrewd guess regarding that which is essential than to accurately measure that which is likely to prove quite irrelevant" (1934:237).

Others, like Mills, have assumed a more cynical explanation. Turning to the sources of research finance, he suggests that: "Many foundation administrators like to give money for projects that are thought to be safe from political or public attack, that are large-scale, hence easier 'to administer' than more numerous handicraft projects, and that are scientific with a capital S, which often only means made 'safe' by trivialization. Accordingly," Mills (1954) concludes, "the big money tends to encourage the large-scale bureaucratic style of research into small-scale problems as carried on by The Scientists."

These explanations have persisted and most of them remain as valid today as they were in the past, but I suspect that they reflect a deeper and perhaps more basic problem. It is possible that the apparent anomaly of acknowledging the correctness of one position while pursuing another can best be explained in terms of the sociology of knowledge.

EPISTEMOLOGY AND RESEARCH METHODS

It has been suggested that the sociology of knowledge "is devoted to digging up the social roots of knowledge, to searching out the ways in which knowledge and thought are affected by the environing social structure" (Merton, 1957:440). We may indeed have some roots to dig in our attempt to understand the directions taken by American sociology during the last three or four decades. The perceptions of knowledge—notions of the proper or appropriate ways of knowing—which were fashionable during the late twenties and early thirties, when sociology had its choices to make, surely impinged upon those choices.

Men like LaPiere, Blumer, and, later, Mills were arguing from a basically anti-positivistic position at a time when a century or more of cumulative positivistic science was resulting in a massive payoff in our knowledge and control of physical forces. And sociology had its alternatives. L. L. Thurstone was giving birth to what was to become modern scaling. Emery Bogardus was translating some of these ideas into sociological scales of contemporary relevance. And the intellectual brilliance of men like George Lundberg and Stuart Chapin was creating the theoretical and methodological rationale for the new "science." Incisive critiques of the new sociology and the logic of its quantitative methods were plentiful (cf. Merton, 1940; Cohen and Nagel, 1934: Ch. 15; Johnson, 1936; Kirkpatrick, 1936), but if we listen to Richard LaPiere's recollections of the temper of the times it becomes apparent that logic may not have been the deciding factor:

What you may not know, or at least not fully appreciate, is that well into the 1930's the status of sociology and hence of sociologists was abominable, both within and outside the academic community. The public image of the sociologist was of a blue-nosed reformer, ever ready to pronounce moral judgments, and against all pleasurable forms of social conduct. In the universities, sociology was generally thought of as an uneasy mixture of social philosophy and social work. . . . Through the 1920's the department at Chicago was the real center of sociology in the United States [but] . . . the men who were to shape sociology during the 1930's were, for the most part, products of one- or two-men departments (e.g., Columbia) of low status within their universities; they were, therefore, to a considerable degree self-trained and without a doctrinaire viewpoint, and they were exceedingly conscious of the low esteem in which sociology was held. Such men, and I was one among them, were determined to prove—at least to themselves—that sociology is a science, that sociologists are not moralists, and that sociology deserves recognition and support comparable to that being given psychology and economics. It was, I think, to this end that toward the end of the '20's, scientific sociology came to be identified with quantitative methods

. . . and by the mid-thirties American sociologists were split into two antagonistic camps—the moralists . . . and the scientists. . . . Now as to my own uncertain part in all this. I was one of the Young Turks, and I shared with Lundberg, Bain, Stouffer, etc., the distaste for sociology as it had been and the hurt of its lowly status. But unlike the majority of the rebels, I did not share their belief that the cure for bad sociology was quantification [although] I did set off in that direction.

LaPiere sees the history of American sociology between the two world wars as an effort, not to build knowledge, but to achieve respectability and acceptability. In terms of this goal we have been successful. "For it has in considerable measure been sociological reliance on quantitative methods that has won for sociology the repute and financial support that it now enjoys. That in gaining fame, sociology may have become a pseudo-science is another, and quite different, matter. Now that sociology is well-established, it may be possible for a new generation of young Turks to evaluate the means through which sociology has won respectability."

With the security of respectability perhaps now we can afford to take a more critical look at alternatives which were neglected at other times for reasons which are no longer cogent. Perhaps now we can begin again to achieve some understanding of the tenuous relationships between men's thoughts and their actions. One strategic point of departure for such a re-evaluation is an examination of some of the consequences of the choices we have made. In attempting to assume the stance of physical science, we have necessarily assumed its epistemology—its assumptions about the nature of knowledge and the appropriate means of knowing, including the rules of scientific evidence. The requirement of clean empirical demonstration of the effects of isolated factors or variables, in a manner which can be replicated, led us to create, by definition, such factors or variables. We knew that human behavior was rarely if ever directly influenced or explained by an isolated variable; we knew that it was impossible to assume that any set of such variables was additive (with or without weighting); we knew that the complex mathematics of the interaction among any set of variables, much less their interaction with external variables, was incomprehensible to us. In effect, although we knew they did not exist, we defined them into being.

But it was not enough just to create sets of variables. They had to be stripped of what little meaning they had in order that they might be operational, i.e., that they have their measurement built into their definition. One consequence, then, was to break down human behavior in a way that was not only artificial but which did not jibe with the manner in which that behavior was observed.

Having laid these foundations and because the accretion of knowledge is a cumulative affair, we began to construct layer upon layer. For example, in three decades we "advanced" from Bogardus to Guttman (1959). Merton (1951) suggests that the cumulative nature of science requires a high degree of consensus among scientists and leads, therefore, to an inevitable enchantment with problems of reliability. He is wrong in his equation of scientific method with maximum concern for problems of reliability: all knowledge, whether scientific or not, is cumulative and all men who think or write stand on the shoulders of those who have thought or have written before. It does, nevertheless, appear that the adoption of the scientific model in the social sciences has resulted in an uncommon concern for methodological problems centering on issues of reliability and to the concomitant neglect of problems of validity.

We have been absorbed in measuring the amounts of error which results from inconsistency among interviewers or inconsistency among items on our instruments. We concentrate on consistency without much concern with what it is we are being consistent about or whether we are consistently right or wrong. As a consequence we may have been learning a great deal about how to pursue an incorrect course with a maximum of precision.

It is not my intent to disparage the importance of reliability per se; it is the obsession with it to which I refer. Certainly zero reliability must result in zero validity. But the relationship is not linear, since infinite perfection of reliability (zero error) may also be associated with zero validity. Whether or not one wishes to emulate the scientist and whatever methods may be applied to the quest for knowledge, we must make estimates of, allowances for, and attempts to reduce the extent to which our methods distort our findings.

This is precisely why C. Wright Mills identifies the "disparities between talk and action" as "the central *methodological* problem of the social sciences" (1940; italics added). Mills's plea for systematic investigations into the differences between words and deeds is based on the need for the "methodologist to build into his methods standard margins of error"—to learn how to appropriately discount variously located sources of data. Just as Mills is concerned about reliability in the historical method, Hyman (1954) has documented the need for estimates of reliability in social anthropological and clinical psychiatric observations. He reminds us, for example, that the village of Tepoztlan as described by Lewis is quite different from the same village as it was described earlier by Robert Redfield. Hyman cites Kluckhohn's lament (1945) that "the limited extent to which ethnologists have been articulate about their field techniques is astonishing to scholars in other disciplines."

One of the few positive consequences of our decades of "scientific" orientation is the incorporation into the sociological mentality of a self-consciousness about methods—regardless of what methods are employed. As a result, those few sociologists who bring ethnological field techniques to bear on their problems are constrained to contemplate methodological issues and to publish methodological observations. I have in mind, specifically, the continuing series of articles by Howard S. Becker and Blanche Geer (e.g., Becker and Geer, 1957; Becker, 1958; Becker and Geer, 1960; Geer, 1964). Regardless of the importance of reliability, there remains a danger that in our obsession with it, the goals—the purposes for which we seek knowledge—and the phenomena about which we seek knowledge, may become obscured.

One of the more regretful consequences of our neglect of the relationship between words and deeds has been the development of a technology which is inappropriate to the understanding of human behavior, and conversely, the almost complete absence of a technology which can facilitate our learning about the conditions under which people in various categories do or do not "put their monies where their mouths are." We still do not know much about the relationship between what people say and what they do —attitudes and behavior, sentiments and acts, verbalizations and interactions, words and deeds. *We know so little that I can't even find an adequate vocabulary to make the distinction!*

Under what conditions will people behave as they talk? Under what conditions is there no relationship? And under what conditions do they say one thing and behave exactly the opposite? In spite of the fact that all of these combinations have been empirically observed and reported few efforts have been made to order such observations. Furthermore, and perhaps of even greater importance, we do not know under what conditions a change in attitude anticipates a change in behavior or under what conditions a change in behavior anticipates a change in attitude. Again, both phenomena have been empirically observed and recorded.

It is important that my comments not be misunderstood as a plea for the simple study of simple behavioral items. This would be a duplication of the same kinds of mistakes we have made in the simple study of simple attitudinal items. Overt action can be understood and interpreted only within the context of its meaning to the actors, just as verbal reports can be understood and interpreted only within the context of their meaning to the respondents. And in large part, the context of each is the other. But the fact remains that one of the methodological consequences of our recent history is that we have not developed a technology for observing, ordering, analyzing, and interpreting overt behavior—especially as it relates to attitudes, norms, opinions, and values.

The development of a new technology could take any of a number of directions. Ideally, we should seek to refine the model provided by LaPiere, whereby we obtain information from the same population on verbal behavior and interaction behavior under natural social conditions. Surely, the kind of cleverness which creates situational apparati for the psychological laboratory could also create refined situational designs for research under conditions which have meaning for the actors. The theoretical and methodological rationalization of participant-observer field techniques, begun by Becker and Geer, is a promising alternative. There may be as yet untapped possibilities in contrived laboratory experiments —if we can learn how to contrive them in such a way that their results are not denuded of any general meaning by the artificial specificity of the situations. If someday reliable and valid projective instruments are developed, we may have made a significant technological step forward. There is considerable developmental work under way at present on instruments which facilitate self-reporting of overt behavior and allow comparisons to be made between attitudes and behavior on the same people, although still on a verbal level (Hardt and Bodine, 1964).

There was a time earlier in this century when we had a choice to make, a choice on the one hand of undertaking neat, orderly studies of measurable phenomena. This alternative carried with it all of the gratifications of conforming to the prestigious methods of pursuing knowledge then in vogue, of having access to considerable sums of monies through the granting procedures of large foundations and governmental agencies, of a comfortable sense of satisfaction derived from dealing rigorously and precisely with small isolated problems which were cleanly defined, of moving for thirty years down one track in an increasingly rigorous, refined, and reliable manner, while simultaneously disposing of the problems of validity by the semantic trickery of operational definitions. On the other hand, we could have tackled the messy world as we knew it to exist, a world where the same people will make different utterances under different conditions and will behave differently in different situations and will say one thing while doing another. We could have tackled a world where control of relevant variables was impossible not only because we didn't know what they were but because we didn't know how they interacted with each other. We could have accepted the conclusion of almost every variant of contemporary philosophy of science, that the notion of cause and effect (and therefore of stimulus and response or of independent and dependent variables) is untenable. We eschewed this formidable challenge. This was the hard way. We chose the easy way.

Yet the easy way provides one set of results and the hard way provides another. The easy way for LaPiere in 1934 would have been to conduct as rigorous as possible a survey of attitudes of hotel and restaurant managers toward Orientals. But this leads to a set of conclusions which are the opposite of what he finds when he does it the hard way, i.e., traveling thousands of miles in order to confront those managers with Orientals. One of our graduate students (Hanson, 1965), after reviewing some of the literature on the relationship between attitudes and overt behavior, concluded that laboratory experimental studies such as those by Scott (1957, 1959), King and Janis (1956), and DeFleur and Westie (1958) tend to show a positive correlation between attitude and behavior, while observational field studies such as those by LaPiere, Kutner, Wilkins, and Yarrow (1952) and Saenger and Gilbert (1950) tend to show no such correlation. Although there are important exceptions to this rule, it serves as a reminder that our choice of methods may not be unrelated to our conclusions.

EMPIRICAL EVIDENCE AND THEORETICAL SUPPORT

Why do I fuss so, largely on the basis of a primitive field study on a Chinese couple done over thirty years ago and the stubborn polemics of a Herbert Blumer? Frankly, that would be sufficient to cause me considerable concern! But there is other empirical evidence as well as a variety of theoretical support for the argument that more attention needs to be directed toward the relationship between what men say and what they do.

There is reason to believe that this problem transcends American attitudes toward Chinese tourists thirty years ago. There is evidence that interracial attitudes and behavior are not identical in Brazil (Bastide and van den Berghe, 1957), that sentiments about Negroes in northern American communities do not coincide with behavior toward Negroes in those communities (Brookover and Holland, 1952), that interracial attitudes and behavior between customers and department store clerks are inconsistent, and that divergences between interracial attitudes and behaviors persist in 1965 as they did in 1934 (Linn, 1965).

Perhaps of even greater importance are the bits of empirical evidence that this discrepancy between what people say and what they do is not limited to the area of racial or ethnic relations: it has been observed that trade union members talk one game and play another (Dean, 1958), that there is no relationship between college students' attitudes toward cheating and their actual cheating behavior (Freeman and Ataov, 1960), that urban teachers' descriptions of classroom behavior are sometimes unrelated to the way teachers behave in the classroom (Henry, 1959), that what rural Missourians say about their health behavior has little connection with their actual health practices (Hassinger and McNamara, 1957), and that the moral and ethical beliefs of students do not conform to their behavior (Putney and Middleton, 1962a, 1962b).

It has also been reported that Kansans who vote for prohibition maintain and use well-equipped bars in their homes (Warriner, 1958), that small-time steel wholesalers mouth patriotism while undercutting the national economy in wartime (Kriesberg, 1956), that employers' attitudes toward hiring the handicapped are not reflected in their hiring practices (Schletzer et al., 1961), and that the behavior of mothers toward their children is unrelated to their attitudes toward them (Zunich, 1962). If it were possible to observe bedroom behavior, I wonder what would be the relationship between Kinsey's survey results and such observations? I don't know, nor does anyone else, but a contemporary novelist has a confused fictional respondent muse about a sex survey, "But what do they expect of me? Do they want to know how I feel or how I act?" (Wallace, 1961).

Students of aging suspect that what older people have to say about retirement has little relationship to their life during that stage of the life cycle (Breen, 1963; Henry and Cumming, 1961) A pair of industrial psychologists, interested in assessing the current state of knowledge regarding the relationship between employee attitudes and employee performance, covered all of the literature in that area through 1954 (Brayfield and Crockett, 1955) Treating various classes of studies separately, they find in every category "minimal or no relationship between employee attitudes and performance."

It would be a serious selective distortion of the existing evidence to suggest that all of it indicates an incongruence between what people say and what they do. Consumers sometimes do change their buying habits in ways that they say they will (Martin, 1963), people frequently do vote as they tell pollsters they will, urban relocation populations may accurately predict to interviewers the type of housing they will obtain (Deutscher and Cagle, 1964), local party politicians do in fact employ the campaign tactics which they believe to be most effective (Frost, 1961), and youngsters will provide survey researchers with reports of their own contact or lack of contact with the police which are borne out by police records.

The empirical evidence can best be summarized as reflecting wide variation in the relationships between attitudes and behaviors. As a result of their review all of the studies on employee attitudes and performance, Brayfield and Crockett (1955) observe, "The scarcity of relationships, either positive or negative, demonstrated to date even among the best designed of the available studies leads us to question whether or not methodological changes alone would lead to a substantial increase in the magnitude of the obtained relationships." Having arrived at the point where they are able to question the assumption that a relationship must obtain between what people say and what they do, these authors can now question whether or not the failure to observe such a relationship is necessarily a consequence of the inefficiency of the measuring instruments. This is an important breakthrough, since it permits them, and us, to look at alternative explanations—especially at conceptual considerations.

A cursory review of the conceptual frameworks within which most of us work suggests that no matter what one's theoretical orientation may be, he has no reason to expect to find congruence between attitudes and actions and every reason to expect to find discrepancies between them. The popular varieties of balance theory in current social science, such as functionalism in sociology and anthropology and cognitive dissonance in psychology, posit a drive or strain toward consistency. This image of man and society must carry with it the assumption that at any given point in time a condition of imbalance or dissonance or inconsistency obtains.

The psychoanalytic concepts of the unconscious and the subconscious assume that people cannot themselves know how they might behave under specified conditions and such mechanisms as repression suggest that they may not be able to tell an interviewer how they have behaved in the past. Such dissimilar sociological ancestors as Charles H. Cooley and Emile Durkheim built their conceptions of man in society around the assumption that human nature is such that it requires the constraints of society. Under such conditions there is an inherent conflict between man's private self and his social self and the area of role theory is developed to help us understand some of the mechanisms by which man is constrained to act as he "ought."

On the gross societal level, such concepts as social disorganization and cultural lag suggest that people can be caught up in discrepant little worlds which make conflicting demands upon them. The immigrant to a new world has been described as assuming new forms of behavior while clinging to older attitudes and beliefs. In the developing countries of Africa, the idea of cultural lag leads us to expect that the rapid acceptance of new behaviors may outrun, at least for a while, the rejection of old norms. Or perhaps behavioral changes may not be able to keep pace with the rapid acceptance of new norms. Either way, the outcome must be inconsistent attitudes and behaviors!

When we consider the behavior of individuals in groups smaller than societies, we frequently think in such terms as situational contingencies, the definition of the situation, public and private behavior, or reference-group theory—all of which relate what one does or what one says to the immediate context, both as it exists objectively and as it exists in the mind of the actor. Do we not expect attitudes and behaviors to vary as the definition of the situation is altered or as different reference groups are brought to bear?

The symbolic interactionists have traditionally exhibited the greatest sensitivity to this problem in sociology. Among others, both Blumer and LaPiere have insisted that we act, either verbally or overtly, in response to the symbolic meaning the confronting object has for us in the given situation. A question put to me by an interviewer concerning how I feel about Armenian women forces me to respond to the words and to the interviewer; standing face-to-face with a real flesh and blood Armenian woman, I find myself constrained to act toward a very different set of symbols. Is there any reason to assume that my behavior should be the same in these two radically different symbolic situations? Arnold Rose (1956) has developed a vigorous symbolic interactionist argument regarding the theoretical independence of attitudes and behaviors.

One conceptual framework which we tend to neglect lies in the undeveloped field of *sociolinguistics*. Although it may be many other things, sociolinguistics should also deal with an analysis of the meanings of verbal communications. It provides an untapped potential for understanding the relation between what people say and what they do. What differences in meaning can be conveyed by different people with the same words? The eloquent teen-age Negro prostitute, Kitten, can find herself involved in a $100 misunderstanding only because she thinks she is listening to someone who speaks the same language (Gover, 1963). The truth of the matter is that, unfortunately, she and her Babbitt-like college sophomore protagonist employ the same vocabulary to speak different languages. Might this not also occur occasionally between interviewer and interviewee? What is the relationship between language and thought and between language and action? Should we assume that a response of "yah," "da," "si," "oui," or "yes" all really mean exactly the same thing in response to the same question? Or may there not be different kinds of affirmative connotations in different languages? And, of course, can we assume that the question itself means the same thing simply because it translates accurately?

We have a great deal to learn from comparative linguistics if we can bring ourselves to view language from the perspective of the symbolic interactionist—as social and cultural symbolism—rather than from the perspective of those psycholinguists who reduce language to mathematical symbols and thus effectively denude it of its socio-cultural context. I would suggest that it is impossible to translate any word in any language to any word in any other language. Words are fragments of linguistic configurations; they mean nothing in isolation from the configuration. The basic linguistic problems of cross-cultural and cross-class survey research have hardly been recognized, much less dealt with.

Let me suggest that, as an intellectual exercise, you take whatever other conceptual frameworks you may be partial to or comfortable with and determine whether or not they permit you to assume that you can expect people to act in accordance with their words. Meanwhile, I will return to Brayfield and Crockett (1955), who helped me earlier with the transition from method to theory: "Foremost among [the] implications," of their review of research, "is the conclusion that it is time to question the strategic and ethical merits of selling to industrial concerns an assumed relationship between employee attitudes and employee performance." It is but a slight extension of this conclusion to question the strategic and ethical merits of selling anything to anyone or to any establishment based on the dubious assumption that what people say is related directly to what they do.

Social Research and Social Policy

If I appear to have belabored some obvious points, it is because it is necessary to build as strong a backdrop as possible to the implications of all of this for the role of social science research in policy recommendations. Research aimed at demonstration and evaluation tends to make precisely the assumption which I have been challenging: the notion that what people say is a predictor of what they will do.

Thus far, I have tried to restrict my attention to the relatively simple question of the relations between attitudes and behaviors —simple as compared to the issues raised when we turn to the relationship between attitudinal and behavioral *changes*. If we are to be relevant to social policy, then we must consider this more complex question. Can we assume that if we are attempting to alter behavior through a training program, an educational campaign, or some sort of information intervention, a measured change in attitude in the "right" direction results in a change in behavior?

Leon Festinger (1964:405), encountering a statement in an unpublished manuscript, reports that he was "slightly skeptical about the assertion that there is a dearth of studies relating attitude or opinion change to behavior." Although no examples occurred to him, he was certain that there must be many such studies. "After prolonged search," he writes, "with the help of many others, I succeeded in locating only three relevant studies, one of which is of dubious relevance and one of which required reanalysis of data. The absence of research and of theoretical thinking, about the effect of attitude change on subsequent behavior is," Festinger concludes, "indeed astonishing."

The three relevant studies all involve study and control populations and pre- and post-tests of attitude. Some form of persuasive communication was injected into the study groups and either self-reports or behavioral observations are obtained. The studies deal with attitudes of mothers of infants toward the age at which toilet training should begin; the training of industrial foremen in human relations; and attitudes of high school students toward proper dental care. *In all three cases the process of persuasive communication resulted in a significant change of attitude in the desired direction. In all three cases there is no evidence of a change in behavior in the desired direction.* To the contrary, Festinger (1964:416) concedes that he has not "grappled with the perplexing question raised by the persistent hint of a slightly inverse relationship," and he confesses his inability to explain the possibility of such a reversal.

It seems to me that we have sufficient grounds to reject any evaluation of an action program which employs attitudinal change as a criterion of "success," except in the unlikely event that the goal of the program is solely to change attitudes without concern for subsequent behavioral changes. And even under these conditions, the validity of our attitudinal measurements can be seriously challenged. For example, Ehrlich and Rinehart (1965) recently reported the results of their analysis of a stereotype-measuring instrument which has been used in identical or slightly modified form in dozens of studies since 1933. They observe that the results achieved in these studies have all been roughly consistent and then proceed to demonstrate that these reliable results are of doubtful validity. In effect, we have achieved over thirty years' worth of cumulative, consistent, and misleading information about prejudice.

If we do not know enough about the behavioral consequences of attitude change to make policy recommendations with confidence in their validity, what do we know about the attitudinal consequences of behavioral change? There is some evidence in the American Soldier studies that the integration of army units may lead to more favorable attitudes toward Negroes on the part of the integrated white soldiers (Stouffer et al., 1949). Integrated public housing projects are reported to increase friendly contacts between races and to reduce stereotyping and prejudice among the white occupants (Deutsch and Collins, 1956; Wilner et al., 1952). In Yarrow's report (1958) of a controlled experiment in a children's camp, the experimental (desegregated) cabins did produce a significant reduction in prejudice as measured by pre- and post-sociometric interviews. But another study in an integrated camp concludes that four weeks of intimate contact on the part of the children produced no change in attitude (Mussen, 1950). Similarly, Bettelheim and Janowitz (1964) found in their study of veterans that intimate contact with members of the minority group does not seem to disintegrate prejudices.

These bits of evidence concerning the attitudinal consequences of behavioral change are all limited to the specific case of coercively integrated residential enclaves, i.e., army units, public housing projects, and children's camps. Although it has been reported that interracial occupational contacts may also result in changed attitudes, the evidence is limited. The invasion-succession process which occurs when people are not coerced in their residential arrangements suggests that, by and large, they prefer flight (avoidance) to attitudinal change. Furthermore, there is some evidence that even when attitudinal changes appear to have occurred in one area, such as the work situation or the housing situation, they are not necessarily generalized to other interactional areas (Lohman and Reitzes, 1954; Rose, 1961; Minard, 1952).

Aside from the case of interracial attitudes and behaviors, there are an infinite number of situations where attitudinal consequences of behavioral change can be studied. In a country such as Britain, where employers are coerced by law under certain conditions to employ handicapped workers, do their attitudes toward such workers change? If a group of Jaycees can be induced to undertake work with delinquent boys, does the experience alter their attitude toward such boys? Does a relatively indifferent adolescent drafted and shipped to Viet Nam consequently develop hostile attitudes toward the Viet Cong?

There can, of course, be no simple "yes" or "no" answer to such simple questions. To polarize attention upon two variables labeled "attitude" and "behavior" and to operationally define them so that we can measure their relationship is to continue down the same track. It is what goes on in between—the process—toward which we must direct our attention. We need to ask what intervenes between the change in behavior and the change in attitude. Such questions need to be reformulated and qualified so that we ask "under what conditions do what kinds of people change their attitudes as a consequence of induced behavior?" We need to recognize that change probably occurs in both directions—from thought to act and from act to thought—sometimes separately, sometimes simultaneously, and sometimes sequentially.

Taking such a balanced position, Bettelheim and Janowitz (1964) reject on theoretical grounds "the view that social practice must invariably precede attitude or personality changes." They argue, "It is a serious oversimplification to assume that changes in overt behavior necessarily bring about desired changes toward increased tolerance," and that "attitude changes often anticipate overt political and social behavior. Thus," they conclude, "it becomes necessary to assess the policy implications of our research on both the levels of social and personal controls."

It would seem that, in spite of our facile use of such concepts as socialization, internalization, re-enforcement—all of which imply attitudinal development as a consequence of behavioral experience —we cannot blandly suggest to the policy maker that if he changes behavior, a change in attitude will follow. Nor can we lead him to assume that if he can alter attitudes, he need only wait patiently for the appropriate behavior to develop.

In view of the arguments and evidence reviewed, I should allude to the possibility that changes in policy are not necessarily related to subsequent changes in behavior. It follows that the process of influencing policy makers may at times have negligible impact on the resolution of social problems. Nevertheless, I am concerned with the consequences of doling out to policy makers wrong advice, based on bad research and justified in the name of science. How many good programs are halted and bad ones continued because of "scientific" evaluations? There are increasing demands being made upon social science. There are expectations that we can be helpful—and we ought to be. We do not know the current extent of our influence or its future limits. No doubt it will increase. It may be that as consultants or advisors or sources of information we are used by policy makers only when our knowledge is expedient to bolster positions they have already arrived at for other reasons. But the fact remains that we are used.

We are all aware of the psychological, sociological, and anthropological documentation of the Supreme Court's historic decisions on segregated education in 1954. We know of the intimate involvement of sociologists as architects of President Kennedy's Committee on Juvenile Delinquency and Youth Crime. We realize the multiple influences of social scientists on President Johnson's "War on Poverty." And our role in local school systems, urban renewal and relocation programs, social agency programs, hospitals, and prisons is probably more pervasive than anyone—including ourselves—realizes.

There are new terms in the language we use to describe ourselves and we ought to be self-conscious about their implications. To what new phenomenon are we referring when we invent the phrase "behavioral science"—and why? What are the implications of beginning to refer to selected disciplines as the "policy sciences"? Why is a new magazine launched in 1965 which is described as concerning itself with "problems of public policy especially," on the grounds "that the social sciences (particularly economics, politics and sociology) have become inextricably linked to issues of public policy?"

The myth of a value-free social science was exploded with finality by Alvin Gouldner (1962). To make such a pretext reflects either hypocrisy or self-delusion. As social scientists, we have responsibility for encouraging and working for social change. The theme of these meetings is based in part upon that assumption and upon the consequent requirement we place upon ourselves to ask, "change for what and why?" The sacred political documents of the United States refer repeatedly to certain kinds of equality and freedoms from constraints in our kind of democracy. There is a discrepancy between the words which most of us honor and the deeds which we all observe. I have no reluctance—in fact, feel an obligation—to bring about a maximum congruence between the word and the deed.

I think that, in large part, this is what the so-called current social revolution in the Untied States (and probably elsewhere) is all about. It is not a revolution in the sense of seeking to replace existing political and social values with new ones; it is the opposite— a conservative movement which demands that we live by old values. It is rebellion, if at all, only against an hypocrisy which claims that there are no inequitable social, political, educational, or economic barriers in our kind of democracy, while in fact there are. It is rebelling against an hypocrisy which claims that universities are establishments where highest values are placed upon teaching and learning, while in fact they are not.

Actually, it makes no difference whether we view the nature of man through the dark lenses of a Hume or a Hobbes—"beastly," with each warring against all others—or through the rose colored glasses of a Locke or Rousseau—as essentially "good" but corrupted by society. It makes no difference since either way man is constrained to behave in ways which are contrary to his supposed nature; either way, the dialect between man's private self and his social self must create occasional and sometimes radical inconsistencies between what he says and what he does; either way, inconsistency between attitudes and behavior may be assumed.

The dilemma of words and deeds is not peculiarly American, as Gunnar Myrdal would have it, nor is it peculiar to the race question. It is a universal condition of human nature. If our inability to recognize and contend with this condition between World War I and World War II was largely a consequence of the scientific temper of the times, perhaps one day it will be written that in the temper of the new times between World War II and World War III, sociology did flourish and come of age.

REFERENCES

BASTIDE, R., and P. L. VAN DEN BERGHE. 1957. "Stereotypes, Norms, and Interracial Behavior in São Paulo, Brazil," *American Sociological Review*, 22 (December), pp. 689–94.

BECKER, HOWARD S. 1958. "Problems of Inference and Proof in Participant Observation," *American Sociological Review*, 23 (December), pp. 652–60.

BECKER, HOWARD S., and BLANCHE GEER. 1957. "Participant Observation and Interviewing: A Comparison," *Human Organization*, 16 (Fall), pp. 28–32.

_____. 1960. "Participant Observation: The Analysis of Qualitative Field Data." In R. N. Adams and J. L. Preiss (eds.), *Human Organization Research*. Homewood, Ill.: The Dorsey Press.

BETTELHEIM, BRUNO, and MORRIS JANOWITZ. 1964. *Social Change and Prejudice Including Dynamics of Prejudice*. New York: The Free Press of Glencoe.

BLUMER, HERBERT. 1931. "Science Without Concepts," *American Journal of Sociology*, 36 (May), pp. 515–33.

_____. 1940. "The Problem of the Concept in Social Psychology," *American Journal of Sociology*, 45 (May), pp. 707–19.

_____. 1947. "Sociological Theory in Industrial Relations," *American Sociological Review*, 12 (February), pp. 271–77.

_____. 1948. "Public Opinion and Public Opinion Polling," *American Sociological Review*, 13 (March), pp. 542–49.

_____. 1954." What Is Wrong with Social Theory," *American Sociological Review*, 19 (February), pp. 3–10.

_____. 1956. "Sociological Analysis and the Variable," *American Sociological Review*, 21 (December).

_____. 1966. "Sociological Implications of the Thought of George Herbert Mead," *American Journal of Sociology*, 71.

BRAYFIELD, A., and D. M. CROCKETT. 1956. "Employee Attitudes and Employee Performance," *Psychological Bulletin*, 52 (September), pp. 396–428.

BREEN, LEONARD Z. 1963. "Retirement: Norms, Behavior, and Functional Aspects of Normative Behavior. In R. H. Williams, C. Tibbetts, and W. Donahue (eds.), *Processes of Aging*. Vol. 2. New York: Atherton Press.

BROOKOVER, WILBUR B., and JOHN B. HOLLAND. 1952. "An Inquiry into the Meaning of Minority Group Attitude Expressions," *American Sociological Review*, 17 (April), pp. 196–202.

COHEN, MORRIS, and ERNEST NAGEL. 1934. *An Introduction to Logic and Scientific Method*. New York: Harcourt, Brace.

DEAN, LOIS. 1958. "Interaction, Reported and Observed: The Case of One Local Union," *Human Organization*, 17 (Fall).

DeFLEUR, MELVIN L., and FRANK R. WESTIE. 1958. "Verbal Attitudes and Overt Acts: An Experiment in the Salience of Attitudes," *American Sociological Review*, 23 (December), pp. 667–73.

DEUTSCH, MORTON, and MAY EVANS COLLINS. 1956. "Interracial Housing." In William Petersen (ed.), *American Social Patterns*. New York: Doubleday Anchor Books.

DEUTSCHER, IRWIN, and LAURENCE CAGLE. 1964. "Housing Aspirations of Low Income Fatherless Families." Syracuse, N.Y.: Syracuse University Youth Development Center. Mimeo.

48   *The Critical Perspective*

EHRLICH, HOWARD J., and JAMES W. RINEHART. 1965. "A Brief Report on the Methodology of Stereotype Research," *Social Forces*, 43 (May).

FESTINGER, LEON. 1964. "Behavioral Support for Opinion Change," *Public Opinion Quarterly*, 28 (Fall).

FREEMAN, LINTON C., and TURKOZ ATAOV. 1960. "Invalidity of Indirect and Direct Measures Toward Cheating," *Journal of Personality*, 28 (December), pp. 443–47.

GEER, BLANCHE. 1964. "First Days in the Field." In P. E. Hammond (ed.), *Sociologists at Work*, pp. 322–44. New York: Basic Books.

GOULDNER, ALVIN. 1962. "Anti-Minotaur: The Myth of a Value-Free Sociology," *Social Problems*, 9 (Winter).

GOVER, ROBERT. 1963. *The One Hundred Dollar Misunderstanding.* New York: Ballantine Books.

GUTTMAN, LOUIS. 1959. "A Structural Theory for Intergroup Beliefs and Action," *American Sociological Review*, 24 (June), pp. 318–28.

HANSON, DAVID J. "Notes on a Bibliography on Attitudes and Behavior," unpublished manuscript.

HARDT, ROBERT H., and GEORGE E. BODINE. 1964. *Development of Self-Report Instruments in Delinquency Research.* Syracuse, N.Y.: Syracuse University Youth Development Center.

HASSINGER, EDWARD, and ROBERT L. McNAMARA. 1957. "Stated Opinion and Actual Practice in Health Behavior in a Rural Area," *The Midwest Sociologist* (May), pp. 93–97.

HENRY, JULES. 1959. "Spontaneity, Initiative, and Creativity in Suburban Classrooms," *American Journal of Orthopsychiatry*, 29, pp. 266–79.

HENRY, WILLIAM E., and ELAINE CUMMING. 1961. *Growing Old: The Process of Disengagement.* New York: Basic Books.

HYMAN, HERBERT, et al. 1954. *Interviewing in Social Research.* Chicago: University of Chicago Press.

JOHNSON, H. M. 1936. "Pseudo-Mathematics in the Mental and Social Sciences," *American Journal of Psychology*, 48, pp. 342–51.

KING, B. T., and I. L. JANIS. 1956. "Comparison of the Effectiveness of Improvised Versus Non-improvised Role-Playing in Producing Opinion Changes," *Human Relations*, 9, pp. 177–86.

KIRKPATRICK, CLIFFORD. 1936. "Assumptions and Methods in Attitude Measurements," *American Sociological Review*, 1, pp. 75–88.

KLUCKHOHN, CLYDE. 1945. "The Personal Document in Anthropological Science," Social Research Council Bulletin, No. 53. New York: SSRC.

KRIESBERG, LOUIS. 1956. "National Security and Conduct in the Steel Gray Market," *Social Forces*, 34 (March), pp. 268–77.

KUTNER, B., C. WILKINS, and P. B. YARROW. 1952. "Verbal Attitudes and Overt Behavior Involving Racial Prejudice," *Journal of Abnormal and Social Psychology*, 47, pp. 649–52.

LAPIERE, RICHARD T. 1928. "Race Prejudice: France and England," *Social Forces*, 7 (September), pp. 102–11.

———. 1934. "Attitudes vs. Actions," *Social Forces*, 13 (March), pp. 230–37.

———. 1936. "Type-Rationalizations of Group Antipathy," *Social Forces*, 15 (December), pp. 232–37.

LINN, LAWRENCE S. 1965. "Verbal Attitude and Overt Behavior: A Study of Racial Discrimination," *Social Forces*, 43 (March), pp. 353–64.

LOHMAN, JOSEPH, and DIETRICK C. REITZES. 1954. "Deliberately Organized

Groups and Racial Behavior," *American Sociological Review*, 19 (June), pp. 342–48.
MARTIN, HAROLD H. 1963. "Why She Really Goes to Market," *Saturday Evening Post* (September 28), pp. 40–43.
MERTON, ROBERT K. 1940. "Fact and Factitiousness in Ethnic Opinionnaires," *American Sociological Review*, 5 (February).
———. 1957. *Social Theory and Social Structure* (rev. ed.). Glencoe, Ill.: The Free Press.
MILLS, C. WRIGHT. 1940. "Methodological Consequences of the Sociology of Knowledge," *American Journal of Sociology*, 46, pp. 316–30.
———. 1954. "IBM Plus Reality Plus Humanism = Sociology," *Saturday Review* (May 1).
MINARD, R. D. 1952. "Race Relationships in the Pocahontas Coal Field," *Journal of Social Issues*, 9, pp. 29–44.
MUSSEN, PAUL H. 1950. "Some Personality and Social Factors Related to Changes in Children's Attitudes Toward Negroes," *Journal of Abnormal and Social Psychology*, 45 (July), pp. 423–41.
PUTNEY, SNELL, and RUSSELL MIDDLETON. 1962a. "Ethical Relativism and Anomia," *American Journal of Sociology*, 67 (January), pp. 430–38.
———. 1962b. "Religion, Normative Standards, and Behavior," *Sociometry*, 25, pp. 141–52.
ROSE, ARNOLD. 1956. "Intergroup Relations vs. Prejudice: Pertinent Theory for the Study of Social Change," *Social Problems*, 4 (October).
———. 1961. "Inconsistencies in Attitudes Toward Negro Housing," *Social Problems*, 8 (Spring), pp. 286–92.
SAENGER, GERHART, and EMILY GILBERT. 1950. "Customer Reactions to the Integration of Negro Sales Personnel," *International Journal of Opinion and Attitude Research*, 4 (Spring), pp. 57–76.
SCHLETZER, VERA MEYERS, et al. 1961. "Attitudinal Barriers to Employment," *Minnesota Studies in Vocational Rehabilitation: XI*, Industrial Relations Center, Bulletin No. 32. Minneapolis: University of Minnesota.
SCOTT, W. A. 1957 "Attitude Change Through Reward of Verbal Behavior," *Journal of Abnormal and Social Psychology*, 55, pp. 72–75.
———. 1959. "Attitude Change by Response Reinforcement: Replication and Extension," *Sociometry*, 22, pp. 328–35.
STOUFFER, SAMUEL A., et al. 1949. *The American Soldier; Adjustment During Army Life*, Studies in Social Psychology in World War II. Vol. 1. Princeton, N.J.: Princeton University Press.
VERNON, P. E. 1938. *The Assessment of Psychological Qualities by Verbal Methods*, Medical Research Council, Industrial Health Research Board, Report No. 83. London: H. M. Stationery.
WALLACE, IRVING. 1961. *The Chapman Report*. New York: New American Library.
WARRINER, CHARLES K. 1958. "The Nature and Functions of Official Morality," *American Journal of Sociology*, 64 (September), pp. 165–68.
WILNER, DANIEL M., ROSABELLE P. WALKLEY, and STUART W. COOK. 1952. "Residential Proximity and Inter-group Relations in Public Housing Projects," *Journal of Social Issues*, 8:1, pp. 45–69.
YARROW, MARIAN RADKE. 1958. "Interpersonal Dynamics in a Desegregation Process," Special Issue, *Journal of Social Issues*, 14:1.
ZUNICH, MICHAEL. 1962. "Relationship Between Maternal Behavior and Attitudes Toward Children," *Journal of Genetic Psychology*, pp. 155–65.

3. Selective Attention

SHERLOCK HOLMES: APPLIED SOCIAL PSYCHOLOGIST
—Marcello Truzzi

THE REALITY AND RELEVANCE OF SHERLOCK HOLMES IN HER REMARKABLE SURVEY OF the history of the detective novel, Alma Elizabeth Murch has noted that:

> There are in literature certain characters who have come to possess a separate and unmistakable identity, whose names and personal qualities are familiar to thousands who may not have read any of the works in which they appear. Among these characters must be included Sherlock Holmes, who has acquired in the minds of countless readers of all nationalities the status of an actual human being, accepted by many in the early years of the twentieth century as a living contemporary, and still surviving fifty years later with all the glamour of an established and unassailable tradition, the most convincing, the most brilliant, the most congenial and well-loved of all detectives of fiction. (Murch, 1958: 167)

In all of English literature, it has been said that the only other three fictional names equally familiar to the "man in the street" might be those of Romeo, Shylock, and Robinson Crusoe (Pearson, 1943: 86).

From Marcello Truzzi, ed., *The Humanities as Sociology* (Columbus, Ohio: Charles E. Merrill Publishing Co., 1973), pp. 93–126.

Although the Holmes saga consists of only sixty narratives[1] by Sir Arthur Conan Doyle,[2] which first appeared between 1887 and 1927,[3] the foothold Sherlock Holmes gained upon the popular imagination has seldom been equalled. The depth of his impact is nowhere better demonstrated than by "the belief, held for years by thousands, that he was an actual living human being—a circumstance that constitutes one of the most unusual chapters in literary history" (Haycraft, 1941: 57–58). Thus, in addition to countless letters from troubled would-be clients addressed to "Mr. Sherlock Holmes, 221-B Baker Street, London" (a nonexistent address, too) and many sent to him care of Scotland Yard, the announcement of Holmes's retirement to a bee farm in a 1904 story brought two offers from would-be employees (one as a housekeeper, the other as bee-keeper). Doyle received several letters from ladies who had been contemplating possible marriages with Holmes (Lamond, 1931: 54–55) and there was even a gentleman (one Stephen Sharp) who believed himself to be Holmes, and he made several attempts to visit Doyle from 1905 onwards (reported by Nordon, 1967: 205).

Aside from those who naively believed the Holmes legend, however, and much more sociologically significant, has been the fact that the "legend of Holmes's reality has been swelled by other enthusiastic if more sophisticated readers who know well enough that their hero has never lived in flesh and blood, but who like to keep up the pretense that he did" (Haycraft, 1941: 58). More has probably been written *about* Holmes's character than any other creation in fiction, and it is remarkable that it is Holmes and not Sir Arthur Conan Doyle who has been the focus of so much attention. Thus, Holmes has been the subject for biographies,[4] encyclopedic works,[5] critical studies,[6] and numerous organizations honoring and studying the Holmes character exist all around the world.[7] Several movements have even been started to get a statue of Holmes erected near his alleged home on Baker Street.[8] As Christopher Morley has often been quoted as saying: "Never, never has so much been written by so many for so few."

Apart from the delightful games of the Sherlockians and their playful mythologies, however, the character of Sherlock Holmes and his exploits touches a deeper reality, for, as has been noted, "this legend fulfills a need beyond the realms of literature"

(Nordon, 1967: 205). Though, as Pearson (1943: 86) has observed, Holmes symbolizes the sportsman and hunter, a modern Galahad hot upon the scent of a bloody trail, the character of Holmes even more clearly epitomizes the attempted application of man's highest faculty—his rationality—in the solution of the problematic situations of everyday life. Most of the plots of the stories came from real life events found by Doyle among the newspaper stories of the 1890s (Nordon, 1967: 236), and remarkably few of the plots deal with bloody violence or murder. In fact, as Pratt (1955) has observed, in fully one-quarter of the stories no legal crime takes place at all. The essentially mundane character of most of the plots clearly demonstrates the observation that the "cycle may be said to be an epic of everyday events" (Nordon, 1967: 247). It is this everyday setting of the applications of Holmes's "science" and rationality that so astounds and gratifies the reader. And it is not so much the superior ability of Holmes to obtain remarkable insights and inferences from simple observations which so impresses the reader; it is the seeming reasonableness and obviousness of his "method" once it has been explained to the reader. One truly believes (at least while under the spell of the narrative) that Holmes's new applied science is possible for the diligent student of his "methods." As has been noted:

> The fictitious world to which Sherlock Holmes belonged, expected of him what the real world of the day expected of its scientists: more light and more justice. As a creation of a doctor who had been soaked in the rationalist thought of the period, the Holmesian cycle offers us for the first time the spectacle of a hero triumphing again and again by means of logic and scientific method. (Nordon, 1967: 247)

This fascination with the possibility of the mundane application of scientific methods to the interpersonal world has captured not only the imagination of the lay readers of the Holmes saga. It has had an appreciable effect upon criminologists and those concerned with the real life problems that parallel those fictionally encountered by Sherlock Holmes. Thus, a representative from the Marseilles Scientific Police Laboratories pointed out that "many of the methods invented by Conan Doyle are today in use in scientific laboratories" (Aston-Wolfe, 1932: 328);

the Director of the Scientific Detective Laboratories and President of the Institute of Scientific Criminology has stated that "the writings of Conan Doyle have done more than any other one thing to stimulate active interest in the scientific and analytical investigation of crime" (May, 1936: x); and, most recently, an expert on firearms has argued that Holmes should be called "Father of Scientific Crime Detection" (Berg 1970). Many famous criminologists, including Alphonse Bertillon and Edmond Locard, have credited Holmes as a teacher and source of ideas, and Holmes's techniques of observation and inference are still presented as a useful model for the criminal investigator (Hogan and Schwartz 1964).[9]

In addition to the very practical consequences of Sherlock Holmes's influence upon modern criminology, the reality of his "method" is even better shown through an understanding of his origins. In his autobiography, *Memories and Adventures* (1924), Doyle clearly states that the character of Holmes was patterned after his memories of his professor of surgery when Doyle was in medical school, Joseph Bell, M.D., F.R.C.S., Edinburgh, whom Doyle recalled as capable of the kind of observation and inference so characteristic of Holmes. Bell's remarkable ability is well exemplified by the following anecdote related by Doyle:

> In one of his best cases he said to a civilian patient: "Well, my man, you've served in the army." "Aye, Sir." "Not long discharged?" "No, Sir." "A Highland regiment?" "Aye, Sir." "A noncom officer?" "Aye, Sir." "Stationed at Barbados?" "Aye, Sir." "You see, gentlemen," he would explain, "the man was a respectful man but did not remove his hat. They do not in the army, but he would have learned civilian ways had he been long discharged. He has an air of authority and he is obviously Scottish. As to Barbados, his complaint is Elephantiasis, which is West Indian, and not British." To his audience of Watsons, it all seemed very miraculous until it was explained, and then it became simple enough. (Doyle, 1930:23)

It is likely, however, that Holmes was only partly patterned after Dr. Bell and is actually a composite of several persons.[10] Ultimately, though, "there is no doubt that the real Holmes was Conan Doyle himself" (Starrett, 1960: 102). As Michael and Mollie Hardwick have shown in their remarkable study *The Man*

Who Was Sherlock Holmes (1964), the parallels in Doyle's life, including the successful solution of several real-life mysteries and Doyle's championing of justice (best seen in his obtaining the ultimate release and clearing of two men falsely convicted of murder, the celebrated cases of George Edalji and Oscar Slater),[11] clearly demonstrate the roots of Holmes's essential character and methods within his creator. Dr. Edmond Locard, Chief of the Surete Police Laboratories at Lyon, stated that "Conan Doyle was an absolutely astonishing scientific investigator," and the criminologist Albert Ullman took the position that "Conan Doyle was a greater criminologist than his creation Sherlock Holmes" (quoted in Anonymous, 1959: 69).

The important point being made here is that the successes of Dr. Bell and Sir Arthur Conan Doyle demonstrate the fact that the methods of scientific analysis exemplified and dramatized by Sherlock Holmes in his adventures have had their counterparts in the real world. As the well-known American detective William Burns put it:

> I often have been asked if the principles outlined by Conan Doyle, in the Sherlock Holmes stories could be applied in real detective work, and my reply to this question is decidedly "yes." (Quoted in Anonymous 1959, p. 68)

What, then, exactly, is the "method" of Sherlock Holmes, and what are its limitations and implications for a modern applied social psychology? We turn now to an examination of Holmes's views of science, and of man and society, and to his prescriptions for the applications of the former to the latter as these are outlined in the canon.

THE METHOD OF SHERLOCK HOLMES

It is unfortunate that, although Holmes's method is central to his character and universal attractiveness, there is no systematic statement of it to be found in the canon. It is also surprising to find that relatively little consideration has been given to his techniques of "deduction" in the massive bibliography of Sherlockiana. Most Sherlockians have been more concerned with their own application of Holmes's techniques to the clues available in the canon than upon an examination of the methods themselves. Therefore, we must turn to a search for the many but scattered statements about his method uttered by Holmes throughout his adventures.

Holmes's "Science of Deduction and Analysis". It has often been stated that science is but refined common sense. With this Holmes would probably agree for he states that his own approach is a "simple art, which is but systematized common sense."[12] But his view is not a simple or mechanical view of the process, for at another point he notes that a "mixture of imagination and reality . . . is the basis of my art."[13] Though Holmes stresses raw empiricism to a degree reminiscent of the archinductionist Francis Bacon, he does not neglect the importance of creative imagination. "It is, I admit, mere imagination," Holmes states, "but how often is imagination the mother of truth?"[14] "One's ideas must be as broad as nature if they are to interpret nature,"[15] he notes, and

> breadth of view . . . is one of the essentials of our profession. The interplay of ideas and the oblique uses of knowledge are often of extraordinary interest.[16]

Although Sir Arthur Conan Doyle was to become a major promoter of spiritualism, Holmes, in a true Comtean manner of positivism and scientific skepticism, refuses to seriously entertain hypotheses of supernatural causation. Recognizing that "the devil's agents may be of flesh and blood,"[17] before considering the possibility that "we are dealing with forces outside the ordinary laws of Nature," he argues that "we are bound to exhaust all other hypotheses before falling back on this one."[18] Holmes states of himself that

> this Agency stands flatfooted upon the ground, and there it must remain. The world is big enough for us. No ghosts need apply.[19]

Holmes's general philosophical assumptions about the universe are somewhat unclear. Although he apparently believed in a purposeful universe,[20] and hoped for the goodness of Providence,[21] he also expressed a more cynical view when he asked Watson:

> But is not all life pathetic and futile? . . . we reach. We grasp. And what is left in our hands at the end? A shadow. Or worse than a shadow—misery.[22]

This view of all knowledge as "shadows," aside from its depressive context here, is very much in keeping with the modern scientific and essentially pragmatic view of man as a creator of "cognitive maps" and theoretical "realities" or "conjectures" rather than as discoverer of objective truths and laws.

Holmes also epitomizes the basically deterministic orientation of most modern social science. As he remarked:

> The ideal reasoner . . . would, when he had once been shown a single fact in all its bearings, deduce from it not only all the chain of events which led up to it but also all the results which would follow from it. As Cuvier could correctly describe a whole animal by the contemplation of a single bone, so the observer who has thoroughly understood one link in a series of incidents should be able to accurately state all the other ones, both before and after.[23]

Or as Holmes put it in his seminal article "The Book of Life" (in a magazine Dr. Watson unfortunately neglected to name):

> From a drop of water . . . a logician could infer the possibility of an Atlantic or a Niagara without having seen or heard of one or the other. So all life is a great chain, the nature of which is known whenever we are shown a single link of it. Like all other arts, the Science of Deduction and Analysis is one which can only be acquired by long and patient study, nor is life long enough to allow any mortal to attain the highest possible perfection in it.[24]

This determinism was seen as present at all levels of life, but Holmes clearly sides with sociology against many psychologists when he states that

> while the individual man is an insoluble puzzle, in the aggregate he becomes a mathematical certainty. You can, for example, never foretell what any one man will do, but you can say with precision what an average member will be up to. Individuals vary, but percentages remain constant.[25]

As with all nomothetic sciences, emphasis is placed upon the search for laws and recurrent events. Holmes is greatly impressed by regularities and repetitions in history, and in speaking of a crime to his friend Inspector Gregson, Holmes echoes Ecclesiastes when he says: "There is nothing new under the sun. It has all been done before."[26] And on another occasion he says of his arch-enemy: "Everything comes in circles, even Professor Moriarty."[27] Holmes seeks out generalizations and will ultimately settle only for universal propositions. As he put it: "I never make exceptions. An exception disproves the rule."[28]

Central to Holmes's basic approach, however, is his concern with the empirical verification of his conjectures. His emphasis on induction—an emphasis more present in his words than in his actual practice, as we shall see—is based on a great fear of conceptual detachment from the "real" world of observable phenomena. "The temptation to form premature theories upon insufficient data is the bane of our profession," he tells Inspector MacDonald.[29] For as Holmes says again and again:

It is a capital mistake to theorize before one has data. Insensibly one begins to twist facts to suit theories, instead of theories to suit facts.[30]

It is a capital mistake to theorize in advance of the facts.[31]

It is a capital mistake to theorize before you have all the evidence.[32]

. . . it is an error to argue in front of your data. You find yourself insensibly twisting them around to fit your theories.[33]

And

how dangerous it always is to reason from insufficient data.[34]

Holmes insists upon the absolute necessity of observable facts.

"Data! data! data!" he cried impatiently. "I can't make bricks without clay."[35]

But he claims even more than this, for his posture is attemptedly atheoretical in an inductive manner remarkably reminiscent of the sort of posture taken today by some behavioristic followers of B.F. Skinner. But like the Skinnerians, Holmes is forced to assert at least provisional hypotheses or "hunches" about the world. Holmes may cry out "No, no: I never guess. It is a shocking habit—destructive to the logical faculty,"[36] but he is forced to acknowledge that

one forms provisional theories and waits for time and fuller knowledge to explode them. A bad habit . . . ; but human nature is weak.[37]

At base, Holmes puts his trust in the empirical world which he sees as the firm and ultimate arbiter. "I can discover facts, Watson, but I cannot change them."[38] And these facts must always be questioned for "it is as well to test everything."[39]

Holmes's Method. Holmes clearly subscribed to the general rule of the modern scientific community that since scientific knowledge is of its definition *public* knowledge (in so far as it must be inter-subjectively communicable), it should ideally be open to public scrutiny. Holmes generally makes no secret of his methods.

It has always been my habit to hide none of my methods either from my friend Watson or from anyone who might take an intelligent interest in them.[40]

Holmes does occasionally fail to inform his astounded clients of his methods, especially in the early stages of his cases, for, as he put it: "I have found it wise to impress clients with a sense of power."[41] Yet, he usually lets us in on his reasonings and points out that the method is basically quite unmysterious.

It is not really difficult to construct a series of inferences, each dependent upon its predecessor and each simple in itself. If, after doing so, one simply knocks out all the central inferences and presents one's audience with the starting-point and the conclusion, one may produce a startling, though possibly a meretricious, effect.[42]

Holmes was very concerned with the clear presentation of his methods, so much so, in fact, that he complained of Watson's romanticizing his adventures:

Your fatal habit of looking at everything from the point of view of a story instead of as a scientific exercise has ruined what might have been an instructive and even classical series of demonstrations.[43]

He even spoke of his plans to do the job properly himself:

I propose to devote my declining years to the composition of a textbook which shall focus the whole art of detection into one volume.[44]

In speaking of the "qualities necessary for the ideal detective," Holmes noted that they were: (1) knowledge, (2) the power of observation, and (3) the power of deduction.[45] We turn now to an examination of each of these.

THE DETECTIVE'S NEED FOR KNOWLEDGE. As we have seen, Holmes stressed the interconnectedness of all elements of the universe in his deterministic view. He also recognized the complexities and sometimes surprising connections that might be found, for he noted that

> for strange effects and extraordinary combinations we must go to life itself, which is always far more daring than any effort of the imagination.[46]

Thus, the effective detective must be well informed about a vast spectrum of potentially relevant bits of information. Holmes's own storehouse of information was astounding. As we noted earlier, he placed a great emphasis on breadth of knowledge.[47] Watson indicates that Holmes's mastery of the topics relevant to his profession (including chemistry, British law, anatomy, botany, geology, and especially the sensational literature) was remarkable.[48] Yet, Watson also notes that Holmes's "ignorance was as remarkable as his knowledge,"[49] for Holmes apparently knew practically nothing of literature, philosophy, astronomy, or politics.[50] Holmes explained his lack of concern with these areas as follows:

> You see . . . I consider that a man's brain originally is like a little empty attic, and you have to stock it with such furniture as you choose. A fool takes in all the lumber of every sort that he comes across, so that the knowledge which might be useful to him gets crowded out, or at best is jumbled up with a lot of other things, so that he has a difficulty in laying his hands upon it. Now the skillful workman is very careful indeed as to what he takes into his brain-attic. He will have nothing but the tools which may help him in doing his work, but of these he has a large assortment, and all in the most perfect order. It is a mistake to think that that little room has elastic walls and can distend to any extent. Depend upon it there comes a time when for every addition of knowledge you forget something that you knew before. It is of the highest importance, therefore, not to have useless facts elbowing out the useful ones.[51]

Despite this avoidance of the irrelevant (based upon a view of memory with which most contemporary experts on cognitive processes would certainly disagree), Holmes still stocked a vast quantity of information in his memory that was not immediately useful; for as he stated on another occasion:

> My mind is like a crowded box-room with packets of all sorts stowed away therein—so many that I may well have but a vague perception of what was there.[52]

What Holmes basically argued for was the need for specialization in the quest for knowledge so that one might gain the maximum in resources relevant to one's analytic needs. The argument is not primarily one for avoiding some areas of knowledge so much as it is for a commitment of one's limited resources to the most efficient ends. As Holmes stated in a somewhat different context:

> Some facts should be suppressed, or at least a just sense of proportion should be observed in treating them.[53]

Thus, not all knowledge is equally useful, a viewpoint certainly the dominant motif in education (not only in the study of social psychology but in most areas) today.

THE DETECTIVE'S NEED FOR OBSERVATION.   Holmes emphasized the need for keen observation, for in detective work "genius is an infinite capacity for taking pains."[54] Openness and receptivity to data are essential.

> I make a point of never having any prejudices and of following docilely wherever fact may lead me.[55]

Holmes was much aware of the need to control for subjective distortions even in relation to his clients.

> It is of the first importance . . . not to allow your judgement to be biased by personal qualities. A client is to me a mere unit, a factor in a problem. The emotional qualities are antagonistic to clear reasoning.[56]

His greatest emphasis, however, was upon "observing" what others merely "see." Thus, though both Dr. Watson and Holmes had walked the steps leading up from the hall to their room hundreds of times, Holmes had "observed" that there were seventeen steps while Watson had merely "seen" them.[57] As Holmes put it:

The world is full of obvious things which nobody by any chance ever observes.[58]

There is nothing more deceptive than an obvious fact.[59]

I have trained myself to notice what I see.[60]

Holmes's observation extended not only to observed facts and events but also to their absence. Negative evidence is frequently regarded as highly significant. Thus, when Inspector MacDonald asks Holmes if he found anything compromising following Holmes's search through Professor Moriarty's papers, Holmes replied, "Absolutely nothing. That was what amazed me."[61] Or, speaking of the absence of international activity following the theft of an important government document, Holmes noted: "Only one important thing has happened in three days, and that is that nothing has happened."[62] But the classic example is the often-quoted instance during Holmes's search for a missing race-horse wherein Inspector Gregory asks Holmes:

"Is there any other point to which you would wish to draw my attention?"
"To the curious incident of the dog in the night-time."
"The dog did nothing in the night-time."
"That was the curious incident," remarked Sherlock Holmes.[63]

Throughout the canon, Holmes emphasizes the importance of what to the less trained might appear to be trifles. But for Holmes, "there is nothing so important as trifles,"[64] and "to a great mind . . . nothing is little."[65]

It has long been an axiom of mine that the little things are infinitely the most important.[66]

You know my method. It is founded upon the observance of trifles.[67]

Never trust to general impressions . . . but concentrate upon the details.[68]

Attention to minutiae is essential, for

as long as the criminal remains upon two legs, so long must there be some identification, some abrasion, some trifling displacement which can be detected by the scientific searcher.[69]

THE DETECTIVE'S NEED FOR DEDUCTION.   Holmes has almost un-
limited faith in the power of scientific analysis to obtain a
reconstruction of human events, for, as he put it: "What one
man can invent, another can discover."[70] For Holmes, "the grand
thing is to be able to reason backwards."[71] Reasoning from a set
of events to their consequences Holmes calls "synthetic" reasoning, whereas reasoning "backwards" from the results to their
causes he calls "analytic" reasoning.

> There are fifty who can reason synthetically for one who can
> reason analytically. . . . There are few people . . . , if you told
> them the result, would be able to evolve from their own inner
> consciousness what the steps were which led up to that result.[72]

The first step Holmes suggests is basic examination and sifting
out from the existing information the definite from the less
definite data.

> The difficulty is to detach the framework of fact—of absolute,
> undeniable fact—from the embellishments of theorists and re-
> porters. Then, having established ourselves upon this sound basis,
> it is our duty to see what inferences may be drawn, and which
> are the special points upon which the whole mystery turns.[73]

> It is of the highest importance in the art of detection to be
> able to recognize out of a number of facts which are incidental and
> which vital.[74]

Following a sorting of the facts for their reliability, Holmes
recommends special inspection of the unique and unusual details present in the situation.

> The more outré and grotesque an incident is, the more carefully
> it deserves to be examined, and the very point which appears to
> complicate a case is, when duly considered and scientifically
> handled, the one which is most likely to elucidate it.[75]

> Singularity is almost invariably a clue. The more featureless
> and commonplace a crime is, the more difficult it is to bring
> home.[76]

> What is out of the common is usually a guide rather than a
> hindrance.[77]

> It is only the colourless, uneventful case which is hopeless.[78]

Yet, Holmes notes that extreme uneventfulness may itself be a singular event which gives a clue to the mystery:

> Depend upon it there is nothing so unnatural as the commonplace.[79]

Holmes is careful in his evaluation of circumstantial evidence. It is not to be ignored for "circumstantial evidence is occasionally very convincing, as when you find a trout in the milk."[80] But the investigator must be very cautious, since

> circumstantial evidence is a very tricky thing . . . ; it may point very straight to one thing, but if you shift your own point of view a little, you may find it pointing in an equally uncompromising manner to something entirely different.[81]

Although Holmes's greatest emphasis is upon the objective gathering of facts, he fully recognizes the heuristic value of imaginative reconstruction through role playing by the investigator.

> You'll get results . . . by always putting yourself in the other fellow's place, and thinking what you would do yourself. It takes some imagination but it pays.[82]

> You know my methods in such cases . . . : I put myself in the man's place, and having first gauged his intelligence, I try to imagine how I should myself have proceeded under the same circumstances.[83]

Holmes emphasizes the need for pursuing several possible lines of explanation any one of which takes account of the facts. Other hypotheses must always be entertained, and when considering an explanation, "you should never lose sight of the alternative."[84]

> One should always look for a possible alternative and provide against it. It is the first rule of criminal investigation.[85]

For

> when you follow two separate chains of thought . . . you will find some point of intersection which should approximate the truth.[86]

From this reconstruction of alternative explanations which fit the facts, one must move next into what might superficially appear to be guessing but is actually the region where we balance probabilities and choose the most likely. It is the scientific use of the imagination, but we have always some material basis on which to start our speculations.[87]

Holmes sees arrival at the truth in terms of setting hypotheses into competition with one another. But the weighing of the alternatives includes not only a comparison of them in terms of *probability*. Explanations must always be considered in terms of their *possibility*. The *possible*, however, is determined not only by the feasibility of the suggested events. It is also the remaining result of elimination of those alternative hypotheses perceived to be impossible. Holmes often repeats "the old axiom that when all other contingencies fail, whatever remains, however improbable, must be the truth."[88]

Though the analytic process described above is primarily an exercise in logic without direct recourse to the empirical world, Holmes next demanded the empirical validation of the resulting hypotheses in terms which closely approximate what is today called the *hypothetico-deductive* method.[89]

> I will give my process of thought. . . . That process . . . starts upon the supposition that when you have eliminated all which is impossible, that whatever remains, however improbable, must be the truth. It may well be that several explanations remain, in which case one tries test after test until one or other of them has a convincing amount of support.[90]

For

> when the original intellectual deduction is confirmed point by point by quite a number of independent accidents, then the subjective becomes objective and we can say confidently that we have reached our goal.[91]

Throughout Holmes's approach, logical (mostly deductive) and empirical (mostly inductive) considerations are in constant inter-relation. The empirical restricts the theoretical, as in the case where Holmes states that

> It *is* impossible as I state it, and therefore I must in some respect have stated it wrong.[92]

But empirical events must be interpreted in terms of established theoretical considerations. Thus, when a fact appears to be opposed to a long train of deductions, it invariably proves to be capable of having some other interpretation.[93]

In a very real and practical sense, Holmes's method anticipated the contemporary emphasis in sociology upon the intertwining relationships between theory and research (cf., Merton, 1957: 85–117).

The Application of Holmes's Method. Thus far, we have outlined Holmes's general approach to the problematic in social life. We turn now to a consideration of the limitations of that approach, especially as exemplified in Holmes's own applications of his method.

HOLMES'S USES OF OBSERVATION. Throughout the adventures, Holmes insists upon intensive familiarization of the investigator with his problem, for familiarity will bring clarification. He notes that "it is a mistake to confound strangeness with mystery." Familiarity is seen as generally reducing the problematic elements in an event. He even states that

as a rule . . . the more bizarre a thing is the less mysterious it proves to be.[95]

Familiarization can also remove fear, for the unfamiliar leaves us room for imagination, and "where there is no imagination, there is no horror."[96]

Holmes attempted to familiarize himself with all possible observable details of life which might have a bearing upon his criminal cases. This familiarization was not just the result of passive observation but includes the active search for new details of meaning which might prove useful in the future. Thus, for example, Holmes was described as having at one time beaten a corpse to discern how bruises might be produced after death.[97]

Holmes argued, as we have noted, that all human actions leave some traces from which the discerning investigator can deduce information. This emphasis on obtaining indirect data from sources through observation of physical traces constitutes an early recognition of the potential uses of what recently have been termed *unobtrusive measures.* (Webb et al., 1966: 35). Again and again, Holmes concerns himself with the small details about those involved in his inquiries.

> I can never bring you to realize the importance of sleeves, the suggestiveness of thumbnails, or the great issues that may hang from a boot lace.

> Always look at the hands first, . . . then cuffs, trouser-knees and boots.[99]

> [T]here is no part of the body which varies so much as the human ear. Each ear is as a rule quite distinctive, and different from all other ones.[100]

> It would be difficult to name any articles which afford a finer field for inference than a pair of glasses.[101]

> Pipes are occasionally of extraordinary interest. . . . Nothing has more individuality save, perhaps, watches and bootlaces.[102]

Nor does Holmes restrict his observations to things seen or heard. The investigator should develop his sense of smell, too, for

> there are seventy-five perfumes, which it is very necessary that a criminal expert should be able to distinguish from each other, and cases have more than once within my own experience depended upon their prompt recognition.[103]

Possibly the most important and frequent among the traces carefully examined by Holmes is the footprint. Of it he says:

> There is no branch of detective science which is so important and so much neglected as the art of tracing footprints.[104]

Even the traces of bicycle tires are not left unconsidered by Holmes, who claims at one point that he can differentiate some forty-two different "tyre impressions."[105]

Though Holmes's uses of the observable differences which he notes and conveys to the reader are often fantastic and hardly practicable in the "real world" outside the pages of the canon, the basic approach represented by these fictional narratives has startling parallels in the actual world of criminalistics and forensic medicine (e.g., cf. Stewart-Gordon, 1961) where true cases of detection through subtle observation and inference are often far more startling than anything ever suggested by Sir Arthur Conan Doyle.

THE CHARACTER OF HOLMES'S INFERENCES. Although examples of Holmes's remarkable uses of inference abound in the Sherlockian literature, as with his basic method, little attention has been given to an examination of the logic of his applications (minor, largely noncritical and merely admiring studies would include those of Hart, 1948; Schenck, 1953; Mackenzie, 1956; Ball, 1958; and, especially, Hitchings, 1946).

Careful examination of the sixty narratives that comprise the canon reveals at least 217 clearly described and discernible cases of inference (unobtrusive measurement) made by Holmes. Many of these are strung together in logical chains with Holmes gathering a great deal of information from a single object or event.[106] Thus, numerous instances appear in one story (at least thirty in "A Study in Scarlet") with few or none (as in "The Adventure of the Dying Detective") in others.

Although Holmes often speaks of his *deductions*, these are actually quite rarely displayed in the canon. Nor are Holmes's most common inferences technically *inductions*. More exactly, Holmes consistently displays what C. S. Peirce has called *abductions*.[107] Following Peirce's distinctions, the differences between deduction, induction, and abduction can be seen as follows:

DEDUCTION

Case All serious knife wounds result in bleeding.
Result This was a serious knife wound.
∴ *Rule* There was bleeding.

INDUCTION

Case This was a serious knife wound.
Result There was bleeding.
∴ *Rule* All serious knife wounds result in bleeding.

ABDUCTION

Rule All serious knife wounds result in bleeding
Result There was bleeding.
∴ *Case* This was a serious knife wound.

Abductions, like inductions, are not logically self-contained, as is the deduction, and they need to be externally validated. Peirce sometimes called abductions *hypotheses* (he also called them *presumptive inferences* at times), and in the modern sense, that is what the conclusion in the abduction represents: a conjecture about reality which needs to be validated through testing.

The great weakness in Holmes's applications of inference—at least as Watson related them to us—was Holmes's failure to test the hypotheses which he obtained through abduction. In most instances, Holmes simply treated the abducted inference as though it were logically valid. (Most of the parodies on Holmes are built upon this weakness in the narratives.) The simple fact is that the vast majority of Holmes's inferences just do not stand up to logical examination. He concludes correctly simply because the author of the stories allows it so.[108] Upon occasion, the abductive inferences are strung together in a long narrative series which the startled client (or Watson) confirms at each step. In a sense, this constitutes a degree of external corroboration of the hypotheses (especially where they are made about things correctly known to the listener, which is often the case). Nonetheless, in the vast majority of instances, the basic reasoning process described by Watson whereby Holmes astounds his listeners must, in the final analysis, be judged logically inadequate if not invalid.

Despite the logical inadequacies of Holmes's abductions, it must be noted that Holmes does actually hypothesis test (i.e., seek external validation) in at least twenty-eight instances (though not even all of these occasions are directly related to the minimum of 217 abductions found in the canon). Several of the stories include more than one case of hypothesis testing ("Silver Blaze" and "A Study in Scarlet" both evidence three such tests), but most of the narratives show no such attempts at external confirmation by Holmes. The best example of such testing by Holmes occurs in the story of Holmes's search for the missing race horse Silver Blaze. Postulating that the horse's leg was to be operated upon by an amateur to damage it, Holmes reasoned that the culprit would probably practice the operation beforehand to gain skill and assure success. Since sheep were nearby, Holmes further conjectured that the culprit might have practiced upon them. Inquiring about the sheep, Holmes learned that several of them had recently and inexplicably gone lame. The sheep's predicted lameness thus acted as a confirmation of Holmes's conjectures.[109]

The reconstruction of Holmes's methods and the extraction of the fundamental ideas in his thought is necessarily incomplete. Holmes relates only bits and pieces to us through the narratives of Dr. Watson, and even these items are stated sparingly. Watson noted of Holmes that "he pushed to an extreme the axiom that the only safe plotter was he who plotted alone."[110] And as Holmes put it:

> I do not waste words or disclose my thoughts while a case is actually under consideration.[111]

> I claim the right to work in my own way and give my results at my own time—complete, rather than in stages.[112]

Despite these obstacles, we have seen that a general reconstruction is possible, and it reveals a systematic and consistent orientation.

HOLMES AND SOCIAL PSYCHOLOGY

Just as with his basic method, examination of the canon reveals a large number of statements and insights, many stated in near-propositional and testable form about many aspects of social and psychological reality. We turn now to a look at some of the observations.

Holmes on Character and Personality. Holmes brings the same skepticism which served him as a detective of crimes into his general orientation towards the social world. As is the case with most social psychologists who term themselves symbolic interactionists (cf. Stone and Farberman, 1970), Holmes was much aware that people's definitions of their situations, their phenomenological perception of their worlds, rather than physical realities, may be the important factors which determine their actions.

> What you do in this world is a matter of no consequence. . . . The question is what can you make people believe you have done.[113]

Holmes's skepticism of appearances bordered upon the paranoic when it came to women. Holmes was especially cautious in his relations with women and found it nearly impossible to correctly assess their motives.

> Women are never to be entirely trusted—not the best of them.[114]

> [T]he motives of women are so inscrutable. . . . Their most trivial action may mean volumes, or their most extraordinary conduct may depend upon a hairpin or a curling-tongs.[115]

He showed special concern about the socially isolated female.

> One of the most dangerous classes in the world . . . is the drifting and friendless woman. She is the most harmless, and often the most useful of mortals, but she is the inevitable inciter of crime in others. She is helpless. She is migratory. She has sufficient means to take her from country to country and from hotel to hotel. She is lost, as often as not, in a maze of obscure pensions and boarding houses. She is a stray chicken in a world of foxes. When she is gobbled up she is hardly missed.[116]

Yet, Holmes was no misogynist (as is well seen in his admiration for Irene Adler who bested him in "A Scandal in Bohemia"), and he placed great value on female intuition.

> I have seen too much not to know that the impression of a woman may be more valuable than the conclusion of an analytic reasoner.[117]

Holmes mentions several generalizations about women which proved valuable to him in successfully analyzing his cases, but these were highly specific to their situations and probably would not stand up under rigorous investigation in other contexts.[118]

In attempting to read a subject's character and motives, Holmes used a variety of subtle indicators. The movement of the subject's eyes and body were carefully noted (such study of "body language" is today called kinesics):

> I can read in a man's eye when it is his own skin that he is frightened for.[119]

And, seeing a young lady client's motions on the street as she approached his apartment, he noted:

> Oscillation upon the pavement always means an affaire du coeur.[120]

Extensive examination was always given not only to the subject under investigation but also to those with whom he associated, including children and animals.

> I have frequently gained my first real insight into the character of parents by studying their children.[121]

And

> I have serious thoughts of writing a small monograph upon the uses of dogs in the work of the detective. . . . A dog reflects the family life. Whoever saw a frisky dog in a gloomy family, or a sad dog in a happy one? Snarling people have snarling dogs, dangerous people have dangerous ones. And their passing moods may reflect the passing moods of others.[122]

Holmes suggested a number of interesting ideas about personality. Thus, he endorsed the idea of complementarity in mate selection:

> You may have noticed how extremes call to each other, the spiritual to the animal, the cave-man to the angel.[123]

He argued that excellence at chess was "one mark of a scheming mind."[124] He claimed that all the misers were jealous men,[125] and that "jealously is a strong transformer of characters."[126] Recognizing the importance of man's inferiorities, Holmes noted that "weakness in one limb is often compensated for by exceptional strength in the others."[127] Regarding the appreciation of subtle variations by those with expertise, he noted that

> to the man who loves art for its own sake, . . . it is frequently in its least important and lowliest manifestations that the keenest pleasure is to be derived.[128]

And of a man's stubborn psychological inertia, he generalized that

> a man always finds it hard to realize that he may have finally lost a woman's love, however badly he may have treated her.[129]

All these generalizations must remain questionable until empirically tested, but these maxims suggest interesting and potentially fruitful directions for future research.

Holmes as Criminologist. Thus far, we have been primarily concerned with Holmes's general orientation to the investigation and perception of the realities of social life. As a consulting detective, however, his primary concern was with legal and moral crimes. We turn now to examine his insights and observations into this more specialized domain.

HOLMES ON JUSTICE AND DECEPTION.   Holmes felt that his personal hardships were "trifling details" that "must never interfere with the investigation of a case."[130] But he was far from the usual stereotype most people have of the daring hero. Though a brave man, Holmes did not ignore adversity, for he thought that "it is stupidity rather than courage to refuse to recognize danger when it is close upon you."[131] Far more contrary to the pure heroic image, however, was the fact that Holmes's activities sometimes ran counter to the law. As an unofficial investigator, he was not bound to the conventions of the police. He had little respect for the abilities of Scotland Yard's men and thought them generally "a bad lot" (though he did display respect for the abilities of the Yard's Inspector Tobias Gregson). He went even further in his disdain for other police, as when he noted that "local aid is always either worthless or biased."[132] Holmes was well aware of the inadequacies of law enforcement and commented that "many men have been wrongfully hanged."[133]

Holmes did apparently have a degree of faith in the ultimate victory of justice, as indicated in his statement that

> violence does, in truth, recoil upon the violent, and the schemer falls into the pit which he digs for another.[134]

But Holmes sometimes finds it necessary to go outside the law to assure justice. Thus, he occasionally commits trespass, burglary, and unlawful detention. Of the most serious of these, burglary, he argues that it

> is morally justifiable so long as our object is to take no articles save those which are used for an illegal purpose.[135]

He adopted this basically vigilante role because, as he put it:

> I think that there are certain crimes which the law cannot touch, and which therefore, to some extent, justify private revenge.[136]

Holmes also recognized that prison was not always an appropriate punishment for a crime, and that it might actually deter the process of reform. Thus, on at least fourteen occasions Holmes actually allowed known felons to go free (Leavitt, 1940: 27), for as he said of one such man he released: "Send him to gaol now, and you make him a gaolbird for life."[137]

Holmes was also not beyond deception if he felt it might suit the ends of justice. This went to rather extreme lengths when he attempted to trap "the worst man in London" by disguising himself as a plumber and becoming engaged to the villain's maid to obtain information.[138] Holmes was aware of the need to obtain the full confidence of his informants, and this he sometimes did by passing himself off as one of them. Thus, on one occasion when he needed certain information, he disguised himself as a groom, explaining to Watson that

> there is a wonderful sympathy and freemasonry among horsey men. Be one of them, and you will know all that there is to know.[139]

On other occasions, Holmes faked illnesses, accidents, information, and even his own death. He often used the newspapers in a manipulative manner[140] and noted that "the press . . . is a most valuable institution, if you only know how to use it."[141]

HOLMES ON CRIME. Sherlock Holmes was well aware of the fact that crime rates normally show only *reported* instances of law violation. Thus, in looking at the pleasant countryside through which he and Dr. Watson were moving by train. Holmes remarked to Watson:

> You look at these scattered houses, and you are impressed by their beauty. I look at them, and the only thought which comes to me is a feeling of their isolation, and of the impunity with which crime may be committed there. . . . They always fill me with a certain horror. It is my belief . . . founded upon my experience, that the lowest and vilest alleys in London do not present a more dreadful record of sin than does the smiling and beautiful countryside. . . . [And] the reason is very obvious. The pressure of public opinion can do in the town what the law cannot accomplish. There is no lane so vile that the scream of a tortured child, or the thud of a drunkard's blow, does not beget sympathy and indignation among the neighbours, that a word of complaint can set it going, and there is but a step between the crime and the dock. But look at these lonely houses, each in its own

fields, filled for the most part with poor ignorant folk who know little of the law. Think of the deeds of hellish cruelty, the hidden wickedness which may go on year in, year out, in such places, and none the wise.[142]

As with his views on personality, Holmes offers us numerous maxims about crime and criminal investigation which the contemporary criminologist might well consider. Thus, Holmes claimed that there was a potential relationship between the unusual and the criminal, as when he pointed out that "there is but one step from the grotesque to the horrible"[143] and "often the grotesque has deepened into the criminal."[144] Yet, he also warned us that we should not assume such a relationship to be automatic for

> the strangest and most unique things are very often connected not with the larger but with the smaller crimes, and occasionally, indeed, where there is room for doubt whether any positive crime has been committed.[145]

Holmes found two types of crime especially difficult to unravel. He found the "senseless" or motiveless crime the greatest challenge for the criminal investigator.

> The most difficult crime to track is the one which is purposeless.[146]

But where a discernible motive is involved, the planned crime presents great difficulties for a detective also, for

> where a crime is coolly premeditated, then the means of covering it are coolly premeditated also.[147]

This realization of the hidden complexities potential within a planned crime led Holmes to be most suspicious in such cases, especially of suspects with seemingly solid alibis, for, he noted, "only a man with a criminal enterprise desires to establish an alibi."[148] Finally, it might be noted that in addition to seeing these two types of crime as formidable, Holmes also recognized special difficulty with cases where the criminal was an M.D.

> When a doctor does go wrong he is the first of criminals. He has nerve and he has knowledge.[149]

CANONICAL ERRORS AND ANTICIPATIONS. As might be expected, the adventures sometimes show Holmes stating scientifically erroneous ideas. These largely reflect the popular notions of his time. Thus, Holmes placed far too great an emphasis on heredity as a causative factor in the creation of criminals. He referred to an hereditary criminal strain in the blood of the arch-villain Professor Moriarty[150] and strongly stated his views when he said:

> There are some trees . . . which grow to a certain height and then suddenly develop some unsightly eccentricity. You will see it often in humans. I have a theory that the individual represents in his development the whole procession of his ancestors, and that such a sudden turn to good or evil stands for some strange influence which came into the life of his pedigree. The person becomes, as it were, the epitome of the history of his own family.[151]

Holmes also seems to share some of the stereotypes and prejudices of his Victorian world as regarded some minority groups. Thus, he displayed mild prejudice towards Negroes and Jews.[152]

He also had some unusual and false ideas about thought processes. We have already mentioned his view of memory as similar to an attic which can become over-crowded.[153] He also showed a degree of misunderstanding of cognitive processes in the following statements:

> To let the brain work without sufficient material is like racing an engine. It racks itself to pieces.[154]

> [T]he faculties become refined when you starve them.[155]

And

> Intense mental concentration has a curious way of blotting out what has passed.[156]

Despite such occasional lapses into the misinformation common to his historical period, Holmes managed to pioneer in the anticipation of several innovations in scientific crime detection. Since the science of ballistics was unknown to police prior to 1909 (cf. Baring-Gould, 1967:II, p. 349, note 51), Holmes's statement about a villain in a story first published in 1903 that "the bullets alone are enough to put his head in a noose"[157] seems to show him to be a true pioneer in this field. Holmes was also an early advocate of the importance of both fingerprints,[158] and the Bertillon system of measurement.[159]

Among the most interesting of his anticipations was his realization of the possibility of distinguishing and identifying different types of communications. He was able to spot identifying differences between a wide variety of printing types in newspapers and magazines, and he stated that

> the detection of types is one of the most elementary branches of knowledge to the special expert of crime.[160]

And, more important, he early recognized that typewriters could be identified.

> It is a curious thing . . . that a typewriter has really quite as much individuality as a man's handwriting. Unless they are quite new, no two of them write exactly alike. Some letters get more worn than others, and some wear only on one side.[161]

But most of all, Holmes strongly believed in the great knowledge which could be gained through the careful examination of handwritings (cf. Christie, 1955; Swanson, 1962). Holmes not only pioneered in this study but went considerably beyond what most graphologists would yet claim for their science when he made the statements that

> the deduction of a man's age from his writing is one which has been brought to a considerable accuracy by experts.[162]

And that

> a family mannerism can be traced in . . . two specimens of writing.[163]

Finally, it should be noted that Holmes may have anticipated some of the devices of later psychoanalysis. Thus, it would appear that he saw the basis for tests of free-association, for in analyzing a coded message which contained seemingly extraneous and meaningless words, he noted of the writer:

> He would naturally use the first words which came to his mind, and if there were so many which referred to sport among them, you may be tolerably sure that he is either an ardent shot or interested in breeding.[164]

Holmes also clearly understood the defense mechanism of projection when he stated of a villain:

It may only be his conscience. Knowing himself to be a traitor, he may have read the accusation in the other's eyes.[165]

And at another point, when speaking of the subtle influences of music, he would seem to have closely paralleled the idea of archetypes within the collective unconscious as later developed by Carl G. Jung when he said:

There are vague memories in our souls of the misty centuries when the world was in its childhood.[166]

Holmes, then, shared many of the errors of the men of his time, but, as we hope has been adequately shown in this essay, he also extended our view of man. Given the extraordinary popularity of the tales of his adventures, created for us through the genius of Sir Arthur Conan Doyle, for many criminologists who recognized the merits of the detective's methods, it is doubtful that Sherlock Holmes could have had a greater impact on the sciences of man had he actually lived.

NOTES

1. The fully accepted Holmes legend appears in four full-length novels and fifty-six short stories. Though a great many editions of the works exist, the most recent and authoritative version of the tales is to be found in William S. Baring-Gould's beautifully edited and introduced *The Annotated Sherlock Holmes* in two volumes (1967). *All reference to the Holmes stories throughout this essay refer to this edition and its pagination.*

   In addition to the above works (called the "canon" or the "sacred writings" by Sherlockian scholars), Holmes is also believed to figure prominently in two other stories by Arthur Conan Doyle ("The Man With the Watches" and "The Lost Special") available as *The Sherlockian Doyle* (1968). There also was published a posthumously discovered manuscript which was at first thought to have been written by Sir Arthur Conan Doyle as "The Case of the Man Who Was Wanted" (1948). The authenticity of this piece has since been challenged with the result being general agreement that the story was actually written by a Mr. Arthur Whittaker, who had sold the story to Conan Doyle in 1913. For full details on this episode, see Brown (1969).

   Within the sixty narratives comprising the canon, mentions are made of at least fifty-five other cases (for a listing, see Starrett, 1960: 90–92). A minority of Sherlockians would therefore be inclined to include twelve other stories among the sacred writings which were written by Sir Arthur's son and official biographer, Adrian Conan Doyle and John Dickson Carr (1954).

In addition to the canon and its apocrypha plus some secondary references to Holmes by Doyle (most notably in several of his plays based on the stories), there is a vast literature based directly on the canon including over twenty-one plays, one Broadway musical, hundreds of radio and television productions, and at least 123 motion pictures. This is not to count the hundreds of books and articles dealing with Sherlockiana or the hundreds of pastiches and parodies of the canon, of which many of the best were anthologized by Ellery Queen (1944).

2. According to Sherlockians, of course, Doyle is not the author of the stories but merely an acquaintance of Holmes's associate, Dr. John Watson, who wrote (narrated) fifty-six of the sixty adventures in the canon. "The Adventure of the Blanched Soldier" and "The Adventure of the Lion's Mane" were apparently written by Holmes himself, and "The Adventure of the Mazarin Stone" and "His Last Bow" were written by person or persons unknown. Sherlockians have speculated about the authorship of these two narratives, suggesting everyone from Mrs. Mary Watson, Inspector Lestrade, a distant relative of Holmes called Dr. Verner, to Dr. Watson himself merely pretending to write in the third person. Even the rather extreme suggestion was made, first by the great Sherlockian scholar, Edgar W. Smith, that these two stories were written by Watson's friend Sir Arthur Conan Doyle. For full details on this controversy, see Baring-Gould (1967:II, pp. 748–50).

For biographical works on Sir Arthur Conan Doyle see: Carr (1949); Nordon (1967); Pearson (1943); Lamond (1931); and M. and M. Hardwick (1964). See also Doyle's autobiography (1924). Re Doyle's writings, see: Locke (1928): Nordon (1967: 347–51); and Carr (1949: 285–95).

3. The adventures themselves have been chronologized differently by numerous Sherlockians, but Baring-Gould (1967) sees them as spanning from 1874 to 1914. Far more controversially, in his biography of Holmes, Baring-Gould (1962) calculated Holmes's birth year as 1854 and placed his death in 1957. For other chronologies, see: Bell (1932); Blackeney (1932); Christ (1947); Brend (1951); Zeisler (1953); Baring-Gould (1955); and Folsom (1964).

4. E.g., Baring-Gould (1967) and Brend (1952). For a biographical study of Dr. John Watson, see Roberts (1931).

5. E.g., Park (1962) and M. and M. Hardwick (1962). Many other reference volumes on the canon exist including: Harrison (1958); Christ (1947); Bigelow (1959); Petersen (1956); Smith (1940); and Wolff (1952 and 1955).

6. Among the many excellent books and collections of Sherlockiana one must include: Bell (1934); Starrett (1934 and 1940); Smith (1944); and Holroyd (1967). A wide variety of such studies appear in the numerous Sherlockian journals. In addition to the best known *The Baker Street Journal*, published in New York, and *The Sherlock Holmes Journal*, published in London, there are many newsletters and other privately printed publications produced by Sherlockian groups around the United States, including: *The Vermissa Herald*, the *Devon County Chronicle*, *Shades of Sherlock*, and the annual *Pontine Dossier*. For an extensive critical bibliography, see Baring-Gould (1967:II, pp. 807–24).

7. The most well-known organization in the United States is the Baker Street Irregulars, born in 1933 in the "Bowling Green" column conducted by Christopher Morley in the *Saturday Review of Literature*.

For a brief history of the B.S.I., see Starrett (1960: 128–36). The B.S.I. has Scion Societies (chapters) all over the world including the Orient. Re the Sherlockian organizations see: Baring-Gould (1967:I, pp. 37–42); and Starrett (1960: 128–36).

8. Though these movements have failed thus far, numerous other memorials have been erected to Holmes's memory including plaques in Piccadilly, at St. Bartholomew's Hospital, at the Rosslei Inn in Meiringen, Switzerland, and even at the Reichenbach Falls. For full information, see Baring-Gould (1967:I, pp. 43–46).

9. For a somewhat more critical view of Holmes as criminologist, see Anderson (1903).

10. Nordon (1967: 214) has argued that Doyle's description of Bell is "too like Holmes to be true," and that the model for Holmes was "invented" by Doyle a *posteriori* to fit the image of a proper man of science. Pearson (1943) suggested that Holmes was largely patterned after one Dr. George Budd, Doyle's eccentric medical partner with whom he briefly practiced at Plymouth. More recently, it has been convincingly argued that Holmes was basically patterned after the private consulting detective Mr. Wendel Shere (Harrison 1971).

11. *The Spectator* said of him: "The fights that he made for victims of perverted justice will stand alongside Voltaire's championship of Jean Calas and Emile Zola's long struggle for Dreyfus" (quoted in Anonymous, 1959: 67).

12. "The Adventure of the Blanched Soldier," II, p. 720.

13. "The Problem of Thor Bridge," II, p. 605.

14. "The Valley of Fear," I, p. 507.

15. "A Study in Scarlet," I, p. 179.

16. "The Valley of Fear," I, p. 512.

17. "The Hound of the Baskervilles," II, p. 20.

18. *Ibid.*

19. "The Adventure of the Sussex Vampire," II, p. 463.

20. " 'What is the meaning of it, Watson,' said Holmes solemnly as he laid down the paper. 'What object is served by this circle of misery and violence and fear? It must tend to some end or else our universe is ruled by chance, which is unthinkable. But what end? There is the great standing perennial problem to which human reason is as far from an answer as ever.' " "The Cardboard Box," II, p. 208.

21. "Our highest assurance of the goodness of Providence seems to me to rest in the flowers. All other things, our powers, our desires, our food, are really necessary for our existence in this first instance. But this rose is an extra. Its smell and its colour are an embellishment of life, not a condition of it. It is only goodness which gives extras, and so I say again that we have much to hope from the flowers." "The Naval Treaty," II, p. 178.

22. "The Adventure of the Retired Colourman," II, p. 546.

23. "The Five Orange Pips," I, p. 398.

24. "A Study in Scarlet," I, p. 159.

25. "The Sign of the Four," I, p. 666. In this passage, Holmes indicates his agreement with Winwood Reade's *The Martyrdom of Man* which Holmes actually misquotes. Cf., Crocker (1964).

26. "A Study in Scarlet," I, p. 168. Re this statement, see W. J. Bell (1947).

27. "The Valley of Fear," I, p. 479.

28. "The Sign of the Four," I, p. 610.
29. "The Valley of Fear," I, pp. 481—82.
30. "A Scandal in Bohemia," I, pp. 349—50.
31. "The Adventure of the Second Stain," I, p. 311.
32. "A Study in Scarlet," I, p. 166.
33. "The Adventure of Wisteria Lodge," II, p. 246.
34. "The Adventure of the Speckled Band," I, p. 261.
35. "The Adventure of the Copper Beeches," II, p. 120.
36. "The Sign of the Four, I, p. 614.
37. "The Adventure of the Sussex Vampire," II, p. 467—68.
38. "The Problem of Thor Bridge," II, p. 589.
39. "The Reigate Squires," I, p. 335.
40. *Ibid.*, p. 341.
41. "The Adventure of the Blanched Soldier," II, p. 707.
42. "The Adventure of the Dancing Men," II, p. 527. Along similar lines, Holmes also stated that "every problem becomes very childish when once it is explained to you" (*Ibid.*, p. 528) and "results without causes are much more impressive" ("The Stockbroker's Clerk," II, p. 154).
43. "The Adventure of the Abbey Grange." II, p. 491. Holmes stated the matter more strongly when he told Watson: "Crime is common. Logic is rare. Therefore it is upon logic rather than upon the crime that you should dwell. You have degraded what should have been a course of lectures into a series of tales." "The Adventure of the Copper Beeches," II, p. 115.
44. *Ibid.*, p. 492.
45. "The Sign of the Four," I, p. 612.
46. "The Red Headed League," I, p. 419.
47. "The Valley of Fear," I, p. 512.
48. "A Study in Scarlet," I, p. 156.
49. *Ibid.*, p. 154.
50. *Ibid.*, p. 156. Holmes's many statements dealing with these very areas in other stories patently contradict Watson's early impressions of Holmes's astounding ignorance in these realms, and Holmes's statement to Watson that he was unaware of the basic Copernican Theory of the solar system is generally taken by most Sherlockians to have been intended as a joke by Holmes which Watson failed to perceive. Cf., Baring-Gould (1967: I, pp. 154—57, notes 30—44).
51. "A Study in Scarlet," I, p. 154.
52. "The Adventure of the Lion's Mane," II, p. 784.
53. "The Sign of the Four," I, p. 611.
54. "A Study in Scarlet," I, p. 171. For an excellent review of Holmes's uses of observations and their implications for modern criminological investigation, see Hogan and Schwartz (1964).
55. "The Reigate Squires," I, p. 341.
56. "The Sign of the Four," I, p. 619.
57. "A Scandal in Bohemia," I, p. 349.
58. "The Hound of the Baskervilles," II, p. 18.
59. "The Boscombe Valley Mystery," II, p. 137.
60. "The Adventure of the Blanched Soldier," II, p. 708.
61. "The Valley of Fear," I, p. 479.
62. "The Adventure of the Second Stain," I, p. 313.
63. "Silver Blaze," II, p. 277.
64. "The Man with the Twisted Lip," I, p. 379.

65. "A Study in Scarlet," I, p. 187.
66. "A Case of Identity," I, p. 409.
67. "The Boscombe Valley Mystery," II, p. 148.
68. "A Case of Identity," I, p. 411.
69. "The Adventure of Black Peter," II, p. 402.
70. "The Adventure of the Dancing Men," II, p. 543.
71. "A Study in Scarlet," I, p. 231.
72. *Ibid.*
73. "Silver Blaze," II, p. 262.
74. "The Reigate Squires," I, p. 34.
75. "The Hound of the Baskervilles," II, p. 109.
76. "The Boscombe Valley Mystery," II, p. 135.
77. "A Study in Scarlet," I, p. 231.
78. "The Adventure of Shoscombe Old Place," II, p. 636.
79. "A Case of Identity," I, p. 404.
80. "The Adventure of the Noble Bachelor," I, p. 291.
81. "The Boscombe Valley Mystery," II, p. 136.
82. "The Adventure of the Retired Colourman," II, p. 556.
83. "The Musgrave Ritual," I, p. 137. Holmes believed that getting into the same environment could facilitate this process for he said: "I shall sit in that room and see its atmosphere brings me inspiration. I'm a believer in the *genius loci*." "The Valley of Fear," I, p. 508.
84. "The Adventure of Black Peter," II, p. 410.
85. *Ibid.*, p. 408.
86. "The Disappearance of Lady Carfax," II, p. 665.
87. "The Hound of the Baskervilles," II, p. 24.
88. "The Adventure of the Bruce-Partington Plans," II, p. 446. Also cf., "The Sign of the Four," I, pp. 613–38; and "The Adventure of the Beryl Coronet," II, p. 299.
89. The hypothetico-deductive method is by no means new, for it can even be seen in the works of the ancient Greek philosopher Parmenides. For an excellent modern statement on this approach to knowledge, see Popper (1968, pp. 215–50).
90. "The Adventure of the Blanched Soldier," II, p. 720.
91. "The Adventure of the Sussex Vampire," II, p. 472.
92. "The Adventure of the Priory School," II, p. 620.
93. "A Study in Scarlet," I, p. 194.
94. *Ibid.* At another point, Holmes quotes Tacitus's Latin maxim that "everything unknown passes for something splendid." "The Red-Headed League," I, p. 421.
95. "The Red-Headed League," I, p. 428.
96. "A Study in Scarlet," I, p. 179.
97. *Ibid.*, p. 149.
98. "A Case of Identity," I, p. 411.
99. "The Adventure of the Creeping Man," pp. 762–63.
100. "The Cardboard Box," II, p. 202.
101. "The Adventure of the Golden Pince-Nez," II, p. 356.
102. "The Yellow Face," I, p. 576.
103. "The Hound of the Baskervilles," II, p. 110.
104. "A Study in Scarlet," I, p. 232.
105. "The Adventure of the Priory School," II, p. 617.
106. According to Ball (1958), this ability is epitomized by what Ball argues are Holmes's twenty-three deductions from a single scrap of

paper in "The Reigate Squires," I, pp. 331–45.

107. For full clarification of Peirce on abduction, the reader is best referred to: Cohen (1949: 131–53); Feibleman (1946: 116–32); Goudge (1950: 195–99); and Buchler (1955: 150–56). For an excellent brief survey of the general problems of induction, see Black, 1967.

108. Noting the logical discrepancies in Holmes's reasoning, one Sherlockian has commented that Holmes's successful conclusions might be accounted for by the suggestion that Holmes had psychic powers of extra-sensory perception (Reed, 1970). Holmes remarkable abilities actually approximate the reading of Watson's mind in "The Cardboard Box," II, pp. 194–95.

109. "Silver Blaze," II, pp. 277–81.

110. "The Adventure of the Illustrious Client," II, p. 684.

111. "The Adventure of the Blanched Soldier," II, p. 715.

112. "The Valley of Fear," I, p. 491.

113. "A Study in Scarlet," I, p. 231.

114. "The Sign of the Four," I, p. 656.

115. "The Adventure of the Second Stain," I, p. 311.

116. "The Disappearance of Lady Carfax," II, p. 657.

117. "The Man with the Twisted Lip," I, p. 380.

118. These include: "[T]here are few wives having any regard for their husbands who would let any man's spoken word stand between them and their husband's dead body." "The Valley of Fear," I, p. 506; "No woman would ever send a reply-paid telegram. She would have come." "The Adventure of Wisteria Lodge," II, p. 238; and "When a woman thinks that her house is on fire, her instinct is at once to rush to the thing which she values most. . . . A married woman grabs at her baby— an unmarried one reaches for her jewel box." "A Scandal in Bohemia," I, p. 364.

119. "The Resident Patient," I, p. 275.

120. "A Case of Identity," I, p. 406.

121. "The Adventure of the Copper Beeches," II, p. 129.

122. "The Adventure of the Creeping Man," II, p. 752. Recent years have seen social psychologists interested in a similar approach, e.g., see Levinson (1966).

123. "The Adventure of the Illustrious Client," II, p. 680. For a modern version of this idea, see Winch (1955).

124. "The Adventure of the Retired Colourman," II, p. 554.

125. Ibid.

126. "The Adventure of the Noble Bachelor," I, p. 291.

127. "The Man with the Twisted Lip," I, p. 376.

128. "The Adventure of the Copper Beeches," II, p. 114.

129. "The Musgrave Ritual," I, p. 137.

130. "The Hound of the Baskervilles," II, p. 110.

131. "The Final Problem," II, p. 302.

132. "The Boscombe Valley Mystery," II, p. 134.

133. Ibid., p. 138.

134. "The Adventure of the Speckled Band," I, p. 261.

135. "The Adventure of Charles Augustus Milverton," II, p. 563.

136. Ibid., p. 570.

137. "The Adventure of the Blue Carbuncle," I, p. 467.

138. "The Adventure of Charles Augustus Milverton," II, pp. 562–63. Holmes commonly obtains information from servants, especially the in-

vestigated subject's ex-employees, for Holmes noted that for information "there are no better instruments than discharged servants with a grievance." "The Adventure of Wisteria Lodge," II, p. 253.

139. "A Scandal in Bohemia," I, p. 356.
140. E.g., in "The Adventure of the Bruce-Partington Plans" (II, p. 449), Holmes planted a false notice in the "agony columns" to get the villain to reveal himself.
141. "The Adventure of the Six Napoleons," II, p. 580.
142. "The Adventure of the Copper Beeches," II, pp. 121–22.
143. "The Adventure of Wisteria Lodge," II, p. 259.
144. *Ibid.,* p. 238.
145. "The Red-Headed League," I, p. 419.
146. "The Naval Treaty," II, p. 179.
147. "The Problem of Thor Bridge," II, p. 600.
148. "The Adventure of Wisteria Lodge," II, p. 252.
149. "The Adventure of the Speckled Band," I, p. 257.
150. "The Final Problem," II, p. 303.
151. "The Adventure of the Empty House," II, p. 347.
152. Holmes apparently accepted the common stereotype of Caucasians that black people have extraordinary body odor for on one occasion he tells the black bruiser Steve Dixie, "I don't like the smell of you," and on another he snidely referred to looking for his scent-bottle. "The Adventure of the Three Gables," II, pp. 723 and 728. Holmes also seems to have accepted an anti-Semitic stereotype for he referred to a client in debt by saying that "He is in the hands of the Jews." "The Adventure of Shoscombe Old Place," I, p. 637.
153. "A Study in Scarlet," I, p. 154.
154. "The Adventure of the Devil's Foot," II, p. 514.
155. "The Adventure of the Mazarin Stone," II, p. 737.
156. "The Hound of the Baskervilles," II, p. 106.
157. "The Adventure of the Empty House," II, p. 348.
158. "The Adventure of the Norwood Builder," II, pp. 425–26.
159. "The Naval Treaty," II, p. 183.
160. "The Hound of the Baskervilles," II, p. 22.
161. "A Case of Identity," I, p. 414.
162. "The Reigate Squires," I, p. 342.
163. *Ibid.,* p. 341.
164. "The Gloria Scott," I, p. 115.
165. "The Valley of Fear," I, p. 473.
166. "A Study in Scarlet," I, pp. 178–79.

References

Anderson, Sir Robert. 1903. "Sherlock Holmes, Detective, as Seen by Scotland Yard." *T.P.'s Weekly* 2 (October 2): 557–58.

Anonymous. 1959. *Sir Arthur Conan Doyle Centenary 1859–1959.* London: John Murray.

Ashton-Wolfe, H. "The Debt of the Police to Detective Fiction." *The Illustrated London News,* February 27, 1932, pp. 320–28.

BALL, JOHN. 1958. "The Twenty-Three Deductions." *The Baker Street Journal* 8, N. S. (October): 234–37.

BARING-GOULD, WILLIAM S. 1955. *The Chronological Holmes*. New York: Privately printed.

————. 1962. *Sherlock Holmes of Baker Street: A Life of the World's First Consulting Detective*. New York: Bramhall House.

————. ed. 1967. *The Annotated Sherlock Holmes*. 2 volumes. New York: Clarkson N. Potter.

BELL, HAROLD W. 1932. *Sherlock Holmes and Dr. Watson: The Chronology of Their Adventures*. London: Constable and Co.

————. 1934. *Baker Street Studies*. London: Constable and Co.

BELL, WHITFIELD J., JR. 1947. "Holmes and History." *The Baker Street Journal* 2, Old Series (October): 447–56.

BERG, STANTON O. 1970. "Sherlock Holmes: Father of Scientific Crime Detection." *Journal of Criminal Law, Criminology, and Police Science* 61: 446–52.

BIGELOW, S. TUPPER. 1959. *An Irregular Anglo-American Glossary of More or Less Familiar Words, Terms and Phrases in the Sherlock Holmes Saga*. Toronto: Castalotte and Zamba.

BLACK, MAX. 1967. "Induction." In Paul Edwards et al., eds. *The Encyclopedia of Philosophy*. New York: Macmillan and Free Press, 169–81.

BLAKENEY, T. S. 1932. *Sherlock Holmes: Fact or Fiction?* London: John Murray.

BREND, GAVIN. 1951. *My Dear Holmes, A Study in Sherlock*. London: George Allen and Unwin.

BROWN, FRANCIS C. 1969. "The Case of the Man Who Was Wanted." *The Vermissa Herald: A Journal of Sherlockian Affairs* [published by the Scowrers, San Francisco, California] 3 (April): 12.

BUCHLER, JUSTUS (ed.). 1955 (1940). *Philosophical Writings of Peirce* [First published in 1940 as: *The Philosophy of Peirce: Selected Writings*]. New York: Dover.

CARR, JOHN DICKSON. 1949. *The Life of Sir Arthur Conan Doyle*. New York: Harper and Bros.

CHRIST, JAY FINLEY. 1947a. *An Irregular Guide to Sherlock Holmes of Baker Street*. New York: The Pamphlet House and Argus Books.

————. 1947. *An Irregular Chronology of Sherlock Holmes of Baker Street*. Ann Arbor, Michigan: Fanlight House.

CHRISTIE, WINIFRED M. 1955. "Sherlock Holmes and Graphology." *The Sherlock Holmes Journal* 2: 28–31.

COHEN, MORRIS R. (ed.). 1949. *Chance, Love and Logic* [First published in 1923]. No address: Peter Smith.

CROCKER, STEPHEN F. 1964. "Sherlock Holmes Recommends Winwood Reade." *The Baker Street Journal* 14, N.S. (September): 142–44.

DOYLE, ADRIAN M. CONAN. 1945. *The True Conan Doyle*. London: John Murray.

DOYLE, ADRIAN M. CONAN, and JOHN DICKSON CARR. 1954. *The Exploits of Sherlock Holmes*. New York: Random House.

DOYLE, SIR ARTHUR CONAN. 1930. *Memories and Adventures* [First published in 1924]. New York: Doubleday, Doran and Co., Crowborough edition.

————. 1948. "The Case of the Man Who Was Wanted." *Cosmopolitan* 125 (August): 48–51 and 92–99.

————. 1968. *The Sherlockian Doyle*. Culver City, California: Luther Norris.

FEIBLEMAN, JAMES. 1946. *An Introduction to Peirce's Philosophy, Interpreted As a System.* New York: Harper and Bros.

FOLSOM, HENRY T. 1964. *Through the Years at Baker Street: A Chronology of Sherlock Holmes.* Washington, New Jersey: Privately printed.

GOUDGE. 1950. *The Thought of C. S. Peirce.* Toronto, Ontario: University of Toronto Press.

HARDWICK, MICHAEL, and MOLLIE HARDWICK. 1962. *The Sherlock Holmes Companion.* London: John Murray.

————. 1964. *The Man Who Was Sherlock Holmes.* London: John Murray.

HARRISON, MICHAEL. 1958. *In the Footsteps of Sherlock Holmes.* London: Cassell and Co.

————. 1971. "A Study in Surmise." *Ellery Queen's Mystery Magazine* 57 (February): 60–79.

HART, ARCHIBALD. 1948. "The Effects of Trades Upon Hands." *The Baker Street Journal* 3, Old Series (October): 418–20.

HAYCRAFT, HOWARD. 1941. *Murder for Pleasure: The Life and Times of the Detective Story.* New York: D. Appleton-Century.

HITCHINGS, J. L. 1946. "Sherlock Holmes the Logician." *The Baker Street Journal* 1, Old Series (April): 113–17.

HOGAN, JOHN C., and MORTIMER D. SCHWARTZ. 1964. "The Manly Art of Observation and Deduction." *Journal of Criminal Law, Criminology and Police Science* 55: 157–64.

HOLROYD, JAMES EDWARD. 1967. *Seventeen Steps to 221B.* London: George Allen and Unwin.

LAMOND, JOHN. 1931. *Arthur Conan Doyle: A Memoir.* London: John Murray.

LEAVITT, R. K. 1940. "Nummi in Arca or The Fiscal Holmes." In VINCENT STARRETT ed. *221B: Studies in Sherlock Holmes.* New York: Macmillan, pp. 16–36.

LEVINSON, BORIS M. 1966. "Some Observations on the Use of Pets in Psychodiagnosis." *Pediatrics Digest* 8: 81–85.

LOCKE, HAROLD. 1928. *A Bibliographical Catalogue of the Writings of Sir Arthur Conan Doyle, M.D., LL.D., 1879–1928.* Tunbridge Wells: D. Webster.

MACKENZIE, J. B. 1956. "Sherlock Holmes' Plots and Strategies." *Baker Street Journal Christmas Annual,* pp. 56–61.

MAY, LUKE S. 1935. *Crime's Nemesis.* New York: Macmillan.

MERTON, ROBERT K. 1957. *Social Theory and Social Structure* [First published in 1949]. Glencoe, Illinois: Free Press.

MURCH, ALMA ELIZABETH. 1958. *The Development of the Detective Novel.* London: Peter Owen.

NORDON, PIERRE. 1967. *Conan Doyle: A Biography.* Translated by FRANCES PARTRIDGE. New York: Holt, Rinehart and Winston.

PARK, ORLANDO. 1962. *Sherlock Holmes, Esq., and John H. Watson, M.D.: An Encyclopedia of Their Affairs.* Evanston, Illinois: Northwestern University Press.

PEARSON, HESKETH. 1943. *Conan Doyle, His Life and Art.* London: Methuen.

PETERSEN, SVEND. 1956. *A Sherlock Holmes Almanac.* Washington, D.C.: Privately printed.

POPPER, KARL R. 1968. *Conjectures and Refutations: The Growth of Scientific Knowledge* [First published in 1962]. New York: Harper and Row, Torchbook edition.

Pratt, Fletcher. 1955. "Very Little Murder." *The Baker Street Journal* 2, N.S. (April): 69–76.

Queen, Ellery (ed.). 1944. *Misadventures of Sherlock Holmes.* Boston: Little, Brown and Co.

Reed, John Shelton. 1970. *The Other Side.* Unpublished manuscript (mimeo), Department of Sociology, University of North Carolina at Chapel Hill.

Roberts, Sir Sidney C. 1931. *Doctor Watson: Prolegomena to the Study of a Biographical Problem.* London: Faber and Faber.

Schenck, Remsen Ten Eyck. 1948. *Occupation Marks.* New York: Grune and Stratton.

――――――. 1953. "The Effect of Trades Upon the Body." *The Baker Street Journal* 3, N.S. (January): 31–36.

Smith, Edgar W. 1940. *Baker Street and Beyond: A Sherlockian Gazeteer,* with Five Detailed and Illustrated Maps by Julian Wolff, M.D. New York: The Pamphlet House.

――――――. 1944. *Profile by Gaslight: An Irregular Reader About the Private Life of Sherlock Holmes.* New York: Simon and Schuster.

Starrett, Vincent. 1940. *221B: Studies in Sherlock Holmes.* New York: Macmillan.

――――――. 1960. *The Private Life of Sherlock Holmes* [First published in a different edition in 1933]. Chicago: University of Chicago Press.

Steward-Gordon, James. 1961. "Real-Life Sherlock Holmes." *Readers Digest* 79 (November): 281–88.

Stone, Gregory, and Harvey A. Farberman (eds.). 1970. *Social Psychology Through Symbolic Interaction.* Waltham, Massachusetts: Ginn-Blaisdell.

Swanson, Martin J. 1962. "Graphologists in the Canon." *The Baker Street Journal* 12, N.S. (June): 73–80.

Webb, Eugene J., et al. 1966. *Unobtrusive Measures: Non-Reactive Research in the Social Sciences.* Chicago: Rand McNally.

Winch, R. F. 1955. "The Theory of Complementary Needs in Mate Selection: Final Results on the Test of the General Hypothesis." *American Sociological Review* 20: 552–55.

Wolff, Julian. 1952. *The Sherlockian Atlas.* New York: Privately printed.

――――――. 1955. *Practical Handbook of Sherlockian Heraldry.* New York: Privately printed.

Zeisler, Ernest B. 1953. *Baker Street Chronology: Commentaries on the Sacred Writings of Dr. John H. Watson.* Chicago: Alexander J. Isaacs.

II: THE SURVEY

DETECTIVES EMPLOY SURVEYS OF A SORT IN DETERMINING WHERE crime is likely to occur. Burglary detectives, for example, place pins on maps for every burglary in a given geographical area. Eventually certain blocks can be identified as being more burglary-prone than others, and various prevention measures can be taken to lower the number of crimes there. Sociological surveys, in the same way, are methods of finding the frequency and distribution of given dimensions in a specified population. *Frequency* refers to the number of times a given dimension can be found, *distribution* refers to where the dimension is found, and *population* or *universe* refers to the group of interest. Thus, the detective in the example above is interested in the dimension of burglary in terms of how often burglaries occur (frequency) in various places (distribution) among various groups (population) in the city where he works (universe).

Surveys are generally characterized by highly structured measurement instruments, most often questionnaires. The questionnaires direct the researcher to ask specific questions about the dimensions of interest or, in the case of an observation survey, to observe specific events and processes. This design serves at least two purposes. On the one hand, by determining the frequency and distribution of certain characteristics in a given population or universe, surveys *describe* social phenomenon (Simon, 1969:244). For example, the researcher can describe a city in terms of its crime rate, birth rate, divorce rate, suicide rate, religious preferences, or any other dimension of interest. Such descriptions can be used in comparing a given society to other societies or to compare the same society at different times, as an indicator of social change. A second use of surveys is a quasi-experimental one (Denzin, 1970:171). Various aspects may be surveyed to find out if there is a *relation* between them. For example, members of various social classes might be questioned about their political preferences. If the researcher finds that members of a lower socio-economic background are more likely to have liberal political preferences than are those of a higher socio-economic class, then he has found a relation between social class and political preferences.

To conduct a survey of a given universe, the researcher rarely observes or interviews every unit in the universe. Rather, he attempts to survey a *sample* that is representative of the entire universe (Goode and Hatt, 1952:209–31). It has been found that if the sample is correctly drawn, what is true for the sample will be true for the entire universe. Thus, instead of having to spend a good deal of time and money surveying the whole population of interest, the researcher can achieve the same results with only a sample of that population.

In order to maximize the probability that the sample is representative of the universe, researchers attempt to ensure that every significant aspect of the universe is proportionately represented. The more nearly homogeneous the population is, the easier it is to draw a representative sample, since most of the members of the population are similar in terms of the aspects of interest. In a heterogeneous and large population, it is more difficult to ensure that all viewpoints and groupings have been proportionately represented in the sample, and the researcher will need a larger sample in order to do so. In either type of universe, however, researchers employ *randomizing* techniques to draw the sample so that every unit, grouping, and variation in a universe is proportionately represented, since they all have the same chance of being part of the sample.

There are a number of sampling techniques employing random sampling (Freund, 1960), and three will be presented here. The *simple random sample* entails determining the number desired for your sample, and selecting all the desired numbers randomly from the units of the universe. If the universe is relatively small, such as all the students in a given major at a given university, you can write each name on a slip of paper, put the slips in a container, and choose the desired number. For a larger universe, such as those listed in a telephone directory, a list of automobile owners, voting registration, or a city directory, you can assign each unit (e.g., name or household) a number and then select a number that, divided into the total number of units, will give you the desired sample size. Then you can take every nth number to be included in your sample. For example, if you have a list of 1,000 names and want 100 in your sample, you take every tenth number on the list. A third method is to use a prepared table of random numbers such as that one provided by L. H. C. Tippett.* After assigning a number to each unit, you draw the units for the sample by going down, across, or diagonally through the table, taking the number corresponding to those in the list.

A second commonly used sample is the *stratified sample*. If you know the different groupings in your universe and you know what proportion of the universe each one represents, you can use a stratified sample effectively. For example, if you know from examining census data that your community is made up of four ethnic groups and you want to draw a sample in which each group is proportionately represented, instead of having to draw a relatively large simple random sample you can draw a relatively small stratified sample. If 40 per cent of the community is of European origin, 20 per cent Asian, 30 per cent African, and 10 per cent Indian, then by randomly selecting a number proportionate to each group's representation in the community, you will have a sample reflecting the ethnic backgrounds of the entire universe without having to take a large simple random sample. Each ethnic group is treated as a subuniverse, and a proportionate simple random sample is taken from each subuniverse.

In the *area* or *cluster sample*, the universe for the research is located geographically and is divided into areas, such as blocks, neighborhoods, or census tracts (Denzin, 1970:88). Each area is assigned a number and the areas to be included in the sample are randomly selected. The assumption is that there is a high degree of homogeneity within each of the areas sampled, and that those

---

* *Tracts for Computers*, Number XV, Karl Pearson (ed.). New York: Cambridge University Press, 1947.

who live in a given area are likely to interact with one another. Thus, for comparative and descriptive purposes, area samples are highly useful, for each grouping can be treated as a real cohort, in that those in the sample are likely to have social relationships with one another rather than simply similar social characteristics.

Often the researcher will want to combine one or more of these sampling techniques with another. In the study by Sanders and McCarthy (Chapter 4), the researchers used a combination of an area sample (cluster sample) and a stratified sample. The areas they used were different police sectors, and they stratified the areas on the amount of crime each area had. Thus, using a relatively small sample, they were able to sample a wide variety of households in terms of their likelihood to be subject to criminal victimization. At the same time they were able to ease the job of the interviewers by clustering the samples in confined areas.

In order to gather the necessary information from his sample, the survey researcher needs an instrument that will give him answers to his questions. This may seem obvious, but many inexperienced researchers construct questionnaires, interview schedules, or observation schedules without giving any thought to the question they are trying to answer. For example, some will automatically include questions about income, marital status, and ethnic background in any survey regardless of whether such information will answer their questions or not. Thus, before choosing or constructing an instrument for a survey, first determine what information is necessary and what questions will need to be asked or observations made to provide it.

Three of the most popular survey instruments are the questionnaire, the interview schedule, and the observation schedule.

The questionnaire is a self-administered set of questions that the researcher gives to the subjects in his sample. The items can either be open-ended (the respondent can give any answer he chooses, of any length he likes) or closed-ended (the respondent chooses from a limited number of responses, such as "true-false," or multiple choice) (Forcese & Richer, 1973:160). For example, a question about the subject's income that provided no categories of income to choose from would be open-ended. If the question asked the respondent to check one of five income groupings, the question would be closed-ended. Generally, open-ended questions are used to elicit new information when the researcher has no firm idea of what the answers might be. In the Ennis survey (Chapter 4), the researchers asked respondents who had been victims of crimes why they had not reported the crimes to the police. From the answers to this open-ended question they were able to derive certain categories that could be used in future surveys as closed-ended questions. In this manner, fixed-choice responses are developed from open-ended questions.

The *interview schedule* is like the questionnaire except that it is administered by an interviewer (Forcese and Richer, 1973:168–69). The advantage of the interview schedule over the questionnaire is that the interviewer can rephrase or explain a question that a respondent does not understand to ensure that the answer he gives is a response to the question intended. Also, an interview schedule can elicit feedback from the respondents. For example, if the interview schedule has a closed-ended question with a set of fixed-choice responses that are not reflective of what the respondents would normally choose as answers, the respondents can tell the interviewer; whereas with a questionnaire the subjects may simply fill in the fixed choices and offer no feedback.

The *observation schedule* is an instrument that directs the researcher to observe certain events in terms of fixed or open categories (Reiss, 1968). For example, in the Wiseman study of a drunk court (Chapter 5), the observer recorded the observed events in terms of a set of social types. Each social type was described in terms of a set of criteria, and the observer noticed the category each defendant fit best. Many items on an observation schedule can be phrased as questions, just like the items on interview schedules. For example, an observation schedule used in observing a court might include such questions as: "What tone of voice did the defendant use?" "What kind of reaction did the judge have to the defendant's story?"

All items on survey instruments should be constructed so that the responses can be compiled and analyzed once the data have been gathered. Generally this involves *coding* the responses and developing items in such a way that they can be coded. If the researcher has a good idea of what typical responses to questions might be, closed-ended questions greatly facilitate coding. For example, consider the following question:

What do you think of the drug laws?
- a. Too strict
- b. About right
- c. Too lenient
- d. Don't know

The researcher can simply compile the number and percentages of replies in terms of the four categories "a," "b," "c," or "d" and compare the responses with other items. However, with open-ended questions the researcher must develop categories after he has gathered the responses and then code the responses in terms of the categories he has developed. For example, if the question "What do you think of the drug laws?" were asked without a set of fixed-choice responses, the content of the responses might vary greatly. By examining the specific responses, the researcher may find that all or most fit one of the categories that we had on the fixed choice question, but we also might find other types of responses we had not considered. For example, we may find respondents saying that the laws regarding marijuana are too strict but the laws governing the sale of heroin are too lenient. Such responses would tell the researcher that the question is too broad, and he should break down the question into several dealing with different types of drugs. In this way, the researcher could develop coded responses for several questions rather than inappropriate fixed choices for a single question.

Once the items are coded and compiled, the researcher can describe his universe in terms of the items. If the survey included items pertaining to socio-economic class and the classes are coded in terms of upper class, middle class, working class, and lower class, the population might be described socio-economically as follows:

Upper class	5%
Middle class	40%
Working class	40%
Lower class	10%

In addition to describing a population, the researcher may want to find whether there is any relationship between certain variables —for example, between attitudes about abortion and social class. To find the effect, if any, of one variable on other, he *holds constant* one variable. That is, the researcher keeps the value of one variable unchanged, then looks to see the values of the other variables in relation to the one held constant. In comparing middle- and working-class respondents in their attitudes toward abortion, he first determines the frequency of attitudes for and against abortion in each class, thus holding social class constant (at the values of middle and working class). The findings may look something like this:

Middle Class
    Favor legalized abortion   70%
    Oppose legalized abortion 30%
Working Class
    Favor legalized abortion   30%
    Oppose legalized abortion 70%

From these figures, the researcher can see that more people who are middle class favor legalized abortion than people who are working class. To get a clearer picture of the relationship, the findings may be charted on a table with the *independent variable* (social class) making up the columns and the *dependent variable* (attitude toward legalized abortion) making up the rows.

Attitude Toward Legalized Abortion	Social Class	
	Working	Middle
Favor	30%	70%
Oppose	70%	30%

Now we can see a relationship between social class and attitudes toward legalized abortion. As the class changes (varies) from working to middle class, so do attitudes.

However, the researcher may not be willing to accept the relationship without further analysis. He may wonder, for example, whether or not religious preference may be more important than social class. To make this determination, the researcher divides the groupings of data so that social class and religion are held constant and observes the variation, if any, in attitudes toward legalized abortion. The following tables illustrate this re-analysis:

Working Class

Attitude Toward Legalized Abortion	Religion	
	Catholic	Protestant
Favor	30%	70%
Oppose	70%	30%

Middle Class

Attitude Toward Legalized Abortion	Religion	
	Catholic	Protestant
Favor	30%	70%
Oppose	70%	30%

Now we can see that 70 per cent of the Protestants favored legalized abortion regardless of social class, and 70 per cent of the Catholics opposed legalized abortion in both the middle and working classes. Therefore, we can see that social class and attitudes toward abortion is a *spurious relationship* (Blalock, 1970:17). What has happened is that there are more Catholics in the working-class sample and more Protestants in the middle-class sample. Assuming there is a relationship between social class and religion, we will always find more favorable attitudes toward abortions in the middle class than in the working class, but the religious variable is the explanatory one and not social class. In this context, religion is the *intervening variable* between social class and attitudes about legalized abortion with the relationship diagramatically looking like this:

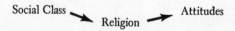

By including questions about more than a single variable, the researcher can design his questionnaire, interview, or observation schedule so that he will be able to determine whether any relationship is spurious or not. The flexibility of survey design allows the researcher to carry out numerous forms of analysis, and for this reason, it has become one of the favorites of sociologists.

The two studies that follow show two different uses for the survey. First, Sanders and McCarthy show how patterns of criminal victimization can be better described by the use of survey research and at the same time locate variations in crime reporting. In the second reading, Wiseman shows how an observation survey was used to test the hypothesis that there was a relationship between social type and court dispositions. These two studies should give an idea of some of the uses of the survey, but keep in mind that the flexibility of survey design limits its application only with one's imagination.

REFERENCES

BLALOCK, HUBERT M., JR. 1970. *An Introduction to Social Research.* Englewood Cliffs, N.J.: Prentice-Hall.

DENZIN, NORMAN K. 1970. *The Research Act.* Chicago: Aldine.

FORCESE, D. P., and STEPHEN RICHER. 1973. *Social Research Methods.* Englewood Cliffs, N.J.: Prentice-Hall.

FREUND, J. E., 1960. *Modern Elementary Statistics.* Englewood Cliffs, N.J.: Prentice-Hall.

GOODE, WILLIAM J., and PAUL K. HATT. 1952. *Methods in Social Research.* New York: McGraw-Hill.

REISS, ALBERT J., JR. 1968. "Stuff and Nonsense About Social Surveys and Observations." In Howard S. Becker et al. (eds.) *Institutions and the Person.* Chicago: Aldine.

SIMON, J. L. 1969. *Basic Research Methods in Social Science.* New York: Random House.

4. Questionnaire Survey

SURVEY OF CRIME VICTIMS
—William B. Sanders and Brian W. McCarthy

EVERY YEAR THE FEDERAL Bureau of Investigation publishes its *Uniform Crime Report*. When the report comes out, there is a general discussion of why crime has gone up in certain areas and down in others, why one type of crime has increased and another has decreased, and, occasionally, why the FBI report is next to worthless in telling us anything about crime. This last area of discussion has been generally limited to grumbling academics in criminology and sociology, but more recently certain police administrators whose towns and cities have been cited in the report as having an unusually high amount of crime have also begun voicing complaints about the FBI's annual report. This chapter discusses the problems with the report, an alternative method to be used, and what the problems with the alternative are.

THE PROBLEM WITH THE FBI UNIFORM CRIME REPORT

To begin with, the *Uniform Crime Report* (UCR) is an honest effort by the FBI to present a national picture of crime in the United States. Before the UCR was first published, our knowledge of crime nationally was next to nonexistent. However, ever since the inception of the UCR, there have been a number of problems that any such report, based on police records, would be bound to have.

This selection was prepared especially for this volume.

Generally, there are six major criticisms of crime statistics generated by the *UCR* (Cressey, 1957: 230–41). We shall discuss each one separately and provide examples of the problems:

1. *Not all crime is known in any given locality at a particular time.* For a crime to be recorded, it must be discovered, reported to the police, and recorded by the police. Consider, for example, a shoplifting. Someone goes into a store, takes something, and leaves without paying. If the shoplift goes unnoticed, as most probably do, there is no discovery, report, or recording of the larceny. Of the shoplifters apprehended, few are reported to the police, and of those reported to the police, not all are recorded. Since shoplifting is recorded under the "larceny" category in the *UCR*, just this one crime is massively underrecorded and the actual amount of larceny is much greater than the *UCR* would lead us to believe.

2. *Crime "indexes" do not maintain a constant ratio with the true crime rate.* Since there is no idea of the actual amount of crime, the crime "index" is not a known sample of the whole. Moreover, it is unknown whether the index is constant for all crimes. As we showed above with shoplifting, there is very little reported, but, on the other hand, we would expect that armed robberies would have a high incidence of report. Therefore, the reported shopliftings reflect one ratio and armed robberies reflect another.

3. *There is a wide variation in conditions affecting published records of crime.* Different jurisdictions have different reporting procedures, and sometimes the same jurisdictions change their procedures, so over a period of two years even in the same jurisdiction we do not know if the rates are comparable. Let's say that we want to compare New York City and Los Angeles. If the two cities have exactly the same report forms, the same reporting procedures, and everything else identical for compiling crime data, then we can compare them equitably. However, since these two cities have different reporting systems, different report forms, and even different state laws, it is nearly impossible to make equitable comparisons. The form turned in to the FBI does give some semblance of order, but since the FBI forms are filled out on the basis of the department's own recording system, even this device fails to make the reports "uniform."

4. *Crime statistics are compiled primarily for administrative purposes and not for scientific research.* Crime statistics are gathered not by trained researchers but by police officers in the course of their daily work. Whatever statistical error may exist is unknown, and often that error can be great. For example, in one jurisdiction an administrative order was sent down stating that all breaking and entering into vending machines would be logged as "vandalism" instead of burglary or larceny. By doing this, the administrator was able to "reduce" the number of index crimes in his jurisdiction, since "vandalism" is not reported in the FBI as an "index crime." Other reporting systems may be for the purposes of investigations; even though a crime is reported to the police, unless there are investigative leads for the detectives to solve the case (See Chapter 8), the crime may not be recorded at all.

5. *Statistics on variations in the recorded rates for some crimes are not routinely compiled.* Certain crimes, notably white-collar crimes, such as consumer fraud, violations of the Sherman Anti-Trust Act, and similar middle- and upper-class violations are never recorded. Since these types of crimes are predominately committed by the middle and upper class, the UCR crime figures make it look as though all of the crime is committed by the lower and working classes. What we get with the UCR report, then, is little more than a compilation of "poor crimes."

6. *The statistics on juvenile delinquency are inadequate because in America we have no precise definition of delinquency.* Delinquency, as a subcategory of crime, is ill defined in that what constitutes a delinquent act varies greatly over time and from place to place (Sanders, 1976). Juvenile status offenses (e.g. runaways, etc.) are applied only to those children under a certain age, but the age of juvenility ranges from fifteen years of age all the way to twenty-one, depending on the state. In order for statistics about juveniles to be of any use, it is necessary to have a single, well-defined conception of juvenile delinquency.

These six criticisms of the UCR crime statistics are only the principal ones. There are other criticisms, but for our purposes it is enough to note these six. What we must discuss now is an alternative to the UCR, a method of gathering crime statistics and data that will give us a clearer view of criminal activity without the pitfalls of the UCR system.

VICTIMIZATION SURVEYS

In 1842 Adolphe Jacques Quetelet noted that crime figures were some unknown ratio of the actual amount of crime (Sylvester, 1972: 28). This, he pointed out, was due primarily to the first of the six criticisms we listed—not all crime is known, not all known crime is reported, and not all reported crime is recorded. It took criminologists more than one hundred years to take this insight and attempt to do something to remedy the problem. The solution to this problem is the victimization survey.

The victimization survey is so simple that it is surprising it took sociologists and criminologists so long to begin using it. Basically, a victimization survey is no more than a survey of a population to determine the frequency and distribution of crime, and the ratio of reported to unreported crime. An interview schedule or questionnaire is used with questions asking whether or not a person has been the victim of various crimes and whether or not it was reported to the police. A sample of the population is surveyed, and the results are compiled much as statistics are compiled by the police.

The findings of victimization surveys have borne out what Quetelet predicted. More crimes are committed than are reported to the police or recorded by the police; different crimes have different likelihoods of being reported; and different jurisdictions have different ratios of known crime to reported crime. For example, of all burglaries and attempted burglaries known to victims in Houston, Texas, only 46 per cent were reported, while in Miami, Florida, 58 per cent of the burglaries and attempted burglaries were reported (U.S. Department of Justice, 1975: 78, 96). In Milwaukee, victims reported only 29 per cent of the thefts other than motor vehicle theft, while they reported 77 per cent of motor vehicle thefts (U.S. Department of Justice, 1975: 114). As can be seen from these figures alone, the criticisms of the UCR are well founded.

In order to find the amount of crime known to victims in a small university city, a class of students conducted a victimization survey. The rest of this chapter deals with how this study was carried out, the findings, and a discussion of the problems that were encountered in the survey. It is a simplified replication of the major victimization surveys, and it can be used, with modifications if necessary, in any town or city where a victimization survey is to be carried out.

METHODOLOGY

The victimization survey discussed here was conducted in a small university city with a population of 72,554. The universe consisted of all the residences or households within the city limits. The survey was performed in July and August as part of a research class project in which thirty-five participating students acted as interviewers. The purposes of the victimization survey were (1) to determine the frequency and distribution of crimes within three representative residential areas; (2) to determine the ratio of reported to unreported crimes; (3) to establish a baseline of crime with which to evaluate community crime prevention programs; and, (4) to determine why crimes are reported or not reported to the police, and which crimes are most likely to be reported or go unreported.

At the time of this study, the local police department used a large city map divided into seventy-two regions to designate the police "beats" within the city. In a previous study completed by a visiting police administrator, in which an overall crime rate had been computed for each of the seventy-two police beats according to their computed crime rates, it was possible to divide the city into high, medium, and low crime rate areas. The twenty-four city areas with the highest rates were designated "high" crime areas. The twenty-four areas immediately following were designated "medium" crime areas, and the lowest twenty-four areas were designated the "low" crime areas. The median area from each of these three categories was selected to be surveyed. Thus, a stratified area sample, based on reported crime, was developed with a high, a medium, and a low crime rate area chosen to be sampled.

In order to survey households, city maps were obtained which showed sufficient detail to be able to locate all individual residences within the selected areas. Each of these maps was then divided into subareas or grids. Each grid was numbered and those grids which did not depict residences were eliminated from the study.

Thirty-five student interviewers were divided into three groups corresponding to the three crime areas to be surveyed. Nine interviewers were assigned to the "low" crime area, fourteen to the "medium" crime area, and twelve to the "high" crime area. Each group member was then randomly assigned a numbered grid and instructed to draw a random sample of ten interviews in the grid. This procedure resulted in a thorough sampling of the households in each crime area.

The interview schedule employed was designed to gather data relevant to the incidence of personal and property crime victimization for the period beginning January 1 and ending June 30. Specifically, the interview schedule was divided into three parts. The first part dealt with demographic particulars, including the respondent's sex, ethnic identification, type of housing, length of time living at residence, and the number of household members. The second part consisted of questions concerning the occurrence and frequency of crimes, specifically larceny, assault, battery, rape, robbery, vandalism, breaking and entering, bicycle theft, assault with a deadly weapon, purse and/or wallet snatching, and consumer fraud. Information with respect to the reporting or nonreporting of each of these crimes was also recorded. The third part of the interview schedule was comprised of open-ended and Likert-scaled questions designed to tap respondents' attitudes regarding the police, their trustworthiness and performance, and crime control, its potential achievability and the specific means of its accomplishment.

Each crime area group was divided into teams of two interviewers (with one interviewer doubling-up team assignments in the uneven numbered "low" crime area group). Team interviewing bolstered the student interviewers' self-confidence and facilitated recording of information during the interview encounter. One team member asked interview questions, and the other recorded responses. In addition, each group member was periodically advised and assisted by a group coordinator and a graduate assistant who were assigned these tasks on the basis of previous interviewing experience.

Aside from being made familiar with the study's objective,

student interviewers were also instructed in the "do's and don'ts of interviewing." Interviewers were encouraged to add their own "do's and don'ts" to the following abbreviated lists:

Do's	Don'ts
1. Do trial interviewing to become familiar with the schedule.	1. Don't give copies of the interview schedule to anyone not working on the study.
2. Practice good opening and closing statements.	2. Don't sell magazines, etc., in combination with interviewing.
3. Keep in touch with group co-ordinator.	3. Don't pass your workload on to anyone else.
4. Organize the availability, handling, numbering and return of interview schedules.	4. Don't let respondent fill out schedule himself.
5. Dress neatly.	5. Don't "overdress" or "underdress" for the occasion—seek to fit into community.
6. Assure respondent that his anonymity will be preserved.	6. Don't ever express anger or surprise over interviewee's responses—seek objective neutrality except when spontaneity contributes to rapport in non-interview-based interaction.
7. Map out interview course for the day—plan ahead.	
8. Use respondent's words when probing for more detail.	7. Don't talk too much or express your views on interview-related topics.
9. Record open-ended responses verbatim when possible.	8. Don't fake the interviews and bias the results.
10. Be poised and treat the occasion seriously.	9. Don't give up on initially reluctant respondents—they can often be assured of anonymity and importance of the study and won over.
11. Always thank the interviewee for his participation in the study.	10. Don't bang at the door and ring bell incessantly—step back from the door.
	11. Don't refer to the interview as part of an "investigation"—use the word "study."
	12. Don't give up on the "don't know" response—give plenty of time, repeat the question, clarify it, etc.

Interviewers were also cautioned to be on the alert for aggressive watchdogs, to carry a dime for telephoning in the event of some emergency, and to be prepared for inclement weather. Interviewer teams consisted of one male and one female member. This procedure was useful in reducing any existing interviewer anxiety, and it served as a partial control for researcher effect. Interviewers also carried a letter of introduction signed by their instructor that explained the general purpose of the study. Teams did not begin interviewing until the interviewer role was confidently learned, and difficulties or problems were managed by the group coordinators. The coordinators and interviewers worked out procedures for reporting and correcting unsatisfactory field work as it occurred.

FINDINGS

When the victimization study was completed, 350 households had been surveyed, comprising a total number of 1,225 persons. Interview data gathered by each student were combined so that specific crime rates could be computed in each of the three surveyed crimes areas (See Tables I, II, and III). The crime rate for each of the eleven crimes in the interview schedule was arrived at by multiplying the incident frequency of each survey-reported crime by 100,000, and then dividing by the appropriate population base.*

For "property" crimes, the total number of households surveyed in each crime area served as the population base, i.e., 90 in the "low" crime area, 140 in the "medium" crime area, and 120 in the "high" crime area. For "person" crimes, the population base was the total number of individuals making up the surveyed household in each of the three crime areas, i.e., 350 in the "low" crime area, 497 in the "medium" crime area, and 378 in the "high" crime area. Specifically, crime rates for breaking and entering, larceny, and vandalism were computed by using the total number of households in each crime area as the population base. Crime rates for assault, rape, battery, robbery, bicycle theft, consumer fraud, assault with a deadly weapon, and wallet and/or purse snatching were computed by using the total number of individuals in the households in each crime area as the population base. This computing procedure was followed since crime rate statistics based on police crime reports are computed in the same manner. That is, police crime reports, in effect, treat "households" as victims in cases of breaking and entering,

---

* The base of 100,000 was used so that the findings could be compared with the UCR figures, which also uses 100,000 as a base. Other victimization surveys use a base of 1,000 for computing rates.

larceny, and vandalism, but these reports treat "individuals" as victims in the eight other crimes cited here.

Table I summarizes the findings for the low crime area. Only 38.4 per cent of survey-reported crime was reported to the police. Therefore, 61.6 per cent of survey-reported crime was not reported to the police in the low crime area. However, notice the wide variation in reporting among the different crimes.

TABLE I   THE LOW CRIME AREA
(The low crime group surveyed 90 households, with a total of 350 individuals.)

Crime	Incident Frequency	Percentage Reported to Police	Rate (Per 100,000)
Breaking and entering	6	100 (6)	6,667
Bicycle theft	7	43 (3)	2,000
Assault	8	25 (2)	2,286
Rape	1	0 (0)	286
Battery	2	100 (2)	571
Assault with a deadly weapon	2	0 (0)	571
Pickpocket/purse snatch	3	33 (1)	857
Robbery	2	50 (1)	571
Vandalism	16	56 (9)	17,778
Larceny	17	24 (4)	18,889
Consumer fraud	22	23 (5)	6,286

Table II summarizes the findings for the medium crime area. Here 47.1 per cent of all survey-reported crime was reported to the police, while 52.9 per cent went unreported.

TABLE II   THE MEDIUM CRIME AREA
(The medium crime group surveyed 140 households, with a total of 497 individuals.)

Crime	Incident Frequency	Percentage Reported to Police	Rate (Per 100,000)
Breaking and entering	27	55 (15)	19,286
Bicycle theft	12	50 (6)	2,415
Assault	9	77 (7)	1,811
Rape	2	100 (2)	402
Battery	11	72 (8)	2,213
Assault wtih a deadly weapon	1	100 (1)	201
Pickpocket/purse snatch	12	25 (3)	2,414
Robbery	4	75 (3)	804
Vandalism	20	45 (9)	14,286
Larceny	35	31 (11)	25,000
Consumer Fraud	7	14 (1)	1,408

Table III summarizes the survey results obtained in the high crime area. While 45.7 per cent of survey-reported crime was reported to the police, 54.3 per cent was not.

TABLE III THE HIGH CRIME AREA
(The high crime group surveyed 120 households, with a total of 378 persons.)

Crime	Incident Frequency	Percentage Reported to Police	Rate (Per 100,000)
Breaking and entering	5	40 (2)	4,167
Bicycle theft	11	64 (7)	2,911
Assault	11	27 (3)	2,911
Rape	3	100 (3)	794
Battery	10	60 (6)	2,646
Assault with a deadly weapon	1	100 (1)	265
Pickpocket/purse snatch	4	50 (2)	1,058
Robbery	0	0 (0)	0
Vandalism	25	40 (10)	20,833
Larceny	5	40 (2)	4,167
Consumer fraud	19	37 (7)	5,028

Table IV shows the overall crime rate for each of the eleven surveyed crimes in the three crime areas combined. This data indicates that 44.4 per cent of all survey-reported crime was reported to the police. Overall, then, 55.6 per cent of survey-reported crime was not reported to the police.

TABLE IV OVERALL CRIME RATE FOR EACH CRIME

Crime	Population Base	Percentage Reported to Police	Rate (Per 100,000)
Breaking and entering	350	61	4,286
Bicycle theft	1,225	53	2,449
Assault	1,225	43	2,286
Rape	1,225	83	490
Battery	1,225	70	1,878
Assault with a deadly weapon	1,225	50	327
Pickpocket/purse snatch	1,225	32	1,551
Robbery	1,225	67	490
Vandalism	350	46	17,429
Larceny	350	30	16,000
Consumer Fraud	1,225	27	3,918

Table V breaks down the survey data into "property" and "person" crimes for the three crime areas, and also shows the combined property versus person crime rates. This table shows that the "medium" crime area had the highest property crime rate, followed by the "low" crime area and then the "high" crime area. In terms of person crimes, the table indicates that the "high" crime area did have the highest person crime rate, followed by the "low" crime area and then the "medium" crime area.

TABLE V   SUMMARY BY TYPE OF CRIME

Area	Property Crimes			Person Crimes		
	Incident Frequency	# of House-holds	Rate (Per 100,000)	Incident Frequency	# of Persons	Rate (Per 100,000)
Low	39	90	43,333	49	350	13,429
Medium	82	140	58,571	58	497	11,670
High	35	120	29,167	59	378	15,608
Combined	156	350	44,571	164	1,225	13,388

With regard to the opinion questions, overall survey figures show that 60 per cent of all respondents believe "the police can be thoroughly trusted." But, "in relation to crime control," 80 per cent of the respondents felt that "there are many problems" associated with effective law enforcement. Eighty per cent of the respondents also felt that "the police should vigorously enforce laws against consumer fraud and white collar crime." Further, 80 per cent believed that "the individual can take steps to safeguard his home" (e.g., dead-bolt locks, watchdogs, alarm systems, fences, lighting, etc.).

Open-ended questions asked respondents to suggest how law enforcement and the criminal justice system as a whole might be improved. Generally, the respondents cited the following: (1) better pay for police officers; (2) more money for overall police operations; (3) more emphasis on police-community relations; (4) harsher judges who give tough sentences; (5) a tightening-up of drug and gun control; (6) less political corruption tied to money-making schemes; and (7) the institution of crime prevention courses for the public.

PROBLEMS IN THE STUDY

Survey research, under the most ideal conditions, faces certain problems in validity. Some of these problems are general to all surveys, and others are specific to a particular survey design or project. First, we will discuss the general problems faced in this survey, which are problems in all survey research, and second, we will look into the problems we faced in this study.

In Chapter 2, Deutcher pointed out that what people say and what they do often do not correspond. When asking people about crime, we do not know whether what they tell the interviewer is true or not. We attempted to minimize this problem by telling respondents that their answers would be confidential and their anonymity was guaranteed, but, even so, we have no way of knowing for certain if the responses to the questions reflected what actually occurred. As we pointed out at the beginning of this chapter, not all crime is reported to the police, and it may be equally true that not all crime is reported to interviewers. However, as we saw in compiling the findings, a good deal more crime was reported to the interviewers than to the police; so even though we may not have the whole truth, it appears that people are more willing to report crime to interviewers than to the authorities.

Another possible problem, one we have no way of knowing for certain, is the overreporting of crime to interviewers. That is, for some reason, people may have reported crime that did not actually occur. If such overreporting did occur, it is unlikely that it amounted to much, for there was no payoff for doing so. It is understandable why people did not report crime to the police (e.g., the police could not do anything about it), and so the fact that the survey found more crime than the police is not surprising. On the other hand, to say a crime had occurred when it did not when talking to an interviewer makes little sense. In all likelihood, if anything, crime in the survey was underreported for respondents may have believed that they would get in trouble for not reporting a crime to the police, or they may have been embarrassed to report certain crimes (e.g., rapes), or they may not have remembered certain petty crimes, such as consumer fraud or petty larceny. Thus, the findings of this survey, like all interview surveys, are subject to humble validity, and even though such data appear to be more accurate than police figures, they are far from perfect reflections of reality.

A second general problem we encountered was the respondents' understanding of the questions. They could not differentiate between burglary (breaking and entering) and a larceny, a theft, or some other kind of crime. In order to overcome this problem, we instructed the interviewers as to the specific sense of the question and told them to rephrase a question if necessary to make sure the respondent understood it. Usually this worked, but occasionally there was still some misunderstanding.

Problems specific to this particular study also occurred. The greatest problem was the time we had to develop the interview schedule and sample and to administer the survey. Since the study was carried out during an academic quarter, and the students had to squeeze in the work they had to do on the survey with their other school work, they were continually pressed for time. For example, if a member of their sample was not at home when they went for the interview, they could not go back time after time until they finally caught someone home. Usually, they would substitute a sample member if they tried a few times to contact a person at home and could not find him. This, of course, affected the random sample.

Another problem that some students experienced was a general distrust of students. Some of the respondents refused to talk to students, expressing a distaste with anything connected with the university, its students in particular. This problem was overcome to some degree when the students explained that the survey was being carried out for a local citizens committee appointed by the mayor, and the findings of the committee could be possibly used to reduce crime. It was fortunate that the instructor was a member of the committee and was in fact conducting the survey under the auspices of the local committee. In small cities and towns where the university is the focus of attention for much of the local citizenry, there is often a gap between "town and gown," and where there is a connection between the university and the locals we find better cooperation.

The last big problem with the survey was the base we used for determining the "high," "medium," and "low" crime areas. The police department had been visited by a "police administrator" who passed himself off as a researcher and planner. The "administrator" had ranked crimes using an interval scale, and then compiled the ranks listing the beats by rank. He made no differentiation between residential and business crimes, and the artificial weighting system he used on the nominal data served to confuse the actual amount and type of crime in the various areas. For example, since he did not differentiate between crimes against businesses and crimes against residences, an area could have a high rate of business crimes and a low rate of residential crimes, with the overall rate being very high since he weighted business crimes more heavily than residential crimes. Our "high crime" area, while high for certain crimes, certainly was not a good representative of the areas with the highest third of crime in the city. The only positive result of this finding was that the police department came to realize the worthlessness of the report by the "administrator" and offered more cooperation with the university in assessing crime in the community.

Several other minor problems cropped up. Many were a result of novice interviewers and linked to the severe time limitations. For the most part, the students overcame these problems with their own devices, and many creative innovations were employed to get the interviews done. For instance, some students told reluctant respondents that if they did not get their interview they would fail their course, picturing the instructor as an impossible ogre. While such practices certainly are not professional, they attest to the resourcefulness of the interviewers. More preparation for interviewers would have been extremely useful, but the experience gained in the field by the interviewers was more valuable than additional classroom instruction, given the limitations the study was conducted under.

Discussion

Given the findings of the study, several important considerations and observations should be noted. The most important use of such surveys is to develop information for testing and constructing theories about crime. Most sociological theories of crime are based on police data, but such data, as we noted, are inadequate for several reasons. Based on police data, we would be led to believe that almost all serious crime is committed by juveniles and the poor. However, as we saw in our findings, the fourth highest incident of victimization was for consumer fraud. Since consumer fraud is typically a crime by the middle and upper classes, we find that crime is not necessarily linked to poverty, as has been believed for years.

A second important use of victimization surveys is to establish ratios of reported to unreported crime. These ratios can be used for adjusting police figures and providing more accurate figures for crime. For example, we found that only 30 per cent of the larcenies were reported to the police, so the ratio of reported to unreported crimes would be 3:7. If the police figures show that there are 90 larcenies in a month, and the ratio of reported to unreported larcenies is 3:7, by multiplying the number of larcenies by three and one-third, we know that the actual number of larcenies is closer to 300. In this way, while our knowledge is not perfect, it is much more valid than it otherwise would be. It is also much cheaper to use these ratios than conduct victimization surveys all the time.

In conclusion, we have seen that victimization surveys are an application of the survey method to one area. They are relatively simple to carry out, and, even though much more sophisticated ones than the one presented here can be used, the basic procedures are the same. They are not perfectly valid, but no single method is. They are, however, one example of how social science methodology can be employed to study a problem and do a better job than existing means. More time and resources will result in a better study, but even with limited means and novice researchers a great deal of knowledge can be gained, and that, after all, is the ultimate purpose of research.

REFERENCES

CRESSEY, DONALD R. 1966. "Crime," in ROBERT K. MERTON and ROBERT A. NISBET (eds.), *Contemporary Social Problems*, 2d ed. New York: Harcourt, Brace & World, pp. 141–45.

SANDERS, WILLIAM B. 1976. *Juvenile Delinquency*. New York: Praeger.

SYLVESTER, SAWYER (ed.). 1972. *The Heritage of Modern Criminology*. Cambridge, Mass.: Schenkman.

U.S. Department of Justice. 1975. *Criminal Victimization Surveys in 13 American Cities*. Washington, D.C.: U.S. Government Printing Office.

EXERCISES

The exercises here are designed to give the student practical experience in drawing samples, constructing questionnaires, and other tasks faced by the survey researcher using a questionnaire. Exercise 4 is a full-scale research project requiring the student to employ all the various techniques of questionnaire surveys; it is suggested that this be done as a class undertaking. It would probably be a good idea to warm up for this final project by completing the other exercises first.

EXERCISE 1

In order to draw a random sample of a universe to be researched, it is generally necessary to begin by having some sort of listing of all the units in the universe. This exercise is designed to give you some practice in locating such listings.

Some universes are familiar and the names of the members readily available, such as the universe of telephone users, which can be found in the telephone directory. Other listings, however, are not so well known or so easily available, such as a list of registered motor-vehicle owners or a list of owners of thoroughbred race horses.

How would you go about finding the universe of students attending your school? Write down everything you must do and everyone you must contact to obtain such a list. Now you should be able to write a set of instructions for locating and obtaining the units for such a universe. Do the same thing for the universe of registered voters, welfare services (not welfare recipients), and local service clubs. Some of these universes contain people as the units; and, in others, organizations or agencies are the universe units. Once you have the lists, draw a simple random sample from each and make up a list of the sample.

EXERCISE 2

For this exercise, you will need a detailed map of your community and a city directory. Your library will have a copy of a city directory, and either the library or your city or county clerk will have a detailed map. (The map should show at least every block in the community and preferably every household.)

Once you have the map and the directory, draw an area sample of your community. First, divide the map into sections based on either political or social boundaries (for example, ethnic, socio-economic, age groups, etc.), or simply make a grid and impose it on the map. Number each of the general sections and randomly choose a 50 per cent sample. Next, from this general sample, draw a 25 per cent sample based on blocks. That is, randomly select 25 per cent of the blocks from each of the sections in your general sample. If you have a map showing individual households, select 20 per cent of the households in each block in the sample. If individual households are not represented on your map or there are several apartment buildings on your sample blocks, simply select every fifth household in each of the sample blocks to be in the sample, and write down the address.

Now you have an area sample of your community based on addresses. To find who lives in each household, use the city directory. This will give you the names and telephone numbers of those in your sample in case you want to use a mail questionnaire or conduct a telephone survey.

Exercise 3

Develop a questionnaire that would provide the information necessary to test the following hypothesis:

The older people are, the more conservative they are.

In developing the questionnaire, consider the following problems: What kinds of items indicate conservatism? What dimensions of conservatism are there (for example, political, sexual, and so on)? What kinds of items should be included to see whether something other than age is the independent variable (for example, social status, ethnic background)? Have other studies been done on this that might be useful in developing the questionnaire? How could such studies be located? How should the questions be worded so that people of different ages understand them in the same way? How should the questions be constructed so that they can be coded? How long should the questionnaire be? Should the questions be open-ended, closed-ended, or both?

Exercise 4

This exercise is intended to test the hypothesis that sex roles influence the career plans of college students. Traditionally, women's role has been domestic and noncareer in orientation, while men's role has been nondomestic and career-oriented. For women, college has been seen largely as an opportunity to meet a prospective husband; while for men, it is seen as a training ground for a future career. Recently, however, more and more women are actively seeking careers and have come to believe that four years of college should prepare them for jobs outside the kitchen and nursery.

To find out the extent to which the traditional sex roles influence women's career plans, develop and administer a questionnaire survey. Take a sample of men and women from different college majors at your school and analyze their responses to determine whether women's career plans are similar to, or different from, men's. If women are less likely to have plans other than for marriage, then the hypothesis will be accepted; but, if there are no differences or very slight differences, the hypothesis will be rejected. Finally, find out which occupations are chosen predominately by women and which by men as well as those that are chosen about equally by both. Then classify the occupations in terms of "women," "men," and "general."

ADDITIONAL READING SUGGESTIONS

BABBIE, EARL R. 1973. *Survey Research Methods*. Belmont, Calif.: Wadsworth. This is an excellent discussion of how survey research is used in conjunction with social science. The different types of designs, problems and logic of survey research are all laid out in a highly readable and coherent fashion. A valuable resource for setting up a survey.

LAZARSFELD, PAUL F. 1954. "The Art of Asking Why: Three Principles Underlying the Formulation of Questionnaires." In Daniel Katz et al. (eds.), *Public Opinion and Propaganda*, pp. 675–86. New York: Holt, Rinehart and Winston. Lazarsfeld's chapter is extremely helpful for constructing a wide variety of questionnaires. He explains that the purpose of questionnaires is to gather information for testing hypotheses, and outlines the principles for doing so.

SIMMONS, ROBERTA G., and MORRIS ROSENBERG. 1971. "Functions of Children's Perceptions of the Stratification System," *American Sociological Review*, 36 (April), pp. 235–49. A good example of the various steps in survey research. Also, it is useful in showing how survey data are laid out in tables. The analysis is relatively simple, but it is done in such a way as to give the researchers the information they need; therefore, it is both understandable and useful.

5. Observation Survey

DRUK COURT:
THE ADULT PARALLEL
TO JUVENILE COURT
—Jacqueline P. Wiseman

THE DISTINCTION THAT PETERSON and Matza (1963:107) draw between two basic types of court procedures—the legalistic court and the so-called socialized court—is especially pertinent to the operation of the drunk court, as will be seen from the following brief outline.

Legalistic courts operate under an adversary system, by which a state attorney and a defense counsel plead a case before a judge and/or jury. The purpose of the trial is to determine whether the defendant in fact committed the crime with which he is charged. Great stress is placed on formal proceedings and rules of evidence, very little on information regarding the defendant's character and background. If he is convicted, the defendant is subject to fine, imprisonment, or execution. The punishment fits the crime, not the particular individual.

Socialized courts usually exercise jurisdiction either over juveniles, both neglected or dependent and delinquent or criminal; or over family law or in some jurisdictions, over both juvenile and domestic problems in one omnibus court. Its methods and procedures have made greatest inroads in the juvenile court. Here, the adversary system is replaced by one or more social workers' reports, which emphasize information regarding the character and background of all

From Jacqueline P. Wiseman, *Stations of the Lost: The Treatment of Skid Row Alcoholics.* © 1970. Reprinted by permission of Prentice-Hall, Inc., Englewood Cliffs, N.J. and the Author.

parties. Judicial procedure is informal; rules of evidence do not apply. The purpose of the hearing is to determine whether a serious problem exists—whether, for example, a child requires help—and to provide the means to meet the needs of the individuals involved.

Although not officially designated as a socialized court in the statutes, drunk court sessions are almost always operated along the latter lines. However, the drunk court judge faces unusual administrative and decisional problems that have a gross distorting effect on its more informal and humanized ideology.

Unlike other cases in other courts, where guilt or innocence of the defendant is the issue, the judge's decision in drunk court is almost always the sentence alone. . . . With but rare exceptions, the men plead guilty. The judge, therefore, has no official reason to assume the men are other than guilty.

Sentencing men who plead guilty to a public drunkenness charge, however, presents a real conflict to a judge who wishes to see himself as compassionate, wise, and just. Because of the widespread discussion of alcoholism as a social problem and a physical illness, a judge must take cognizance of both the need for efficient administration of sentences for public drunks and the theoretical causes of alcoholism. As a collateral matter, he is also aware that ordinary male citizens sometimes "tie one on," perhaps do damage to themselves or others, and are arrested by police. Such men usually have jobs and a family. A jail sentence for public drunkenness would be a severe blow, both socially and economically.

In other words, with each man who appears before him the judge must ask himself whether he should view the defendant as merely an "overindulgent social drinker," or as a "chronic drunken bum," or as a "sick alcoholic."

In the first of these possible definitions, the judge must make a decision about whether the defendant is a wayward, but basically solid, citizen. If this is the case, the sentence can be suspended and the person let off with a warning. On the other hand, if the defendant is the type the judge tends to mentally characterize as a "childlike, hedonistic, willful, chronic drunk," he must be dried out for his own good, since he is a menace to himself and society. All the while, the third possible definition creates great decisional pressures, because the judge is aware that he must consider the prevailing public opinion that alcoholism per se is an illness, even if some of the acts of the person who drinks too much may legally be defined as a crime. (See Stem, 1967.) If the judge accepts this latter view, he is forced to consider the possibility he is sentencing a man who may be ill to jail. The implied inhumanity of this act must be explained and justified, even if only self-justification is involved.

This decisional picture is further confused by the fact that the judge must consider not one but two types of illness. The first type is the temporary, acute *physical distress* caused by repeated over-indulgence in alcohol which, in cases of continuous heavy drinking, is serious enough to cause death if left unattended. The second type is based on the assumption that some mysterious psychological compulsion forces a man to drink and, like the plea "not guilty by reason of insanity," the chronic alcoholic is not responsible for his excessive drinking. Each type of illness demands a different kind of concern and treatment, although in judicial discussions these are often blurred together.

If a judge were to think aloud, he might explain the chronic drunk sentence dilemma and his solution to it something like this:

Alcoholism may be an illness or it may be a weakness. Whatever it is, all alcoholics need help to quit drinking. One of the surest ways to help an alcoholic quit drinking is to separate him forcibly from any supply of liquor. However, jail is a drastic penalty for being found drunk and therefore should be used only after other methods fail. This is because if a man is sent to jail, he may suffer undesirable social consequences, such as jeopardizing his job or causing his wife and children great embarrassment. Some men are so upset about being arrested, that is all the punishment they need. It serves as adequate warning. Others should be educated about the dangers of overindulgence through forced attendance at Alcoholism School. Others need a short sentence, but suspended, to scare them a bit; still others need a short sentence to see what jail is like so they don't want ever to go back; and some repeaters need aid in getting off the bottle which can be supplied by a longer separation from it —say 30, 60 or 90 days. The jail is set up to give these men both medical and psychological therapy through the Jail Branch Clinic of the Out-Patient Therapy Center, so they are well taken care of. Transients can be handled by telling them to leave town.

Matching sentences with men who plead guilty is thus the

judge's true concern. This task must be handled within the pressures created by restricting drunk court to a morning session in one courtroom, regardless of the number of men scheduled to be seen that day.

Up until last year (when drunk arrests were temporarily reduced because of the large number of hippies and civil rights demonstrators in jail), 50 to 250 men were often sentenced within a few hours. Appearance before the judge was handled in platoons of five to 50. This meant the judge decided the fate of each defendant within a few short minutes. Thus judicial compassion attained assembly-line organization and speed.

As a court observer noted:

> The Court generally disposes of between 50 and 100 cases per day, but on any Monday there are 200 to 250 and on Monday mornings after holiday weekends the Court may handle as many as 350 cases. I would estimate that, on the average, cases take between 45 seconds and one minute to dispose of (LeClercq, 1966:1).

Later, with drunk arrests drastically curtailed, the court handled no more than 50 cases in an average morning, and perhaps 125 on the weekends, according to the observer. Right after a civil rights demonstration that resulted in many arrests, only 33 persons were observed in drunk court. This reduction in the quantity of defendants, however, did not appear to increase the length of time spent on each person. Rather, it seemed to reduce it. The observer noted the average length of time per person was 30 seconds, although the size of platoons was reduced from 50 to 15 or 20.

SENTENCING CRITERIA

How is the judge able to classify and sentence a large, unwieldy group of defendants so quickly? The answer is he utilizes social characteristics as indicators to signify drinking status—just as in an arrest situation the policeman looked for socal characteristics to identify alcoholic troublemaking potential, combined with the arrestee's legal impotence. The effect is essentially the same: the men are objectified into social types for easy classification. In the case of the judge, the legal decision process must be more refined than for a policeman's arrest, no-arrest decision. Therefore, the judge's sentencing criteria are more complex, as they must include all possible decision combinations.

From court observations, plus interviews with court officers and judges, three primary criteria for typing defendants in drunk court emerge:

The General Physical Appearance of the Man. Is he shaky and obviously in need of drying out? Here, some of the judges ask the men to extend their hands before sentencing and decide the sentence on the degree of trembling.

Physical appearance may actually be the most potent deciding factor. As one court officer put it, when asked how the judges decide on a sentence:

> Primarily by appearance. You can tell what kind of shape they're in. If they're shaking and obviously need drying out, you know some are on the verge of the DT's so these get 10 or 15 days [in jail] to dry out.

One of the seasoned judges said that his criteria were as follows:

> I rely on his record and also his "looks." Their "looks" are very important. I make them put their hands out—see if they are dirty and bloody in appearance (LeClercq, 1966:12).

Past Performance. How many times have they been up before the court on a drunk charge before? A record of past arrests is considered to be indicative of the defendant's general attitude toward drinking. The longer and more recent the record, the greater the need for a sentence to aid the defendant to improve his outlook on excessive liquor consumption. (This is in some contradiction to the presumed greater need the man must have for drying out, since previous recent jailings mean that he could not have been drinking for long.)

The previous comment, plus the answer by a court officer to the question "Who gets dismissed?", illustrates this criterion for sentencing:

> A person with no previous arrests [gets dismissed]. If they have had no arrests, then the judge hates for them to have a conviction on their record. *The more arrests they've had and the more recently they've had them, the more likely they are to get another sentence.* (Emphasis mine.)

The Man's Social Position. Does he have a job he could go to? Is he married? Does he have a permanent address, or will he literally be on the streets if he receives a dismissal?

For these data, dress is an all-important clue, age a secondary one. A man who looks down-and-out is more likely to receive a sentence than the well-dressed man. According to a court officer:

If they look pretty beat—clothes dirty and in rags, then you figure that they need some help to stop drinking before they kill themselves.

If they're under 21 we usually give them a kick-out. If they are a business man or a lawyer we have them sign a civil release so they can't sue and let them go.

An observer reports that a judge freed a young man with the following remarks:

I am going to give you a suspended sentence and hope that this experience will be a warning to you. I don't want you to get caught up in this cycle.

Transients form a category of their own and get a special package deal—if they will promise to leave town, they draw a suspended sentence or probation. The parallel between this practice and the police policy of telling some Skid Row drunks to "take a walk" need only be mentioned. The following interchanges are illustrative:

Judge: I thought you told me the last time you were in here that you were going to leave Pacific City.
Defendant: I was supposed to have left town yesterday. I just got through doing time.
Judge: Go back to Woodland. Don't let me see you in here again or we are going to put you away. Thirty days suspended.
Defendant: I am supposed to leave with the circus tomorrow. If I don't go, I will be out of work for the whole season.
Judge: You promised to leave three times before. Thirty days in the County Jail.

By combining the variables of physical appearance, past performance, and social position, a rough description of the social types expected in drunk court and matching sentences for each type are shown in Table I.

These first two categories in Table I, and sometimes the third, have not been, in Garfinkel's terms, "made strange" (1967). They are treated as though they are full-fledged persons who may have

TABLE I   PARADIGM OF SOCIAL TYPES AND SENTENCES IN DRUNK COURT

Social Type	Probable Sentence
A young man who drank too much: a man under 40, with a job, and perhaps a wife, who has not appeared in court before	A kick-out or a suspended sentence
The young repeater: same as above, but has been before judge several times (may be on way to being an alcoholic)	Suspended sentence or short sentence (5-10 days) to scare him, or possible attendance at Alcoholism School
The repeater who still looks fairly respectable. (Image vacillating between an alcoholic and a drunk)	30-day suspended sentence, with possible attendance at Alcoholism School
Out-of-towner (social characteristics not important as they have nonlocal roots). Therefore not important whether overindulged, a chronic drunk, or an alcoholic	Suspended sentence on condition he leave town. Purpose is to discourage him from getting on local loop and adding to taxpayer's load
The middle-aged repeater who has not been up for some time. (May be an alcoholic who has relapsed)	Suspended sentence with required attendance at Alcholism School or given to custody of Christian missionaries
The derelict-drunk who looks "rough," i.e., suffering withdrawal, a hangover, has cuts and bruises, may have malnutrition or some diseases connected with heavy drinking and little eating; a chronic drunk; seedy clothing, stubble beard, etc.	30–60–90-day sentence depending on number of prior arrests and physical condition at time of arrest. (Has probably attended Alcoholism School already)
The man who looks gravely ill (probably a chronic alcoholic)	County hospital under suspended sentence

over-indulged. The remaining types are stripped-down persons, on the "other side," so far as they are perceived by the judge.

A total of 180 men were observed in drunk court and tabulated according to the social types outlined in the table. Observations were spread over three days. Two different judges presided. The results are shown in Table II.

Of the total tabulated, the Skid Row alcoholics category would include the derelict (38 per cent), the middle-aged repeater who has not been arrested for some time, probably having been in the loop (11 per cent), the out-of-towner (8 per cent), and the man who looks gravely ill (2 per cent), for a total of 59 per cent. This

TABLE II   Distribution of Drunk Ordinance Social Types in Court

Social Types	Per cent (N = 180)
Derelict who looks "rough"	38
Young repeater	15
Recent repeater who looks respectable	15
Middle-aged repeater who has not been arrested for some time	11
Young man with wife, job, first offense	11
Out-of-towner	8
Man who looks gravely ill	2
Total	100

TABLE III   Distribution of Sentences in Drunk Court

Sentences	Per cent of defendants (N = 180)	
Kick-out (no sentence, warned only)	2	
County hospital		
With hold	—	
No hold	2	74 (non-jail sentence)
Suspended sentence		
10 days or less	—	
11 to 30 days	23	
31 to 60 days	28	
61 to 90 days	19	
Over 90 days	—	
Sentence to County Jail		
10 days or less	1	
11 to 30 days	23	26 (jail sentence)
31 to 60 days	2	
61 to 90 days	—	
Over 90 days	—	
Total	100	

is quite near the usual 40 to 45 per cent of Skid Row men represented in the total arrests for drunkenness in Pacific City.

The detailed pattern of sentencing was also tabulated and is illustrated in Table III. As can be seen in the table, only 26 per cent of the men received sentences to be served in County Jail. This is quite close to the yearly average of 20 to 25 per cent.

Most pertinent to this study, however, is the distribution of sentences among social types of defendants. From Table IV, it

TABLE IV DISTRIBUTION OF SENTENCES AMONG SOCIAL TYPES OF DEFENDANTS IN DRUNK COURT

Sentences	Per cent of defendants by social types						
	Young man with job, wife, 1st offense (N=19)	Young repeater (N=27)	Middle-aged respectable repeater (N=26)	Out-of-towner (N=15)	Middle-aged repeater, not recent (N=20)	Derelict who looks rough (N=69)	Man looking gravely ill (N=4)
Kick-out (no sentence, warned only)	21	—	—	—	—	—	—
County hospital							
With hold	—	—	—	—	—	—	—
No hold	—	—	—	—	—	—	75
Suspended sentence							
10 days or less	59	—	—	—	—	—	—
11 to 30 days	10	22	11	60	15	13	25
31 to 60 days	10	22	35	—	60	30	—
61 to 90 days	—	37	35	33	25	3	—
Over 90 days	—	—	—	—	—	—	—
Sentenced to County Jail							
10 days or less	—	4	4	7	—	—	—
11 to 30 days	—	15	15	—	—	54	—
31 to 60 days	—	—	—	—	—	—	—
61 to 90 days	—	—	—	—	—	—	—
Over 90 days	—	—	—	—	—	—	—
Totals	100	100	100	100	100	100	100

can be seen that the derelicts who look rough or men who are repeaters (regardless of age or appearance), are most likely to serve time and get the longest sentences. Furthermore, the derelict who looks rough is the least likely of any social type to escape jail.

A word should be said about the suspended sentence. Judges sometimes give exceedingly long suspended sentences to drunk ordinance defendants—often 90 days or more to repeaters. This places a weapon in the hands of the court that is greatly feared. If at any time within the following 90 days (or whatever the length of the sentence), the man is picked up on a drunk charge, he may be sent directly to jail without trial for the entire length of the suspended sentence. Many men, upon receiving a long suspended sentence, and realizing their vulnerability to arrest, will "take out insurance" against being incarcerated for that length of time by seeking admission to another "more desirable" station on the loop. Favorite "hideouts" while waiting for the suspended sentence to run out are (in approximate rank order): Welfare Home for Homeless Men, State Mental Hospital, and the Christian Missionaries.

OTHER SENTENCING ASSISTANCE

Even with the aid of a simplified mental guide, the judge cannot be expected to assemble and assimilate sufficient material on each man, review it, mentally type the man, and then make a sentencing decision in less than a minute. Thus, it is not surprising that almost all drunk court judges employ the aid of one assistant and sometimes two court attachés who are familiar with the Row and its inhabitants. These men are known as court liaison officers. Because of personal familiarity with chronic drunkenness offenders, the liaison officers are able to answer questions about each accused person quickly and to recommend a case disposition. Such persons obviously operate as an informal screening board.

The most important court helper in Pacific City is a man who knows most of the Row men by sight and claims also to know their general outlook on alcohol and life. Known to the defendants as "the Rapper," this man often sits behind the judge and suggests informally who would benefit most from probation and assignment to Alcoholism School, who might need the "shaking-up" that jail provides, and who ought to be sent to alcoholic screening at City Hospital and perhaps on to State Mental Hospital. As each man is named, the Rapper whispers to the judge, who then passes sentence. (See Bogue, 1963:414.)

In Pacific City, the man who was the Rapper for a period of time was an ex-alcoholic who could claim intimate knowledge of the chronic drunkenness offender because he had drunk with them. A relative of the Rapper was highly placed in city politics, and the Rapper made no secret of the fact that his appointment was politically engineered. During the course of the study (several times in fact), the Rapper himself "fell off the wagon" and underwent treatment at Northern State Mental Hospital, one of the stations on the loop. While there, the Rapper told about his recent job with the court and how he helped the judge:

> Each man arrested has a card with the whole record on it. We would go over the cards before the case came up. We see how many times he's been arrested. I could advise the judge to give them probation or a sentence. Many times, the family would call and request a sentence. I would often arrange for them to get probation plus clothes and a place to stay at one of the halfway houses. Oh, I'll help and help, but when they keep falling off—I get disgusted.

The Christian Missionaries also send a liaison man to the drunk court sessions. He acts as Rapper at special times and thereby also serves in an informal screening capacity. Sponsorship by this organization appears to guarantee that the defendant will get a suspended sentence. For instance, this interchange was observed in court several times:

> *Judge,* turning to Missionary representative: "Do you want him [this defendant]?" (Meaning, "Will you take him at one of your facilities?")
> *Missionary:* (Nods "Yes.")
> *Judge:* "Suspended sentence."

Another observer discussed this arrangement with a veteran judge:

> *Interviewer: Isn't there any attempt made to consider the men for rehabilitation?*
> The men are screened by the Christian Missionaries usually. The Christian Missionaries send someone down to the jail who tries to help them. They talk with the men and screen them. Nobody does the job that the Christian Missionaries do in the jails.

Interviewer: The Court abdicates the screening of defendants to the Christian Missionaries, then?

Not completely. We try to keep a record. Some of these men we can help, but most we can't. I know by heart all of their alibis and stories [LeClercq, 1966:11].

Another important informal court post is filled by an employee who is known to some of the men as "the Knocker." The job of the Knocker is to maintain the personal records of the men who appear before drunk court and to supply the judge with this information. A court observer reported the following:

The Knocker spoke to the judge in just about every case. However, I do not know what he said. He may just be reading to the judge the official records, or he may be giving his personal judgment about the possibility of the defendant being picked up again in the near future. One thing seems clear: the judge receives his information from the Knocker just before he hands out the sentence.

Sometimes it is difficult to distinguish the Knocker (who merely gives information to the judge) from the Rapper (who "suggests" the proper sentence.) In 1963, two of these court liaison officers worked together. An interview with one partner is quoted below:

Interviewer: What do you do?

Up here we act as a *combination district attorney and public defender* [emphasis mine]. We are more familiar with these guys than the judges are. The judges alternate. We have the previous arrest records. A lot of times, guys will give phony names. It may take us a while to catch up with them. We try to remember if we have seen a guy before.

Interviewer: How does a judge decide whether to sentence the men and if so, for how long?

We help him out on that. If a guy has been in three times in four weeks, they should get a minimum of 30 days. They need to dry out. You know, if a man has been arrested three times in four weeks, you ask yourself the question: "How many times has he been drunk that he wasn't arrested?" Also, you look at the condition of a man—he may even need hospitalization.

Interviewer: You mean you can tell whether a man ought to be sent to jail by looking at him?

Some of them look a lot more rough looking than others. You can tell they have been on a drunk for more than one day. They are heavily bearded. They have probably been sleeping in doorways or on the street. You can tell they have been on a long drunk [LeClercq, 1966:6–7].

Thus perhaps the most revealing aspect of the sentencing procedure is the virtual absence of interest in the charge and the judge's role as spokesman for the court officer's decision. This may account for the fact the judge seldom discusses the case with the defendant, except in a jocular, disparaging way. The following interchanges, which illustrate this attitude, were witnessed by observers:

Defendant: I was sleeping in a basement when a man attacked me with a can opener.
Judge: Did you also see elephants?

Judge: What is your story this time?
Defendant: (As he begins to speak, Judge interrupts.)
Judge: You gave me that line yesterday; 30 days in the County Jail.

Court Atmosphere

The above exchanges between the judge and the defendant would seem to suggest the atmosphere of drunk court is more informal than most courts of law. From the reports obtained from all observers, this is true. Drunk court is not taken as seriously as other sessions of the municipal court, or other departments, and a great deal of levity and antic behavior is tolerated (in full view of defendants), an attitude not allowed in other Pacific City courts. Excerpts from observers' notes illustrate this unserious aspect of drunk court:

Bailiff came in today and asked other court officers in voice audible to all, "When does the parade [of defendants] begin?"

There is open flirting between a police matron and police before court starts.

The Knocker and bailiff put a sign, "The Flying Nun," over the judge's name before court started. Removed it when judge appeared.

Judge comes in the front door of the court, walks very casually, often presides without robe. Unlike other courts, bailiff asks everyone to remain seated when judge appears. Judge is always five to ten minutes late.

Just as the judge was about ready to start, there was a gasp and a thud. (This didn't seem to shake anyone except me.) One of the defendants had fallen over near the front of the line, and the other defendants stood there like this wasn't anything to get upset about.

The judge asked, "What was his number?" and the Knocker told him. Then one of the court policemen said that he thought the guy was dead. "This man has had an alcoholic seizure. We're going to take him to the hospital," the judge said.

The bailiff asked what should be done about the man's case. The judge dismissed it. It was the only kick-out that day.

From this it can be seen that the operational ideology of the judge in drunk court, although much like that of juvenile court, is lacking in the compassion often shown for juveniles. An attempt is made to sentence the man in terms of his characteristics and not the criminal act he is accused of. Extenuating circumstances of all types are used in arriving at decisions. There is no lawyer or advocacy system in operation. The defendant may be discharged to "responsible" persons in the community (this means some member of his family if he has one, or the Christian Missionaries if they exhibit an interest in him).

Far from freeing the judge to make idiosyncratic personalized decisions, the result of the drunk court system is to standardize drunks on the basis of social types and then with the assistance of court aides objectify them in such a way as to fit the predetermined types. Thus the decision of the patrolman in typification of the Skid Row drinker is not only accepted in the court without question—it is reinforced and embellished.

Justifying the Sentencing Process

How does the municipal court judge, serving in drunk court sessions, allow himself to be a party to such extra-legal activities as platoon sentencing, the heavy reliance on advice from "friends of the court," and the utilization of extraneous social characteristics in setting the sentence? Why is there not a conflict with his self-image of judicial compassion for the individual and scrupulous attention to legal niceties?

For some judges, the conflict is resolved by falling back on the alcoholism-as-an-illness view of drunkenness, and by redefining many of the men who appear before him as *patients* rather than defendants. Thus, when asked to describe their duties, drunk court judges often sound like physicians dealing with troublesome patients for whom they must prescribe unpleasant but necessary medicine, rather than judges punishing men for being a public annoyance. As an example of this:

> I know that jail isn't the best place for these men, but we have to do something for them. We need to put them someplace where they can dry out. You can't just let a man go out and kill himself.

> This is a grave and almost hopeless problem. But you have to try some kind of treatment. Often they are better off in jail than out on the street.

The drunk court judges sometimes add the wish that the city provided a more palatable alternative to the County Jail, but then reiterate the view that it is better than no help at all.

Court attachés have essentially the same attitude:

> Some of these guys are so loaded that they will fall and break their skull if you don't lock them up. Half of these guys have no place to stay anyway except a dingy heap. They are better off in jail.

> The whole purpose of the law is to try to help them. It's for the protection of themselves and for others, that's the way the law reads. For example, say you're driving through here [Skid Row] and you hit a drunk. He could get killed and if you don't stop and render aid, you could become a criminal.

> Giving them 30 days in County Jail is sometimes a kindness. You are *doing them a favor, like a diabetic who won't take his insulin. Sometimes you must hurt him to help him.* (Emphasis mine.)

Like the Skid Row police, the officers, the judge and his coterie are reinforced in their definition of the situation as clinical, and of themselves as diagnosticians and social internists, by the fact that relatives often call the court and ask that a man be given time in jail for his own good. The judge usually complies. Furthermore, as has been mentioned, there is at the jail a branch of the Out-Patient Therapy Center that was originally established to work for the rehabilitation of alcoholics. Having this jail clinic allows the drunk court judge to say:

I sentence you to 30 days and I will get in touch with the social worker at the County Jail and she will help you.

I sentence you to therapy with the psychologists at the County Jail (Also reported by court observers.)

Creation of the Pacific City Alcoholism School also allows the judge to feel that he is fulfilling both judicial and therapeutic duties, giving the defendant a suspended sentence on the condition that he will attend the lecture sessions.

Where the name of the social worker or psychologist of Alcoholism School is not invoked as part of the sentence, an awareness of alcoholism as an illness is frequently used as an introductory statement to indicate the reasoning of the courts for giving a jail sentence.

We realize that you men are sick and need help. Any action I might take, therefore, should not in any sense be construed as punishment. Jail in this case is not a punitive measure, but to help you with your alcoholism problem.

However, the uneasiness of the judge with the jailing of alcoholics has other indicators. The captain of the County Jail, for instance, reports that inmates serving time for public drunkenness have only to write a letter requesting modification and it is almost automatically forthcoming, something not true for modification requests of prisoners convicted of other misdemeanors.

That drunk court's methods and procedures of handling the Row men go against the judicial grain also seems to be indicated by the fact court officers claims a new judge must be "broken in" to drunk court before he operates efficiently. When the judge first arrives, he will sentence differently from an experienced judge and in the direction of greater leniency. This upsets the established pattern.

The result is he is taken in hand and guided to do "the right thing" by the veteran court aides. As one court aide put it:

Most of the judges are pretty good—they rely on us. Sometimes you get a new judge who wants to do things his way. We have to break them in, train them. This court is very different. We have to break new judges in. It takes some of them some time to get adjusted to the way we do things.

The high rate of recidivism of chronic drunkenness offenders leads some experts to question the value of jail as a cure for alcoholism or chronic drunkenness. Publicly, at least, the judges appear to hold to the view that the current arrest and incarceration process can be helpful, but that often the alcoholic simply does not respond to "treatment" permanently and needs periodic "doses" of jail-therapy. As one judge put it:

> Some men have simply gone so far that you can't do anything for them. They are hopeless. All we can do is send them to jail to dry out from time to time.

SENTENCING AS AN ASSEMBLY-LINE OUTRAGE

Although the chronic drunkenness offender makes many trips through drunk court, it is not too surprising that he never becomes completely accustomed to the way he is treated there. The mass sentencing, the arbitrariness of the judge, the extraneous factors that seem to go into sentencing decisions, all these shock and embitter him.

Of the group-sentencing procedures, the Row men have this to say:

> It's law on the assembly line. That's how it really is. No judge would admit it, though. He's got a nice, soft, plush $15,000 or $18,000 job which hinges on this.
>
> I mean there's no concept on the part of anybody that goes into drunk court, that this is a court of law, that the judge is going to weigh the pros and cons. . . .
>
> Let me tell you, he's handling 50 guys in a period of an hour or less. Do you think he has time to, uh, to say, "Well now, why do you drink?" and like that?
>
> The situation here [in jail] could stand a lot of improvement, but the court situation is much worse. When you go down there to court each individual in the courts of the United States is entitled to individual and separate trial. You go down there and they run you into these courts, 30 or 40 at a time, and they sentence you accordingly. The front row first.
>
> I was in there one time, I don't remember who the judge was, when we got in he ran off about seven or eight names, "You people have 30 days in the County Jail." Then he says, "The rest of you in the front row can plead guilty, not guilty, trial by court, trial by jury."

Here is how they describe the seemingly unrelated factors that appear to go into the judge's decision:

If you haven't been picked up for a long time and you've been in town all that time, you'll get a kick-out; but if you've been out of town, you get a sentence, because they figure you were probably drinking all the time.

. . . If you've been [picked up], say, a couple of times in a week or more, why you're subject to be sent to County Jail.

On Monday before court, we all 15 of us shaved on one razor after being picked up on Friday because we knew that if we were whiskery we'd go to County Jail for sure.

Of those arrested before Christmas, everyone who had an address other than Skid Row—even a Beatnik area—got a kick-out. Others like us went to County Jail.

Judge Darlington is a no good son-of-a-bitch. He says to us, "Hold your hands out." They have been holding you in the drunk tank for about eight hours, no beds there, just concrete. After that you go to a holding cell. They line them up ten at a time in front and ten in back. After three days in there, worrying what's going to happen to you, you shake a bit. If you do, Judge Darlington says, "Sixty days."

The fact the judge acts on advice from an ex-alcoholic, a non-professional who clearly is drawing his views from personal (and possibly petty) recollections of the men, further confirms the picture of totally arbitrary power with little concern for justice.

There's this guy they call "the Rapper" and he has the ear of the judge. He actually sets the sentence whenever he's there. I'd like to get my hands on him sometime.

We call him "the Rapper." He has the power of life and death for the men. He sat up next to the judge and would say, "probation," "30 days," "90 days," and that's what you'd get. Is that legal? I don't think anyone should be allowed to play God like that.

We were all glad when he slipped. He looked for the worst of himself in others. (Comment on the fact that the Rapper had recently fallen off the wagon himself and was at State Mental Hospital.)

The Christian Missionary Rapper was no more popular with the men:

Jim Brown, a reformed alcoholic who has no use for another alcoholic, is the Rapper. He will hang a man if he doesn't like him. I was at Barabas Abode and Beacon in the Darkness. We speak to each other, but he's a double-crossing, no-good son-of-a-bitch. Absolutely no good! At 6 A.M. he and the court liaison officer go through the records and *they* decide what each man shall get. They see my name and say, "Give that bastard 60 days!"

The Row men are also aware that there are sometimes drastic differences between the sentences received one day in court and those received another. Empirical evidence of this can be seen in Table V, where sentences received during a time when County Jail was normally full, and during a time when it was beyond normal capacity because of a recent demonstration, are compared. (Arrests were also below average for that day, as well.)

TABLE V   COMPARISON OF SENTENCES GIVEN IN DRUNK COURT WHEN JAIL WAS FULL AND WHEN IT WAS BEYOND CAPACITY

Sentences	State of County Jail	
	Full (N=180) Per cent	Beyond capacity (N=36) Per cent
Kick-out (no sentence, warned only)	2	8
County Hospital		
With hold	—	—
No hold	2	—
	74	91
Suspended sentence		
10 days or less	—	5
11 to 30 days	23	70
31 to 60 days	28	8
61 to 90 days	19	—
Over 90 days	—	—
Sentenced to County Jail		
10 days or less	1	3
11 to 30 days	23	6
31 to 60 days	2	—
61 to 90 days	—	—
Over 90 days	—	—
	26	9
Total	100	100

As shown in Table V, only 9 per cent of the men received a County Jail sentence when the jail was beyond capacity (as compared to 26 per cent when it was merely very full).

Skid Row drunks explain such disparity not as a function of jail capacity but as evidence of graft among agents of social control. Collusion is assumed to exist among the police, City Hospital, the Christian Missionaries, the jailers, and the judges in the Municipal Court, and among the judges, the police, the jailers, and the social workers in the Superior Courts. This reinforces the idea of a power ful system beyond the control of a penniless individual. The Row men cite the following evidence (so far as they are concerned) as proof of this.

Sometimes, if you get smart with the policeman, he tells the judge and you get a bigger sentence.

When I was arrested for drunk, they took me first to the hospital. A social worker came around, and she had a folder, and she said, "Let's see now, uh, you won't have any way to pay for your stay here." I'd only been there [in the hospital] a day and a half, and I says, "Well, how do you know?" And she said, "Well, where you're going, you won't be able to pay anyway." So I says, "Well, how do you know where I'm goin'?" She says, "Well, you're goin' to County Jail for 60 days." I says, "Well, how do you know? I haven't even been before the judge yet!" She said, "Oh, it's right here in your folder." I hadn't been to court yet, see, and sure enough, as soon as I went before the judge—60 days at County Jail. I told the judge about it after he sentenced me and he said, "You're being irrelevant," or something like that. In other words you're going for 60 days, and you just don't argue. He said also, "Well, sometimes that's court procedure."

This cooperation is oftentimes suspected by embittered Row men to serve the purpose of enriching unscrupulous agents of social control or at the very least maintain them in their jobs by keeping the jail population at an assigned level:

The key to the whole situation is the cut on the food taken by Sheriff Smith and Captain Jackson and the judges. They are all get ting their cut by stealing from the food appropriations to the jail They make $1.50 a day on each one of us. I think they have a quota at County Jail. If they are down 50 men, you can bet that 50 will go out on the next bus.

What a lot of people don't realize is that this institution and most jails need labor and the alcoholic furnishes that. When I was a trusty in Minneapolis, I'd hear the superintendent call the judge and say, "We are short 150 men here"—and in three days the courts would send us our 150 men (Bittner, 1967).

Maneuvers to Escape County Jail

Lacking the power to fight a drunk charge legally or by means of forfeiting bail, the Skid Row alcoholic has developed other ways of avoiding the County Jail, which is hated more than any other locale on the loop. It should be emphasized that if such avoidance tactics are successful the Row man is still incarcerated, but in another (and more desirable) area.

For instance, a "regular" (i.e., chronic drunkenness offender) may get a job at the City Jail as trusty if he is known to be a good worker and is popular with guards.

> After you're sentenced, then you go see the head man there [at City Jail], and if you've been there before, which most of 'em have, then he'll say, "Yeah, you can stay here and work for me." It's who you know that counts.

A second means of avoiding County Jail is for a man to act psychotic so that he is referred to the City Screening Facility at the hospital, and perhaps even to the psychiatric ward there. Often this results in a five-day hospitalization or a sojourn in the Northern State Mental Hospital rather than a jail sentence. As one man put it:

> One good way is to act or talk suicidal. That scares them sometimes. Do a lot of yelling and pretend to hear voices. This will often break them [the jailers] down and you'll get to go to City Hospital.

The Feeling of Unfairness

The judge may feel righteous because he is saving a man from drinking himself to death by sending him to jail to dry out, but the Skid Row alcoholic is neither convinced this alleged judicial "good will" exists, nor is he grateful even if it does. With the exception of those Row men who have settled on the jail as a second home, most believe there is great inequity in the way Pacific City courts are operated. They point to other state jurisdictions that deal with the drunk far less harshly:

> You take Alabama, Georgia, any place, they'll give you a ten dollar fine. Texas, you get two days in jail. You can get in jail ten times and you'll still only get two days and more chance the judge'll let you go.

Chicago doesn't treat its alcoholics like this city, neither does New York. Most of the time they keep you overnight or a couple of days. They don't send you to jail for a month or more.

The alcoholics' opinion of being sent to jail for drunkenness is perhaps best summed up in this quote:

As far as the jail goes, all jails are the same. Nobody likes to be in 'em regardless of whether they give you steak or, uh, filet mignons, or whatever it is, nobody likes to be in jail. They don't beat you or nothin' like that. Like any place, it's a place of detention; that's their job, that's what the judge said; we're just taken away from the public. As far as gettin' here, it's for drunk, and as far as the sentence goes I believe that's quite a price to pay. Even if it's ten days, I think it's too much myself—even ten days, takin' ten days away from your life for gettin' drunk.

REFERENCES

BITTNER, EGON. 1967. "The Police on Skid Row: A Study of Peace-Keeping," American Sociological Review, 32 (October).

BOGUE, DONALD J. 1963. Skid Row in American Cities. Chicago: University of Chicago.

GARFINKEL, HAROLD. 1956. "Conditions of a Successful Degradation Ceremony," American Journal of Sociology, 61 (March), pp. 420–22.

LeCLERCQ, FREDERIC S. 1966. "Field Observations in Drunk Court of the Pacific Municipal Court," unpublished memorandum, p. 1.

PETERSEN, WILLIAM, and DAVID MATZA. 1963. "Does the Juvenile Court Exercise Justice?" In Petersen and Matza (eds.), Social Controversy. Belmont, Calif.: Wadsworth.

STEM, GERALD. 1967. "Public Drunkenness: Crime or Health Problem?" Annals of American Academy of Political and Social Science, 374 (November), pp. 147–56.

EXERCISES   Like the observation survey, the questionnaire survey requires the researcher to draw
a sample and analyze quantitative data. However, some of the
issues and problems are different, and this set of exercises is designed to give the student some experience in the tasks of observation survey. Exercise 4, however, is a research project, and most
of the analysis it requires is similar to that in questionnaire surveys.

EXERCISE 1

This exercise is designed to give the student a feel for recording
observations and finding a spot from which to observe. The purpose is to identify windowshoppers in terms of easily observable
features—sex, age, and race.

Make a simple observation schedule by establishing categories of
sex, age, and race. Find a display window where there is frequent
pedestrian traffic, preferably near a place where you can sit down
and take notes, such as a bus stop. Record the characteristics of
those who stop and look at the display. It is not important that
you guess the exact age of a person. Rather, this exercise is intended
to give you some experience in observing different categories of
people.

EXERCISE 2

This exercise is to give you experience in designing an observation schedule to test a hypothesis. If your police department
has a program allowing citizens to accompany police officers, you
might even be able to do a little research with the schedule you
develop. However, the main purpose of this exercise is to deal
with the problems of making an observation schedule that will
test two competing hypotheses.

In observational surveys on the police, some researchers have
found that the decision to make an arrest is based on the demeanor
of the subject under suspicion. Other studies have found that a
more important causal variable is the complaining party's attitude
toward having the police make an arrest. Is the suspect's demeanor
more important in a potential arrest situation, or is it the com-
plainant's desire to have the police take the suspect to jail? Design
an observation schedule that would resolve this argument. Remember, though, that the schedule is based on what can be seen and
heard by the observer without asking questions.

EXERCISE 3

The samples considered in questionnaire surveys generally involve such units as individuals and households; while in observation surveys, time samples and situation samples are more important. The purpose of this exercise is to demonstrate the importance of sampling at different times of the day and days of the week.

Choose a public place frequented by different groups at all times of the day, such as a public park, a bowling alley, or a downtown street. On slips of paper write all the hours of day. Put the slips in a box and draw a 25 per cent sample. Observe the setting you have chosen during the sample hours to see whether there are different groups or forms of activities during the different times. Also, compare weekdays and weekends.

EXERCISE 4

The purpose of this exercise is to determine, using an observation survey, whether there is a relationship between the way in which a person presents himself in traffic court and what the judge decides to do with the case. This exercise is very much like Wiseman's study, which found a relationship between social type and sentencing, except that a traffic court, instead of a drunk court, is the observational setting.

The observation schedules should be typed on duplication masters and several copies made, so that there is a sheet for each case to be observed. Below is an example of what the observation sheet might look like; but, since state and local traffic laws differ depending on where you live, be sure that the observation schedule reflects your particular court.

Traffic Court Observation Schedule

Date _____ Judge _____ Violation _____

Researcher _____ Case # _____

   1. Appearance
      a. Dressed up _____
      b. Casual _____
      c. Sloppy _____

2. Sex
   a. Female   _____
   b. Male   _____
3. Ethnic Background
   a. White   _____
   b. Black   _____
   c. Other   _____
      (specify)
4. Demeanor
   a. Antagonistic   _____
   b. Polite   _____
   c. Humble   _____
5. Age
   a. Juvenile (under 18)   _____
   b. Young adult (18–25)   _____
   c. Adult (26–40)   _____
   d. Middle age (40–60)   _____
   e. Senior citizen (60+)   _____
6. Plea
   a. Guilty   _____
   b. Not guilty   _____
7. Type of Explanation
   a. Apology   _____
   b. Police officer's
      fault   _____
   c. Accident   _____
   d. Road or traffic
      conditions   _____
   e. Ignorance   _____
   f. Other (specify) _____
8. Outcome (what the judge decided)

   _____
   _____
   _____

Once the data have been collected, categorize the open-ended observations—the offences and the outcomes. For example, violations can be grouped into "speeding," "illegal maneuver," and other such categories. Outcomes should be dichotimized into relative "win" and "lose" categories. A small fine, for example, might be seen as a "win" in a case where the possible fine is high. Then code the data and analyze the results, using multivariate analysis.

Treat the "outcome" as the dependent variable and each of the other items as the independent variable. Keep the analysis simple by taking only a single item at a time, as the independent variable to be compared to the dependent variable. Finally, see which item has the highest relationship with the courtroom outcome.

ADDITIONAL READING SUGGESTIONS

CUMMING, ELAINE, IAN CUMMING, and LAURA EDELL. 1965. "Policeman as Philosopher, Guide and Friend," *Social Problems*, 12, pp. 276–86. This observation survey provides a useful model for the student. Instead of using an observation sheet or note pad, the researchers recorded their observations of incoming police calls on tape. The analysis of these data was then done in the same way as any other survey.

REISS, ALBERT J., JR. 1968. "Stuff and Nonsense about Social Surveys and Observation," in Howard S. Becker et al. (eds.), *Institutions and the Person*, Chicago: Aldine, pp. 351–67. In this discussion of a large-scale study of the police, Reiss explains how many of the elements of survey research can be accomplished with observers in the place of questionnaires. He also discusses the problems that observers have in overidentifying with their subjects—a problem not found when questionnaire surveys are used.

III: THE EXPERIMENT

In the adventures of Sherlock Holmes, the detective often encountered problems that he resolved by the use of experiments. In one case chronicled by Dr. Watson, known as "The Problem of Thor Bridge," Holmes was attempting to account for the shooting death of a woman found on a bridge. The only clue was a chip on the stone balustrade of the bridge next to the place where the dead woman was found. Taking his cane, Holmes struck the bridge several times without succeeding in replicating a mark like the chip. This experiment showed Holmes that it was unlikely that the dead woman had been attacked by someone with a cane or stick who had used more than a single weapon in killing her. Using his famous analytic imagination, Holmes proposed another hypothesis and experiment. He reasoned that if the woman had killed herself and wanted to frame someone for her death, she would have had to do it in a way that would make the weapon disappear so it would not look like suicide. To test this hypothesis, Sherlock Holmes borrowed Dr. Watson's revolver and tied a string to it. On the other end of the string he tied a large rock. He then suspended the rock over the edge of the bridge and held the gun next to his head standing near where the woman was found. Then Holmes released the gun and it was pulled over the side of the bridge and into the water by the rock attached to the other end of the string. As the gun was pulled into the water, it hit against the stone balustrade of the bridge and left a chip similar to the first one he found. Thus

Holmes demonstrated, using a simple experiment, that, instead of being murdered, the woman had committed suicide.

Like surveys, experiments are also used to find relationships between variables. Unlike surveys, however, experiments are designs in which the researcher manipulates variables intentionally in order to locate such relationships (Simon, 1969:228). Specifically, the researcher manipulates an independent variable to find what effect it has on a dependent variable. In the Moriarty experiment (Chapter 6), the independent variables of stigma and public and secret status were manipulated to assess their relationship to attraction and conformity, the dependent variables.

The basic logic behind experiments is that if, in the presence of a given variable, certain changes are seen to occur in another variable, and if these changes do not occur in the absence of the given variable, then the changes, all other elements being equal, must have been due to the given variable. In other words, if the dependent variable changes when the independent variable is present but does not when it is absent, then the independent variable caused the change in the dependent variable. For example, if a class of students talks noisily while the instructor is out of the class but becomes quiet when he enters the room, the change in the level of classroom noise (dependent variable) is caused by the instructor's presence (independent variable).

In order to create a situation in which the effect of an independent variable can be tested, two similar groups are observed or tested at two different times. The first test is intended to establish their similarity. Then one group is exposed to the independent variable and the other is not. The results of a post-test of the two groups indicate the effect of the independent variable. This design is the *classical experiment* (Phillips, 1971:113–115). The elements of the classical experiment include a *pretest* and a *post-test*, a *control group* and an *experimental group*, and an *experimental variable*.

The sequence of operation for the classical experiment begins with a hypothesis. For example, an educator might hypothesize that, if students are given positive encouragement, they will perform better in a learning task—say, mastering a list of spelling words. In order to test this hypothesis experimentally, the researcher would take a group of students who were equal in academic ability and divide them into a control group and an experimental group. Next, the researcher would test each group to make sure they were equal. This is the pretest. In this case, the researcher might use a spelling test as a pretest. Next, the researcher introduces the experimental variable, positive encouragement—for instance, saying a kind word—but only to the experimental group. He would not give the control group positive encouragement of any sort. Both groups would be treated the same in every other way, with the sole exception that *only* members of the experimental group would receive encouragement. Finally, the two groups would be tested a second time on the list of spelling words to find whether there were any performance differences between them. If there is a difference, and all other aspects of the composition of the group and the experimental procedure were held constant, the difference can be attributed to the experimental variable—that is, the experimental variable can be said to have *caused* the difference.

The classical experimental design has been highly successful in the natural sciences, and it has therefore been widely used in social research as well. Unlike natural scientists, however, sociologists deal with a subject matter that has a mind of its own, and they have therefore encountered problems not found in the natural sciences. For example, when people enter an experimental setting or situation, they are generally aware that the experimenter is attempting to find experimentally induced change, and they often attempt to "help" the experimenter by responding "properly" (Webb et al., 1966:12–21). Awareness that they are subjects in an experiment, in other words, becomes the causal factor in their behavior, instead of the experimental variable. Sometimes, the pretest itself will raise questions in the subjects' minds that themselves cause the subjects later to change their minds on the post-test. Middleton (1960), in his experiment, found, for example, that anti-Semitic attitudes for both the experimental and the control group was less on the post-test than on the pretest. Apparently, once the subjects realized that they were anti-Semitic, they re-evaluated their attitudes; and the realization was prompted by the pretest, not by the experimental variable.

In order to determine the effect of the pretest on subjects, the Solomon four-group design was developed (Solomon, 1949). Besides having all the elements of a classical experiment, the Solomon four-group design has an additional control group and experimental group that are not given pretests. All four groups are randomly selected and are therefore equal. If there are any differences in the post-tests of the two control groups or the two experimental groups, these differences are attributed to the effect of the pretest. If, however, both control groups are the same in the post-test but different from the experimental groups, the difference can be attributed solely to the experimental variable. Diagrammatically, the Solomon four-group appears as follows:

	Pretest	*Experimental variable*	*Post-test*
Control Group 1	Yes	No	Yes
Control Group 2	No	No	Yes
Experimental Group 1	Yes	Yes	Yes
Experimental Group 2	No	Yes	Yes

An attempt to offset the artificiality of a laboratory setting is the *natural* or *field experiment* (Swingle, 1973). Basically, a field experiment is one in which the researcher introduces the experimental variable into a natural setting to see what effect it has on behavior in the setting. In such experiments, the researcher lacks the control he has in experiments that take place in a small group laboratory or in other settings he arranges; but they have greater external validity, because they take place in naturally occurring social life. For example, to find whether there is a relationship between having a Black Panther bumper sticker and being cited for traffic violations, a researcher selected 15 subjects who had no traffic violations in twelve months and had them affix Black Panther bumper stickers to their cars (Heussenstamm, 1971). The subjects began receiving so many tickets that the experiment had to be discontinued. The results thus confirmed the relationship hypothesized (Heussenstamm, 1971). The "pretest" in this experiment, as in many other field experiments, consisted of the events preceding the introduction of the experimental variable—the absence of traffic violations—and the "post-test" consisted of the events subsequent to the introduction of the experimental variable.

The two selections that follow represent a laboratory experiment and a field experiment. Moriarty's experiment provides an example of- how the experimental researcher can manipulate a controlled setting to test a hypothesis. The study by Russo and Sommer, on the other hand, is a creative example of a field experiment taking place in a natural setting, introducing "sitting too close" as an experimental variable to test the maintenance of personal space.

REFERENCES

HEUSSENSTAMM, F. K. 1971. "Bumper Stickers and the Cops," *Trans-action* 8, pp. 32–33.

MIDDLETON, RUSSEL. 1960. "Ethnic Prejudice and Susceptibility to Persuasion," *The American Sociological Review*, 25 (October) pp. 679–86.

PHILLIPS, B. S. 1971. *Social Research: Strategy and Tactics.* New York: Macmillan.

SIMON, J. L. 1969. *Basic Research Methods in Social Science.* New York: Random House.

SOLOMON, R. L. 1949. "Extension of Control Group Design," *Psychological Bulletin*, 46, pp. 137–50.

SWINGLE, P. G. 1973. *Social Psychology in Natural Settings.* Chicago: Aldine.

WEBB, EUGENE, D. T. CAMPBELL, R. D. SCHWARTZ, and L. SECHREST. 1966. *Unobtrusive Measures: Nonreactive Research in the Social Sciences.* Chicago: Rand McNally.

6. Laboratory Experiment

ROLE OF STIGMA IN THE EXPERIENCE OF DEVIANCE
—Thomas Moriarty

DEVIANCE, AS A SOCIAL CATEGORY, includes diverse types of individuals and groups. A contemporary listing (Goffman, 1963) includes "prostitutes, drug addicts, delinquents, criminals, jazz musicians, bohemians, gypsies, carnival workers, hobos, winos, show people, full-time gamblers, beach dwellers, homosexuals, and the urban unrepentant poor [pp. 143–44]." More general lists (e.g., Clinard, 1963) have included the mentally ill and members of racial and ethnic minorities.

Although it is agreed that there are special consequences for those included in this category, the necessary and sufficient conditions for placement are subject to debate. Becker (1963) and Clinard (1963) suggest that deviance involves two factors—being different from the majority and being devalued (or, in Goffman's terms, stigmatized) for the difference. Taking an apparently more parsimonious view, Freedman and Doob (1968) suggest that simple minority status is sufficient to produce feelings of deviance in the individual. The effects of the stigma factor are examined in the present study. To the extent that stigma is important, the phenomena usually associated with social deviance will be present when stigma is involved and absent when minority status is not devalued.

Journal of Personality and Social Psychology 1974, Vol. 29, No. 6, 849–55.

Phenomena of Social Deviance.   Deviancy, at least initially, is unpleasant for the individual. For Goffman (1963), the deviant's major problem is acceptance by nondeviants, and the tendency for unanimous majorities to reject and ridicule deviants has been experimentally demonstrated (Asch, 1952; Schachter, 1951). Individuals, therefore, may try to avoid being deviant or at least avoid being recognized by others as deviant. Becker (1963) suggests that "secret deviants" are quite numerous, and Goffman has many conjectures about the problems of "passing," techniques the deviant uses to control and conceal information that would signal his deviation and discredit him in the eyes of others.

In the event that neither change nor secrecy is possible or desirable, the individual may seek out others who share his deviancy. The new reference group may help the individual validate his deviant aspect as natural and good (Festinger, 1954) while satisfying needs for acceptance and providing skills for dealing with the problems of being deviant. (In the case of racial and ethnic minorities, this is usually accomplished during socialization.)

Membership in a deviant group has psychological consequences for the individual, especially in his relations with fellow deviants. On a simple level, one might assume that a deviant individual would like his fellow deviants more than he would nondeviants. Much psychological theory (e.g., Heider, 1958) as well as research (e.g., Byrne, 1961) have been devoted to the simple proposition that interpersonal attraction is a function of similarity. On the other hand, it has occasionally been suggested that ambivalence is common among deviants, which in the extreme, becomes self-hatred. For Lewin (1948), self-hatred toward similar others stems from the fact that being identified with the group may limit the individual's opportunities, engendering frustration and aggression; the latter cannot be directed against the majority (which is highly valued because of the opportunities it offers), and so it is directed against the self and similar others.

Conformity (the tendency to be influenced in one's judgments by the judgments of others) is a fact of group life. As Festinger (1954) has suggested, the costs and difficulties involved in performing reality tests often necessitate reliance on group wisdom. Members of deviant groups are not exempt from this fact, although the majority may cease to function as the appropriate reference group. As Cooley (1902) pointed out, nonconformity to the majority may reflect conformity to a deviant reference group rather than independence on the part of the individual. It seems likely that an individual who has adopted a deviant reference group will conform more to fellow deviants than to nondeviants. In a study using a similar methodology, Darley, Moriarty, Darley, and Berscheid (1974) found support for this hypothesis.

The Present Study. Assuming a minority-majority situation arises, under what conditions will the minority individual *feel* deviant? It is assumed that feelings of deviance are revealed in the following way: (a) attempts to change the deviant aspect, thereby avoiding the unpleasantness of deviant status; (b) ambivalence toward similar others, that is, fellow deviants; (c) a change in reference group, indicated by greater reliance on the judgments of fellow deviants than on those of the majority; and (d) an attempt to pass as nondeviant when the individual's deviance is unknown to others.

In the present experiment, an attempt was made to create deviance in the laboratory, based on opinion divergence. Each subject discovered during the course of an opinion exchange that his opinions on important political and social issues were at variance with those of the majority of others present. One of the others in the group consistently agreed with his opinions, thereby providing social support. To assess the effects of stigma, the minority was derogated in half of the cases; to assess the consequences of secret deviance, the subject either announced his opinions publicly to the group or merely listened to the opinions of the others. The variables were manipulated orthogonally, giving rise to four conditions under which opinion divergence occurred. After indicating first impressions of each of the other members of the group, the subject was paired with one of them in a disguised test of susceptibility to social influence. Finally, after completing a questionnaire designed to elicit his feelings about the experience, the subject was fully debriefed and was thanked for his cooperation.

METHOD

Subjects. The subjects were white males, drawn from the Introductory Psychology courses at New York University and

Fairleigh Dickinson. The original design called for 80 subjects (10 per cell), and the experiment continued until that quota was met.[1]

Procedure. Each subject received a telephone call inviting him to take part in a human relations study scheduled for the following day. He was told that the study would take about one hour of his time and, while providing information about how people work together, would enable him to fulfill part of the research requirement in the Introductory Psychology course. The subject was told to be on time since the study could not begin until all participants had arrived.

Upon arrival, the subject was ushered into one of a series of small rooms containing a desk and chair, a set of headphones, and a wall sign that stated, "You are Subject No. 6." When seated, the subject was directed to fill out an opinion inventory that consisted of 10 attitudinal statements dealing with the war in Viet Nam, the wisdom of capital punishment, freedom of the press, etc. After indicating agreement or disagreement with each item, the subject was directed to don the headphones through which he would receive all subsequent instructions. The experimenter then left, and the opinion exchange began.

Via the headphone set, the subject was told that the purpose of the experiment was to see how first impressions are formed. The experimenter would read each item and the subject, when his number was called, was to announce his opinion on the issue by reading the answer he had written on the opinion inventory, which he still had before him. During the exchange, the subject was to form an impression of each of the others in the group.

By the time the exchange had ended, the subject had learned that on 8 of the 10 issues, four of the five others (the majority) consistently disagreed with his views; one of the five (the fellow minority member) consistently agreed with him on those 8 issues.

---

[1] Actually, 90 subjects participated in the experiment. Ten subjects (11% of the total sample) expressed strong doubts about the true purpose of the auditory acuity test during the debriefing. Suspicious subjects were excluded prior to the data analysis, which was based on 80 subjects; however, subsequent analyses based on all 90 subjects revealed no major departures from the findings reported here.

Of course, each subject was "Subject No. 6." Following the suggestions of Blake and Brehm (1954), a tape recording was used to simulate the presence of the group. By means of a dual-track stereo tape recording, all subjects heard the identical pattern of disagreement, regardless of the opinions they held.[2]

INDEPENDENT VARIABLES

Stigma. Halfway through the opinion exchange "Subject No. 1" (the voice of an experimental confederate) interrupted the proceedings:

> May I ask a question . . . without spoiling anything? I've been thinking about what's been going on and . . . it's hard to believe anybody would have answers different from ours—I mean they're *obvious*, a guy would have to be *weird!*

At that point, other voices joined in, muttering agreement with Subject No. 1. The experimenter then cautioned all subjects against talking out of turn and resumed the exchange.

Public Versus Secret Status. All subjects were instructed to announce their opinions to the group; however, in the secret conditions, the subjects did not. On the very first item of the opinion exchange, the experimenter announced that Subject No. 6's reply was not audible and attributed it to a probable malfunction in the latter's microphone that would be corrected later. The experimenter resumed the exchange, suggesting that if Subject No. 6 could hear the proceedings, he was to try to form an impression of the others.

DEPENDENT VARIABLES

Attraction. At the end of the exchange, the subject rated each of the others on a series of 20-point scales. The scale designed to measure attraction provided the subject with verbal anchors that corresponded to the scale values as follows: 17–20 points (extreme liking), 13–16 points (moderate liking), 9–12 points (neither like nor dislike), 5–8 points (moderate dis-

[2] The technical details of the procedure are outlined in: J. Darley and T. Moriarty, "Techniques for the experimental study of conformity." Unpublished manuscript, 1965 (available from the author on request).

liking), and 1–4 points (extreme disliking). The experimenter entered the subject's room briefly to make sure the rating instructions were clear. (In the secret conditions, the experimenter used this opportunity to replace the subject's "defective" microphone.)

Conformity. After completing the first-impressions inventory, the subject took part in a test allegedly designed to measure auditory acuity. The test (again conducted with headphones) involved judging the number of clicks over a series of 12 trials.[3] Subjects worked on the test in pairs, and after each trial the real subject (who was always preceded by a confederate of the experimenter) announced his judgment. The pairing of confederate and subject was made to appear as though determined by chance.[4] In fact, the subject was paired either with Subject No. 4 (the fellow minority member) or Subject No. 5 (one of the former majority). In either case, the auditory judgments of the confederates were identical, with confederates systematically overestimating on 11 of the 12 trials. (On the first trial, the confederate gave the correct answer.) Overestimates ranged from 1 to 15 points, and on 7 of the 11 trials the confederate's estimates were 10 points over the correct answer.

The test just described was intended as a measure of susceptibility to social influence, and the index of conformity was the number of times the subject overestimated on the 11 critical trials.

Results

Feelings of Deviance and Avoidance Behavior. It has been suggested that the feeling of deviance is unpleasant and that the individual tries to avoid deviant status when possible. The feeling of deviance should evidence itself in the desire to change one's

[3] The clicks were produced by an electric metronome and recorded at a speed of 360 beats per minute. The average number of clicks per trial was 45, the range, from 31 to 65. The task was difficult, and correct judgments were infrequent. Baseline (no influence) data for an accidental sample of 10 male students indicated that errors of underestimation were most common; errors of overestimation occurred on 2.1 of the 11 critical trials. In this experiment, concern was not with accuracy but with errors of overestimation.

[4] When the subject arrived for the experiment, he signed a form for the experimenter's records that had already been "signed" by the others in the group. The purpose of this procedure was twofold: It added credibility to the pretense that there really were others in the group and predetermined work pairs for the auditory acuity study. The pairing was pointed out to the subject as he signed the form.

deviant aspect and, in some cases, in actual change. Two sources of data are relevant to this issue.

1. On the postexperimental questionnaire (before debriefing), subjects were asked to reflect on the opinion exchange and to report whatever feelings they had experiencd at that time. Specifically, they were asked: "On those occasions when there was disagreement did you experience, even for just a brief moment, a desire to change your opinion, to make it more like the others?" Of the 80 subjects, 27 (34%) reported experiencing a desire to change. Thus, about one third of the subjects found minority status unpleasant enough to want to change. However, this tendency was not randomly distributed throughout conditions. While 20% of those in the nonstigma conditions reported this desire, 48% in the stigma conditions did so ($z = 2.77$, $p < .01$). Stated differently, 19 of the 27 subjects (70%) who reported wanting to change were in the stigma conditions.

2. The experimental instructions were designed to discourage the occurrence of opinion change during the exchange since the latter, if it occurred to any large extent, would weaken the opinion divergence manipulation. The subjects were told that, during the exchange, they were simply to read aloud the opinions they had indicated on the opinion inventory. Violation of this instruction was infrequent in the public conditions. Fortunately, when it did occur subjects spontaneously "corrected" the opinion inventory to bring it up to date with their public statements. Of course, those in the secret conditions did not announce their opinions publicly, but an examination of the opinion inventories after the exchange indicated that they too changed some opinions during the exchange.

Of the 80 subjects, 13 (16%) made one or more changes on the opinion inventory after the exchange had begun, and 11 of the 13 were in the stigma conditions. Thus, when overt opinion change occurs in the minority situation, it does so primarily when the minority is derogated ($p = .04$).[5]

[5] In manipulating opinion divergence, it was arranged that subjects hear disagreement from the majority on 8 of the 10 opinion items. It is unlikely that changes during the opinion exchange materially reduced the impact of the manipulation. There were only 20 instances of opinion change for the 13 subjects who did change; change typically involved only 1 of the 8 critical items.

Interpersonal Attraction. At the conclusion of the opinion exchange, each subject indicated his liking for the fellow minority member and the four majority members. For each subject, the rating given the fellow minority member was compared with the best rating given the majority members.

The overall rating assigned to the fellow minority member was 14.8, clearly in that range of the scale labeled moderate liking. For the majority, the overall rating was, on the average, 11.3, which corresponds to the neutral range on the scale. This difference was reliable (for paired observations, $t = 7.45, p < .01$) and large ($r = .64$), accounting for roughly 41% of the variance in ratings. Thus, the subject typically views the fellow minority member with warm regard, while the majority, at best, is viewed with neutrality.

TABLE I LIKING SCORES FOR THE FELLOW MINORITY MEMBER

Condition	Nonstigma	Stigma
Public	16.7	14.5
Secret	15.0	12.9

NOTE: The higher the liking score, the more positive the rating.

The analysis of variance (Winer, 1962) was performed on the ratings of the fellow minority member to assess the effects of stigma on liking. As can be seen in Tables I and II, stigma had a pronounced effect on liking for the fellow minority member: When the minority members were derogated by the majority, attraction between them was significantly lowered, though still in the positive range. The public–secret variable also produced a main effect: Liking for the fellow minority member was greater in the public than in the secret conditions. The absence of an interaction indicates that the two effects were additive, and the

TABLE II ANALYSIS OF VARIANCE: LIKING SCORES FOR THE
FELLOW MINORITY MEMBER

Source	df	MS	F
Public (A)	1	54.50	6.00*
Stigma (B)	1	92.50	10.18†
A × B	1	.00	<1
Within	76	9.09	

* $p < .05$.
† $p < .01$.

fellow minority member was liked least in the case in which difference was stigmatized and the subject's own position was unknown to others.

Susceptibility to Social Influence. After completing the first-impressions inventory, subjects were paired with one of the confederates in a disguised test of social influence. One half of the subjects in each condition ·were paired with the fellow minority

TABLE III   CONFORMITY TO A MAJORITY MEMBER

Condition	Nonstigma	Stigma
Public	3.0	3.8
Secret	2.5	2.6

TABLE IV   ANALYSIS OF VARIANCE:
CONFORMITY TO A MAJORITY MEMBER

Source	df	MS	F
Public (A)	1	7.23	<1
Stigma (B)	1	2.03	<1
A×B	1	1.23	<1
Within	36	8.79	

member and the other half, with a former majority member. (At this point in the analysis, then, there are eight cells.) For subjects paired with the fellow majority member, the conformity rate was 5.1; for those paired with the former majority member, 3.0. The difference was reliable ($t = 3.09$, $p < .01$). Thus, it would appear that the fellow minority member is, in general able to exert more influence than is a former majority member.[6]

As can be seen in Tables III and IV, conformity to the former majority member was relatively unaffected by either the public or the stigma variable. Conformity to the fellow minority member was, however, affected by the experimental factors: Conformity was more frequent in the stigma than in the nonstigma conditions and was more frequent in the public than in the secret conditions (see Tables V and VI). The presence of a significant interaction suggests that the obtained effects were largely due to the high rate of conformity in the public-stigma

[6] A comparison between this data and data obtained in the no-influence situation reveals that the subject was relatively immune to influence emanating from a former majority member ($t=.92$, $p>.05$) but was quite open to influence from a fellow minority member ($t=2.96$, $p<.01$).

condition. Duncan's new multiple-range test, contrasting all eight groups, reveals that conformity to the fellow minority member was more frequent in the public-stigma condition than in all the other conditions ($p < .01$). The remaining seven conditions did not differ reliably from each other ($p > .05$, in all cases). Thus, conformity to a fellow minority member was heightened only when the minority status of the subject was known to the group and when stigma was involved.

TABLE V CONFORMITY TO THE FELLOW MINORITY MEMBER

Condition	Nonstigma	Stigma
Public	3.4	8.8
Secret	3.8	4.2

TABLE VI ANALYSIS OF VARIANCE: CONFORMITY TO THE FELLOW MINORITY MEMBER

Source	df	MS	F
Public (A)	1	44.10	4.63*
Stigma (B)	1	84.10	8.82†
A×B	1	62.50	6.56*
Within	36	9.53	

* $p < .05$.
† $p < .01$.

DISCUSSION

The major focus of the present study is on the role of stigma in the experience of deviance, and current beliefs about "real-world" deviant individuals serve as criteria for assessing the importance of this variable. Specifically, to the extent that stigma is important, the feelings and behavior usually attributed to deviant individuals should be present in the stigma conditions and absent (or weak) in the nonstigma conditions.

The discovery that one is deviant is unpleasant, and individuals try to avoid being deviant, or at least avoid appearing deviant to others. In the present experiment, there were two manifestations of this avoidance: the desire to change one's opinions during the change and actual change (in spite of instructions to the contrary). The opinion items were selected to insure a lack of novelty, and it was assumed that most subjects would have clear opinions on the issues. Therefore, instances of change are viewed as attempts to avoid appearing deviant by reducing the overt discrepancy between the subject and the majority. While minority status in this experiment was unpleasant enough to produce these effects, they occurred primarily in the stigma conditions and only to a trivial degree in the nonstigma conditions.

The expected relationship between opinion similarity and attraction was confirmed: Agreers (fellow minority members) were liked more than were disagreers (the majority). An exception to this well-established rule is that deviants, despite similarity on the deviance dimension, feel ambivalence toward fellow deviants. Data in the present study suggest that stigma is responsible for ambivalence: While subjects in the nonstigma conditions viewed the fellow minority member with warm regard, these feelings were considerably dampened by the occurrence of stigma.

The significant main effect of the public—secret variable on the attractiveness of the fellow minority member indicates that liking for the latter is less when the subject's status is unknown to the group. Perhaps this phenomenon may be understood in terms of Heider's (1958) suggestion that interaction leads to increased liking. In the public conditions the subject took part in the exchange, while in the secret conditions the subject was merely a passive observer. The absence of a significant interaction, however, indicates that stigma decreases the attractiveness of the fellow minority member, whether the subject's own minority status is known or unknown to the others in the group.

The conformity data are consistent with the notion that deviants conform more to fellow deviants than to the majority. As we have seen, this is true only in the public-stigma condition. In all other conditions there was no difference between conformity to the fellow minority member and conformity to the majority. Again, the importance of the stigma factor is evident.

It has been proposed that secret deviants feel deviant but generally try to pass as nondeviant in the eyes of others. The responses of subjects in the secret-stigma condition fit this pattern rather nicely: Private feelings toward the fellow minority member are characterized by the ambivalence usually associated with deviants, while public behavior is marked by independence of others known to be deviant.

The implications of these findings for the study of social deviance should be clear. Freedman and Doob (1968) have suggested that "if someone is different enough on any dimension regardless of whether the difference is evaluated positively or negatively he will be considered and consider himself a deviant [p. 4]." The opinion divergence created in the present experiment is quite extreme, and the present data indicates that although there may be consequences of being different from others, the reaction of the others is a critical determinant of the experience of deviance.

Of course, the anticipation of stigma on the part of an individual who discovers he is different may produce similar effects. This is especially true if the difference is novel and salient for the individual. As suggested in social comparison theory, the individual will most likely try to evaluate the difference. In the absence of physical and social reality-testing opportunities, he will probably assign some meaning to the difference, based on the anticipated reactions of others to the discrepancy. The interesting findings of Freedman and Doob (1968), attributed to nonevaluative but extreme difference, may in fact be due to anticipated evaluations on the part of the subjects. One disadvantage of creating novel differences for the study of social deviance lies in the fact that anticipated evaluations (positive or negative) are likely to be affected by a host of factors not under experimental control. In the absence of information to the contrary, the neutrality of opinion differences is usually taken for granted. As many subjects in this experiment asserted, everyone is entitled to his own opinion.

The present study may also add to our knowledge of small groups. When a difference of opinion exists in a group, the majority may try to change minority opinion by derogating dissenters. As we have seen in this experiment, derogation of a minority that can be publicly identified may have quite opposite effects. Rather than changing the minority, derogation may serve to increase polarization and foster schism within the group.

REFERENCES

ASCH, S. E. 1952. *Social psychology.* Englewood Cliffs, N.J.: Prentice-Hall.
BECKER, H. S. 1963. *Outsiders.* New York: Free Press.

BLAKE, R. R., and BREHM, J. W. 1954. The use of tape recording to simulate a group atmosphere. *Journal of Abnormal and Social Psychology*, 49: 311–13.

BYRNE, D. 1961. Interpersonal attraction and attitudinal similarity. *Journal of Abnormal and Social Psychology*, 62: 713–15.

CLINARD, M. B. 1963. *Sociology of deviant behavior*. New York: Holt, Rinehart & Winston.

COOLEY, C. H. 1902. *Human nature and the social order*. New York: Scribner.

DARLEY, J., MORIARTY, T., DARLEY, S., & BERSCHEID, E. 1974. Increased conformity to a fellow deviant as a function of prior deviation. *Journal of Experimental Social Psychology*, 10:211–23.

FESTINGER, L. 1954. A theory of social comparison processes. *Human Relations*, 117–140.

FREEDMAN, J. L., and DOOB, A. N. 1968. *Deviancy*. New York: Academic Press.

GOFFMAN, E. 1963. *Stigma*. Englewood Cliffs, N.J.: Prentice-Hall.

HEIDER, F. 1958. *The psychology of interpersonal relations*. New York: Wiley.

LEWIN, K. 1948. *Resolving social conflicts*. New York: Harper and Row.

SCHACHTER, S. 1951. Deviation, rejection and communication. *Journal of Abnormal and Social Psychology*, 46, 190–208.

WINER, B. J. 1962. *Statistical principles in experimental design*. New York: McGraw-Hill.

EXERCISES   Many laboratory experiments are conducted in elaborate settings with two-way mirrors, special rooms for control and experimental groups, and a vast array of hardware to ensure total environmental control. While such facilities are desirable for experiments, they are not mandatory. The following exercises are designed to require minimal laboratory facilities. The first two exercises deal with problems in experimental design and require no facilities of any sort; the second two require only a room in which the experiments can be conducted. A small room or even an office will suffice for Exercise 3, and a larger room where a group presentation can be made is necessary for Exercise 4. These facilities should be available at your school.

EXERCISE 1

In the introduction to this section, we described an experiment in which the researcher introduced as the experimental variable "positive encouragement", defined, in this case, as a "kind word." In fact, a great many other things could be regarded as positive encouragement. The purpose of this exercise is to develop experimental variables in terms of concrete actions to be introduced in experiments. Consider the following as experimental variables:

1. Positive Encouragement
2. Threat
3. Authority
4. Disorganization

Now take each one of these variables and write a set of actions that will be introduced in an experiment. It will help to consider each variable in terms of a hypothesis stating its causal effect on social behavior. For example, you might think of the variable "authority" (such as a police officer, a dean, or a boss) as causing more or less group interaction. The important thing is not what the experimental variable will cause but, rather, what concrete actions can be introduced as representing the variable.

EXERCISE 2

The purpose of this exercise is much like that of Exercise 1, except that, rather than develop a set of actions that can be introduced as an experimental variable, here you are to develop a measurement for a dependent variable. The task should be done in groups of three or four, each of which will attempt to develop an observable or testable measure of "group cohesiveness." Group cohesiveness, or group solidarity, refers to the strength of the relationships in a group and of ties to the group. For example, during prolonged periods of combat, fighting units develop very strong ties and have a high amount of solidarity. The problem is to measure such cohesiveness. If a researcher has the hypothesis that group solidarity increases as threat to the group increases, he needs some measure to find whether the group's cohesiveness increases or decreases. By working with a group, the student will discuss what might be observed or tested. Each member of the group is to write a set of observations or questions that would serve as such a measure. He will then compare his list with the list of other members in an effort to develop a measurement that the group agrees on. Each group will present its measurement to the other groups for discussion. (The purpose of working in groups is so that the measurement that is developed can be tested in the group.)

Exercise 3

This exercise is a simple experiment to test whether there is a relationship between negative images and presentations of self. Using an experimental group and a control group and a one-time observation, present the following set of symbols to both groups:

The experimental group will be told that two of these symbols have a high preference among mental patients (negative image); the control group will simply be shown the drawings and told nothing. Each group will be told to rank the drawings on a continuum from most intuitively pleasing to least pleasing. If the hypothesis is correct, the experimental group will have a lower ranking of preference for the two symbols (presentation of self) that were said to have a high preference among mental patients than will the control group.

If there is no difference between experimental and control groups in preferences, take the two figures most preferred by the two groups combined and do the experiment again with different subjects, telling the experimental group that the two new figures were highly preferred by mental patients. If there is still no difference, reject the hypothesis.

EXERCISE 4

This exercise is designed to test whether there is a relationship between antismoking propaganda and smoking behavior. Design the experiment along those of the classical form. Using a film or slide presentation that describes the damage caused by smoking, see if there is a change in smoking behavior in the experimental group. (Your local chapter of the American Cancer Society or the Heart Association should have films or slide presentations; but a speech by a local physician or someone from the health department would serve the same function.) Pretest the control and experimental groups for similarity in smoking behavior; all subjects in both groups must be smokers. After the introduction of the experimental variable, use several post-tests over a period of time to determine whether the propaganda has had any effect on smoking behavior. You might find that there is an immediate effect, or there may be no effect for some time, if at all; by administering post-tests over a period of time, any delayed effects can be found.

ADDITIONAL READING SUGGESTIONS

ASCH, SOLOMON E. 1956. "Studies of Independence and Conformity: A Minority of One Against a Unanimous Majority," *Psychological Monographs*, Vol. 70, No. 9. Describes a now-famous experiment. In a unique design, Asch showed how group pressure affected decision-making. A good example of an innovative experiment.

MILGRAM, S. 1963. "Behavioral Study of Obedience," *Journal of Abnormal Social Psychology*, 67 (October), pp. 371–78. Another example of innovation in experimental design. Milgram found that experimental subjects were quite obedient when told to give another subject an electric shock. Among other things, this experiment suggests that researchers have a good deal of influence in defining the experimental situation.

Ross, John, and Perry Smith. 1968. "Orthodox Experimental Designs." In Hubert M. Blalock and Ann B. Blalock (eds.), *Methodology in Social Research*, Chapter 9. New York: McGraw-Hill. A brief discussion of designs, variables, and analyses used in experiments in sociology and other disciplines. Points out many of the problems and pitfalls awaiting the experimental researcher in the collection and analysis of data.

Weubben, P., B.C. Straits, and G. Schulman. 1974. *The Experiment as a Social Occasion*. Berkeley, Calif.: Glenessary Press. Provides a well-rounded discussion and analysis of different types of research designs using experimental formats. It gives the novice an excellent idea of what to expect when planning an experiment.

7. Field Experiment

INVASIONS OF PERSONAL SPACE
—Nancy Jo Felipe Russo and Robert Sommer

THE LAST DECADE HAS BROUGHT an increase in empirical studies of deviance. One line of investigation has used the case study approach with individuals whom society has classified as deviants—prostitutes, drug addicts, homosexuals, mental patients, etc. The other approach, practiced less frequently, has involved staged situations in which one individual, usually the investigator or one of his students, violates the norm or "routine ground" in a given situation and observes the results. (See, for example, Garfinkel, 1964.) The latter approach is in the category of an experiment in that it is the investigator himself who creates the situation he observes and therefore has the possibility of systematically varying the parameters of social intercourse singly or in combinations. From this standpoint these studies have great promise for the development of an experimental sociology following the model set down by Greenwood (1945). With topics such as human migration, collective disturbance, social class, the investigator observes events and phenomena already in existence. Control of conditions refers to modes of observations and is largely on an *ex post facto* statistical or correlational basis. On the other hand, few staged studies of deviance have realized

From *Social Problems*, Vol. 14, No. 2 (Fall, 1966), pp. 206–14. Reprinted by permission of the authors and The Society for the Study of Social Problems.

their promise as experimental investigations. Generally they are more in the category of demonstrations, involving single gross variations of one parameter and crude and impressionistic measurement of effect without control data from a matched sample not subject to the norm violation. Of more theoretical importance is the lack of systematic variation in degree and kind of the many facets of norm violation. The reader is left with the impression that deviancy is an all-or-none phenomenon caused by improper dress, impertinent answers, naive questions, etc. It cannot be denied that a graduate student washing her clothes in the town swimming pool is breaking certain norms. But we cannot be sure of the norms that are violated or the sanctions attached to each violation without some attempt at isolating and varying single elements in the situation.

The present paper describes a series of studies of one norm violation, sitting too close to another individual. Conversational distance is affected by many things including room density, the acquaintance of the individuals, the personal relevance of the topic discussed, the cultural backgrounds of the individuals, the personalities of the individuals, etc. (Hall, 1959). There are a dozen studies of conversational distance which have shown that people from Latin countries stand closer together than North Americans (Hall, 1960), eye contact has important effect on conversational distance (Argyle and Dean, 1965), introverts stand farther apart than extroverts (Williams, 1963), friends place themselves closer together than strangers (Little, 1960), and so on, but there is still, under any set of conditions, a range of conversational distance which is considered normal for that situation. Several of these investigators, notably Birdwhistell (1952), Garfinkel (1964), Goffman (1963), and Sommer (1959) have described the effects of intruding into this distance or personal space that surrounds each individual. The interest shown in the human spacing mechanisms as well as the possibilities of objective measurement of both norm violation and defensive postures suggests that this is an excellent area in which to systematically study norm violations.

The present paper describes several studies of invasions of personal space that took place over a two-year period. The first was done during the summer of 1963 in a mental hospital. At the time it seemed that systematic studies of spatial invasions could only take place in a "crazy place" where norm violation would escape some of the usual sanctions applied in the outside world. Though there is a strong normative control system that regulates the conduct of mental patients toward one another and toward staff, the rules governing staff conduct toward patients (except cases of brutality, rape, or murder), and particularly higher status staff, such as psychiatrists, physicians, and psychologists, are much less clear. At times, it seems that almost anything can be done in a mental hospital provided it is called research, and one can cite such examples as psychosurgery, various drug experiments, and recent investigations of operant conditioning as instances where unusual and sometimes unproven or even harmful procedures were employed with the blessings of hospital officialdom. To call a procedure "research" is a way of "bracketing" it in time and space and thus excluding it from the usual rules and mores. This is one reason why we supposed that spatial invasions would be more feasible inside a mental hospital than outside. We had visions of a spatial invasion on a Central Park bench resulting in bodily assault or arrest on a sex deviant or "suspicious character" charge. It seemed that some studies of norm violation were deliberately on a one-shot basis to avoid such difficulties. After the first study of spatial invasions in a mental hospital had been completed, however, it became apparent that the method could be adapted for use in more typical settings. We were then able to undertake similar intrusions on a systematic basis in a university library without any untoward consequences, though the possibilities of such problems arising were never far beyond the reaches of consciousness in any of the experimental sessions.

METHOD

The first study took place on the grounds of Mendocino State Hospital, a 1,500-bed mental institution situated in parklike surroundings. Most wards were unlocked and many patients spent considerable time outdoors. In wooded areas it was common to see patients seated beneath trees, one to a bench. Because of the easy access to the outside as well as the number of patients involved in hospital industry, the ward areas were relatively empty during the day. This made it possible for the patients to isolate themselves from other people by finding a deserted area on the grounds or remaining in the almost empty wards. The invasions of personal space took place both indoors and outdoors. The victims were chosen on the basis of these criteria: the victim would be a male, sitting alone, and not engaged in any clearly defined activities such as reading, card playing, etc. All sessions took place near the long-stay wards, which meant that newly admitted patients were largely omitted from the study. When a patient meeting these criteria was located, E walked over and sat beside the patient without saying a word. If the victim moved his chair or moved farther down the bench, E would move a like distance to keep the space between them about six inches. There were two experimental conditions. In one, E sat alongside a patient and took complete notes of what ensued. He also jiggled his keys occasionally and looked at the patient in order to assert his dominance. In the second experimental condition, E simply sat down next to the victim and three or four times during the twenty-minute session, jiggled his keys. Control subjects were selected from other patients seated at some distance from E but still within E's visual field. To be eligible for the control group, a patient had to be sitting by himself and not reading or otherwise engaged in an activity as well as be visible to E.

Each session took a maximum of twenty minutes. There were 64 individual sessions with different patients; 39 involved the procedure in which E took notes, and 25 involved no writing.* One ward dayroom was chosen for additional, more intensive observations. During the daylight hours this large room was sparsely populated and the same five patients occupied the same chairs. These patients would meet Esser's (Esser *et al.*, 1965) criteria of territoriality in that each spent more than 75 per cent of his time in one particular area.

RESULTS

The major data of the study consist of records of how long each patient remained seated in his chair following the invasion. This

---

* Four incomplete sessions are omitted from this total. On two occasions, a patient was called away by a nurse, and, on two other occasions, the session was terminated when the patient showed signs of acute stress. The intruder in Study One was the junior author, a thirty-five-year-old male of slight build. It is likely that invasions by a husky six-footer would have produced more immediate flight reactions.

can be compared with the length of time the control patients remained seated. Figure 1 shows the cumulative number of patients who had departed at each one-minute interval of the twenty-minute session. Within two minutes, all of the controls were still seated but 36 per cent of the experimental subjects had been driven away. Within nine minutes fully half of the victims had departed compared with only 8 per cent of the controls. At the end of the twenty-minute session, 64 per cent of the experimental subjects had departed, compared with 33 per cent of the controls. Further analysis showed that the writing condition was more potent than the no-writing condition but that this difference was significant only at the .10 level ($\chi^2 = 4.61$, df $= 2$). The patient's actual departure from his chair was the most obvious reaction to the intrusion. Many more subtle indications of the patient's discomfort were evident. Typically the victim would immediately face away from E, pull in his shoulders, and place his elbows at his sides. Mumbling, irrelevant laughter, and delusional talk also seemed to be used by the victim to keep E at a distance.

Repeated observation of the same patients took place on one particular ward where the patients were extremely territorial in their behavior. Five patients generally inhabited this large room and sat in the same chairs day after day. There were gross differences in the way these particular territorial patients reacted to the writer's presence. In only one case (S_3) was E clearly dominant. At the other extreme with S_1 and S_2, it was like trying to move the Rock of Gibraltar. E invariably left these sessions defeated, with his tail between his legs, often feeling the need to return to his colleagues and drink a cup of coffee before attempting another experimental session. S_5 is a peculiar case in that sometimes he was budged but other times he wasn't.

Study Two

These sessions took place in the study hall of a university library, a large room with high ceilings and book-lined walls. The room contains fourteen large tables in two equal rows. Each table is 4 x 16 feet, and accommodates six chairs on each long side. Because of its use as a study area, students typically try to space themselves as far as possible from others. Each victim was the first female sitting alone in a pre-determined part of the room with at least one

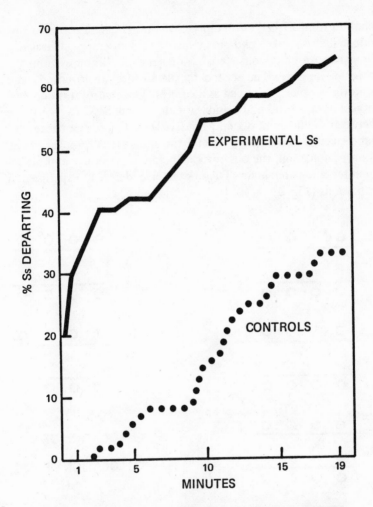

Figure 1. CUMULATIVE PERCENTAGE OF PATIENTS
HAVING DEPARTED AT ONE-MINUTE INTERVALS

book in front of her, two empty chairs on either side (or on one side if she was at the end of the table), and an empty chair across from her. An empty chair was also required to be across from E's point of invasion. The second female to meet these criteria and who was visible to E served as a control. The control was observed from a distance and no invasion was attempted. Sessions took place between the hours of 8-5 on Mondays through Fridays; because of time changes between classes and the subsequent turnover of the library population, the observations began between five and fifteen minutes after the hour. There were five different experimental conditions (Fig. 2).

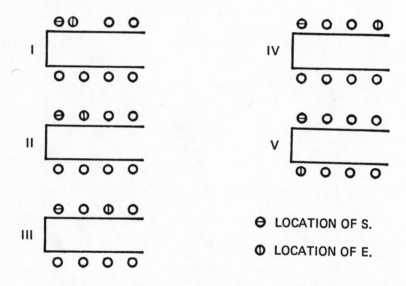

Figure 2. SEATING OF INTRUDER VIS-À-VIS
VICTIM IN EACH EXPERIMENTAL CONDITION

Condition I: E walked up to an empty chair beside an S, pulling the chair out at an angle, and sat down, completely ignoring S's presence. As E sat down, she unobtrusively moved the chair close to the table and to S, so that the chairs were approximately within three inches from one another. Then E would lean over her book.

in which she surreptitiously took notes, and tried to maintain constant shoulder distance of about 12 inches between E and S. To use Crook's (1961:125–49) terms, E tried to maintain the arrival distance, and to keep the S from adjusting to a settled distance. This was sometimes difficult to do because the chairs were 18½ inches wide and an S would sometimes sit on the other half of her chair, utilizing its width as an effective barrier. However, E tried to get as close to the Ss as possible without actually having any physical contact. If the S moved her chair away, E would follow by pushing her chair backward at an angle and then forward again, under the pretense of adjusting her skirt. At no time did she consciously acknowledge S's presence. In this condition E took detailed notes of the S's behavior, as well as noting time of departure.

Condition II: E went through the same procedure, except instead of moving the adjacent chair closer to S, E sat in the adjacent chair at the expected distance, which left about 15 inches between the chairs or about two feet between the shoulders of E and S.

Condition III: One empty seat was left between E and S, with a resulting shoulder distance of approximately three and a half feet.

Condition IV: Two empty seats were left between E and S with a resulting shoulder distance of about five feet.

Condition V: E sat directly across from S, a distance of about four feet.

In all conditions E noted the time of initial invasion, the time of the S's departure (or the end of the thirty-minute session, depending on which came first), and any observable accommodation to E's presence such as moving books or the chair. For the controls E noted the time the session began and the time of the C's departure if it occurred within thirty minutes after the start of the session.

RESULTS

Figure 3 shows the number of subjects remaining after successive five minute periods. Since there was no significant difference between the scores in Conditions II–V, these were combined in the analysis. At the end of the thirty minute session, 87 per cent of the controls, 73 per cent of the Ss in the combined conditions

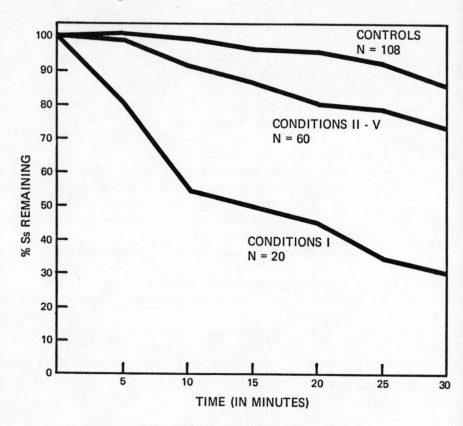

Figure 3. PER CENT OF VICTIMS REMAINING AT
FIVE MINUTE INTERVALS AFTER THE INVASION

remained, compared to only 30 per cent of the experimental Ss
in Condition I. Statistical analysis shows that Condition I produced significantly more flight than any of the other conditions,
while there was a slight but also significant difference between the
combined conditions (II–V) and the control condition. Although
flight was the most clearly defined reaction to the invasion, many
more subtle signs of the victim's discomfort were evident. Frequently an S drew in her arm and head, turned away from E
exposing her shoulder and back, with her elbow on the table, her
face resting on her hand. The victims used objects including

books, notebooks, purses, and coats as barriers, and some made the
wide chair into a barrier.

Discussion

These results show clearly that spatial invasions have a disruptive
effect and can produce reactions ranging from flight at one extreme
to agonistic display at the other. The individual differences in
reacting to the invasion are evident; there was no single reaction
among our subjects to someone "sitting too close." The victim
can attempt to accommodate himself to the invasion in numerous
ways, including a shift in position, interposing a barrier between
himself and the invader, or moving farther away. If these are pre-
cluded by the situation or fail because the invader shifts positions
too, the victim may eventually take to flight. The methods we
used did not permit the victim to achieve a comfortable *settled
distance*. Crook (1961:125–49) studied the spacing mechanisms
in birds, and found three component factors that maintain individual distance, which he defined as the area around an individual
within which the approach of a neighboring bird is reacted to with
either avoidance or attack. A number of measurements may be
taken when studying individual distance—the arrival distance (how
far away from settled birds a newcomer will land), settled distance
(the resultant distance after adjustments have occurred), and the
distance after departure. The conditions in Study One and in Condition I of the second study called for E to maintain the arrival
distance, and to keep the victim from adjusting to a settled distance. In these conditions, the victim was unable to increase the
arrival distance by moving away (since the invader followed him
down the bench in Study One and moved her chair closer in
Study Two), and the greatest number of flight reactions was produced by these conditions. McBride (1964; also McBride et al.,
1963), who has studied the spatial behaviors of animals in confine-
ment, has found that avoidance movements and turning aside are
common reactions to crowding, particularly when a submissive
animal is close to a dominant animal. Literally the dominant bird
in a flock has more space and the other birds will move aside and
look away when the dominant bird approaches. Looking away to
avoid extensive eye contact was also a common reaction in the

present studies. This probably would not have occurred if a subordinate or lower status individual had invaded the personal space of a dominant or higher status individual. There was also a dearth of direct verbal responses to the invasions. Only two of the mental patients spoke directly to E although he sat right beside them, and only one of the 80 student victims asked E to move over. This is some support for Hall's (1959) view that "we treat space somewhat as we treat sex. It is there but we don't talk about it."

We see then that a violation of expected conversational distance produces, first of all, various accommodations on the part of the victim. The intensity of his reaction is influenced by many factors including territoriality, the dominance-submission relationship between invader and victim, the locus of the invasion, the victim's attribution of sexual motives to the intruder (in this case all victims and intruders were like-sex individuals), etc. All of these factors influence the victim's definition of the situation and consequently his reaction to it. In the present situation the first reaction to the invasion was accommodation or adaptation: the individual attempted to "live with" the invasion by turning aside, interposing a notebook between himself and the stranger, and pulling in his elbows. When this failed to relieve the tension produced by the norm violation, flight reactions occurred.

There are other elements in the invasion sequence that can be varied systematically. We have not yet attempted heterosexual invasion sequences, or used invaders of lower social standing, or explored more than two unusual and contrasting environments. We are making a start toward using visual rather than spatial invasions, in this case staring at a person rather than moving too close to him. Preliminary data indicate that visual invasions are relatively ineffective in a library where the victims can easily retreat into their books and avoid a direct visual confrontation. There are many other types of intrusions, including tactile and olfactory, that have intriguing research potentialities. It is important to realize that the use of staged norm violations permits these elements to be varied singly and in combination, and in this sense to go beyond the methods of *ex post facto* or "natural experiments" or single-point demonstrations. It is noteworthy that the area of norm violation provides one of the most fruitful applications for the experimental method.

REFERENCES

ARGYLE, MICHAEL, and JANET DEAN. 1965. "Eye-Contact, Distance, and Affiliation," *Sociometry*, 28 (September), pp. 289–304.

BIRDWHISTELL, R. L. 1952. *Introduction to Kinesics*. Washington, D.C.: Foreign Service Institute.

CROOK, J. H. 1961. "The Basis of Flock Organization in Birds." In W. H. Thorpe and O. L. Zangwill (eds.), *Current Problems in Animal Behaviour*. Cambridge: Cambridge University Press.

ESSER, ARISTIDE H., et al. 1965. "Territoriality of Patients on a Research Ward." In Joseph Wortis (ed.), *Recent Advances in Biological Psychiatry*. Vol. 8. New York: Plenum Press.

GARFINKEL, HAROLD. 1964. "Studies of the Routine Grounds of Everyday Activities," *Social Problems*, 11 (Winter), pp. 225–50.

GOFFMAN, ERVING. 1963. *Behavior in Public Places*. Glencoe, Ill.: The Free Press.

GREENWOOD, ERNEST. 1945. *Experimental Sociology*. New York: Kings Crown Press.

HALL, EDWARD T. 1959. *The Silent Language*. Garden City, N.Y.: Doubleday.
———. 1960. "The Language of Space," *Landscape*, 10 (Autumn), pp. 41–44.

LITTLE, KENNETH B. 1960. "Personal Space," *Journal of Experimental Social Psychology*, 1 (August), pp. 237–47.

MCBRIDE, GLEN. 1964. *A General Theory of Social Organization and Behaviour*. St. Lucia, Australia: University of Queensland Press.

MCBRIDE, GLEN, et al. 1963. "Social Forces Determining Spacing and Head Orientation in a Flock of Domestic Hens," *Nature*, 197, pp. 1272–73.

SOMMER, ROBERT. 1959. "Studies in Personal Space," *Sociometry*, 22 (September), pp. 247–60.

WILLIAMS, JOHN L. 1963. "Personal Space and Its Relation to Extraversion-Introversion," unpublished M.A. thesis. Edmonton, Alberta, Canada: University of Alberta.

EXERCISES

The essential difference between field and laboratory experiments is control. In the latter, the researcher can control the situation, while, in the former, all the researcher controls is the experimental variable. Both experiments, however, use the introduction of an experimental variable to test a hypothesis. The following exercises will provide experience in working with field experiments. While the student should understand the differences in the administration of laboratory and field experiments, it is important to look for the similarities as well.

EXERCISE 1

The purpose of this exercise is to sensitize the student to indicators that the experimental variable has caused change in the observed situation. Indicators in field experiments are generally inferred from the differences in patterned behavior before and after the introduction of the experimental variable. For example, in the television program "Candid Camera," the producers wondered what would happen if they had people face the back instead of the front of elevators. They found that the more people there were facing the back, the more likely other riders on the elevator would be to conform and do likewise. The indicator of change here was the degree of variation from the norm that people face the front of elevators. In a situation when a social norm has been violated, people may laugh, become angry, demand explanations, or make snide comments about the violator. For this exercise, simply become cognizant of such reactions in everyday interactions. Whenever you observe someone reacting to another's behavior, write down what caused the reaction and what the content of the reaction was. Actually, what you will be doing is observing naturally occurring field experiments. This will not only give you several ideas for your own experiments, it will also provide you with a set of indicators for norm violations.

EXERCISE 2

For this exercise, you are to design some simple field experiments to test the following hypothesis:

Individuals will conform to the group in situations where a substantial number of people behave in a manner contrary to normal behavior in that situation.

In the "Candid Camera" situation, for example, when several people faced the back of the elevator, individuals who entered the elevator did the same even though people normally face the front. What other situations could be designed to show the same thing? Make up four and discuss them with the class.

EXERCISE 3

Some social norms are matters of etiquette, some matters of law, and some matters of special group behavior. Such norms are easily seen and understood, but other norms are so ingrained that we do not think of them as norms but as "natural" ways of doing things. One such norm is the rule of pace. As children, we learn not to do things too slowly or too quickly, and, as we develop and mature, we take on a certain pace—a "normal" pace—in everything we do. To see this, and to see the reactions to one who breaks normal pace, conduct the following field experiment.

Go through some motion you normally engage in, but do it in slow motion. For example, eat dinner in slow motion. Do not act as though it is a joke or anything out of the ordinary. After you have sufficient reactions from others (and yourself!), explain the action in terms of the experiment. Record both the reactions of others and how you felt while engaging in the action. This will give you insight into the force of social control, as both an external and an internal phenomenon.

EXERCISE 4

This exercise is designed to find, using a field experiment, whether there is a relationship between how people present themselves and how they are treated. In the observation survey (Chapter 5), it was seen that the way a drunk presented himself in court may have affected his sentence. Here, you will discover whether the way you present yourself has any effect on your treatment as a customer.

Using a new- or used-car dealer as the experimental setting, different students will present themselves in different dress, demeanor, and style to see whether they are treated with the same attention. Students should conduct the experiment both singly and in pairs. The continuum for appearances and types of pairs should be broad enough to ensure that they are seen by the car dealers as clearly different types. On one end of the continuum, the presentation should be that of the socially unconventional and irresponsible, while, on the other end, it should be that of the well-to-do. Different groups in the class can be used to find whether there is a difference between dealers in inexpensive cars and those in luxury cars.

ADDITIONAL READING SUGGESTIONS

CAMPBELL, D. T., and J. C. STANLEY. 1963. "Experimental and Quasi-experimental Designs for Research on Teaching." In N. L. Gage (ed.), *Handbook of Research on Teaching*, pp. 171–246. Chicago: Rand McNally. Discusses "quasi-experimental" designs, offering a solid grounding in "field experiments."

ROSS, H. L., and D. T. CAMPBELL. 1968. "The Connecticut Speed Crackdown: A Study of the Effects of Legal Change." In H. Laurence Ross (ed.), *Perspectives on the Social Order*, pp. 30–35. 2d ed. New York: McGraw Hill. A good example of experimental design.

SWINGLE, PAUL G. (ED.). 1973. *Social Psychology in Natural Settings*. Chicago: Aldine. This collection provides numerous examples of field experiments. The role and importance of field experiments are discussed in the Introduction. A valuable resource.

IV: THE ETHNOGRAPHY

In order to be effective in their work, police officers have to "know" their beat. By "knowing" a beat, a police officer can tell when things are proceeding normally and when something is out of place and requires special attention. Similarly, detectives come to know and understand the character of various neighborhoods, and they realize that they must approach people in different neighborhoods in terms of what is considered proper for the people who live there. The methods used in "getting to know" a group of people include observing and participating in their activities, talking with them, and noting various signs and artifacts typically associated with one group or another. The methods employed in obtaining such understandings are called *ethnographies*.

The purpose of ethnographic methods is to uncover social, cultural, or normative patterns of a group of people. Generally, this involves an analytic description of a cohort's behavior in terms of a social setting, organization, or culture. For example, Cavan (1966) studied the patterns of behavior in bar settings, showing that there were standardized forms of sanctioned behavior for people who entered various types of bars. Sudnow (1967) described and explained the organization of hospitals in terms of how death was routinely handled, and Zimmerman and Wieder (1974) studied a drug subculture in terms of the group's beliefs and values pertaining to drug use. All these studies incorporated participant observation, intensive interviewing, and qualitative analysis in order to arrive at an understanding of the observed patterns of behavior engaged in by those being studied.

Of the numerous methods used by ethnographers, three will be discussed here. While each will be discussed separately, it is not uncommon that they are used in conjunction with one another. For example, in the study described in Chapter 8, participant observation was the primary method employed, but intensive interviewing was also used in gathering data.

PARTICIPANT OBSERVATION

Participant observation can be defined as a method in which the researcher spends time in the normal flow of social life in a setting, organization, or culture. Thus, William Foote Whyte (1943) lived in a lower-class Italian neighborhood, participating in the daily life of a street-corner gang. He boarded with a neighborhood family; spent his time with a gang, engaging in most of their activities; and made notes of what he observed and experienced. In this way, he developed an understanding of the way of life of the people who lived in the neighborhood.

The greatest problem encountered in participant-observation research is deciding what to observe. In any observational setting, innumerable activities are taking place; unlike a researcher doing an observation survey, who has a list of items to look for, the participant observer has a much less specific guide. He is attempting to come to terms with a complex set of relationships, norms, and beliefs, all of which are being acted out in front of his nose. Until he develops a sense of what meanings the swirl of activities has for the subjects, it is difficult to distinguish between significant and insignificant behavior.

To guide his observations, the researcher uses his conceptual framework. For instance, if a sociologist is using a normative framework, he assumes that behavior is regulated by a set of sanctioned rules. If a rule is broken, it is expected that those who observe the rule violation will become upset and will impose sanctions. With such a framework, the participant observer may begin to look for behavior that upsets those around him. For instance, at the race track there are rules regulating sitting and standing in the audience (Scott, 1968). If someone stands up at the beginning of the race, members of the audience may tell him to sit down or even swat him with a racing program. However, the same sanctions against standing are not imposed as the horses come down the home stretch.

In this way, the observer can begin to hypothesize about normative patterns of behavior and start looking for behavior in terms of these patterns. The researcher at the race track found that there were definite, observable patterns regarding standing and sitting, depending on where the horses were. From the beginning of the race to the first turn, the audience remained seated; as the horses entered the back stretch, the crowd began standing; and, as the horses came down the home stretch, they began standing on their seats.

Not all patterns, however, are social patterns. Some may be idiosyncratic or individual forms of behavior and are not reflective of the social milieu. In order to determine social patterns, the participant observer attempts to find behavior that is (1) typical, (2) persistent, (3) trans-situational, and (4) transpersonal. A behavior is *typical* if it occurs in a standardized, regular fashion. For example, in their study of a drug culture, Zimmerman and Wieder (1974) found that "passing the joint" (passing a marijuana cigarette from one person to another) characteristically occurred whenever marijuana smokers came together to smoke marijuana. Similarly, the pattern of passing a joint was *persistent* in that it was observed repeatedly over a period of time. Third, the act was *trans-situational* in that it was distributed in several different situations. Finally, the act was *transpersonal* in that various groups engaged in the same behavior.

Before the researcher can begin his research, he must gain access. On the one hand, there is an ethical problem involved in whether the researcher should tell his subjects of the study. (As was pointed out in Chapter 1, such announcements depend on the situation.) On the other hand, there is an interpersonal problem in gaining access to the subjects. If the owner of a factory gives a researcher free reign to research anything he desires but the workers in the factory shun the researcher, very little data can be gathered, even though access to the setting is gained. Winning the trust and confidence of subjects is a matter of rapport, and, in participant observation more than any other method, rapport is essential, for the researcher must spend a great deal of time with his subjects; if the subjects would rather not have the researcher around, the project is doomed to failure (Douglas, 1972). Generally, rapport is a matter of being noncritical, interested in what the subjects do and say, and, most important, genuinely open to an understanding of how they see and experience their social world. There is a danger of overrapport if the researcher becomes so much a part of what he is studying that he ceases to function as a researcher; but, if the participant observer attempts to bear his purpose in mind, this will not be a problem.

A final matter of importance is note-taking. Good notes will later bring back to memory that which was observed. The more detailed the notes, the more will be remembered. Therefore, participant observers attempt to write as much as possible about their observations as soon afterwards as possible. In some situations, very little on-the-scene note-taking is possible, and the researcher must frequently leave the scene to write up his notes. Other situations, especially those where the subjects know that the observer is engaged in research and expect note-taking, provide lulls in activity when notes can be taken. However, any notes taken in the field should be expanded after the researcher leaves the field and should be typed for ease in later reference.

The notes should include the time and date of the observations, for some patterns may take place only at certain times or on certain days. For instance, we have noted that, in observations of public parks, especially in urban areas, different patterns are observed during different times of the day and different days of the week. Children's play patterns are certain to be different during the hours school is in session and after school. After dark, a park setting belongs to such groups as muggers and the police, and their patterned behavior is substantially different from that observed during the day.

Notes not only serve as a record of observations but are also used as a guide to further observations. For instance, if certain activities are found to occur only at certain times of the day or days of the week, these findings can be used to schedule subsequent observations. This is especially important when one group supplants another, or when one behavior pattern begins and another one ends. In order to know when such a shift occurs, the time will have to be in your notes.

INTENSIVE INTERVIEWING

Intensive interviewing is much like a conversation one might have with a friend not seen for a long time. Unlike more structured interview schedules, where the researcher has a list of questions he asks the respondents, the intensive interview begins with a general question, and the interviewer's subsequent questions are developed in terms of the respondent's replies. For example, if a researcher wanted to know why policemen chose their careers, he might begin simply by asking what influenced them to become police officers and then ask further questions in terms of the response. The following interchanges are hypothetical examples of how an interview might go in different directions:

INTERVIEW 1

Q. What made you decide to become a policeman?

A. The pay seemed good, and the department has a good pension program.

Q. Well, a lot of jobs have good pay and pension plans. There are a number of office jobs and factory jobs with the same pay and pension. Why didn't you take one of them?

A. It's not just the pay. I like the work. In a factory or an office, you've gotta stay indoors all day.

INTERVIEW 2

Q. What made you decide to become a policeman?

A. The work is interesting. You get to work with people, and every day is different. Not the same old nine-to-five.

Q. Well, a social worker has a variety of unusual tasks and gets to work with people; and, besides, a social worker's job is a lot safer.

A. Well, you see, that's part of it. If it's safe, it's not as interesting. Look, what's the kind of days you remember and talk about the most? The safe, routine days, or the ones where something dangerous happens? Like the earthquake. I'll bet you can remember everything that happened that morning, but I'll bet that if someone asks you about today next month, you won't remember. Right?

Q. Okay, then you're saying that it's exciting and interesting because of the danger?

A. Right.

INTERVIEW 3

Q. What made you decide to become a policeman?

A. Well, I don't know. Let me think. I guess I felt I'd be doing something important by enforcing the law.

Q. There are a lot of important jobs. Why did you decide that enforcing the law was more important than, say, building houses?

A. I didn't say that building houses wasn't important.

Q. I know. I was just using that as an example of something that was important. Why do you think being a policeman and enforcing the law is the most important?

A. I don't know if it's the most important thing. I think doctors do the most important thing in saving lives.

Q. Okay, but why law enforcement?

A. It's something like doctors in a way. If you prevent somebody from hurting someone else, then it's even better than patching them up after someone has hurt them.

In each of the interviews, the interviewer pressed for specifics in the responses. Instead of merely accepting such general responses as "good pay," "interesting," or "important," he attempted to find concrete answers and the meanings of general responses (Cicourel, 1964:73–104). Moreover, the intereviewer simultaneously built his questions on the responses and, at the same time, pressed for an answer to the original question.

Sometimes in an interview situation, the respondent will not have really thought about the kinds of things the interviewer wants to know. For example, in Interview 3, the respondent was vague and evasive. In such cases, if the interviewer probes enough, he may eventually find that the respondent actually has only the vaguest sense of an answer to his question. If this is the case, rather than attempting to supply a concrete response for the subject, the researcher should simply note that the respondent was unsure or ambiguous. It is important, however, to keep the respondent on the right track if his talk begins to wander or becomes evasive. In Interview 3, it can be seen that the interviewer has to keep returning to questions that the respondent evades.

It is important to remember that intensive interviewing involves a skill in listening. If the respondent does not think you are interested, or if he feels that you disapprove of what he says, he is unlikely to give you the information you need. On the one hand, if the respondent believes that the interviewer is not interested, he is likely to give short, choppy replies; if he believes that the interviewer is interested, he is likely to elaborate his answers so that there is a complete sense of his meaning. On the other hand, if the respondent feels that the interviewer disapproves of his beliefs, the interview data will be invalid, for the respondent may attempt to impress the interviewer with replies manufactured for the situation.

UNOBTRUSIVE MEASURES

Every research method discussed so far has had the problem of controlling the effect of the method on the subjects. In surveys and interviews, the subject's responses may be a reaction to the way a questionnaire was worded or how the interviewer combed his hair; in experiments, the subjects may try to "help" the experimenter prove his hypothesis; in participant observation, the subjects may act in one way when the observer is present and another way when he is not. All such methods have potential reactive capacities, in that the data collected may be tainted by the reaction to the method (Webb et al., 1966). Unobtrusive measures are nonreactive, in that they are taken from signs that are given off by social actors in normal, everyday interaction. For example, to estimate liquor consumption, a researcher simply counted the number of liquor bottles discarded in the trash (Sawyer, 1961). Such measurements avoid researcher-produced reactions, in that those who provide the information do so unintentionally.

In addition to being nonreactive and serving as checks on other measurements, these types of measures serve as legitimate measures in their own right. They can be used to describe characteristics of social phenomena, and they can be used to measure relationships between variables. For example, to measure a community's perception of criminal activity, the number of large locks and alarm systems installed might be used. In looking for a relationship between religious-oriented college education and smoking behavior, the researcher can simply note whether religious-oriented colleges have fewer ashtrays, cigarette-vending machines, or cigarette butts on campus.

QUALITATIVE ANALYSIS

In looking for causal explanations, researchers using ethnographic techniques are more likely to describe social processes and forms of behavior verbally than to show statistical relationships or use statistical description. Some refer to data used in statistical analysis as "hard data" and data used in qualitative analysis as "soft data," but this dichotomy belies the fact that both types of data are equally "hard" or "soft." The difference is simply that one type has been transformed into numbers and the other has not.

Since qualitative data are not transformable into numbers, statistical analysis is impossible. This does not mean, however, that the analysis used is invalid. Rather, the focus of the analysis is different. For example, a survey researcher may show a statistical relationship between voting behavior and ethnic background. He may find that 90 per cent of all blacks in his sample voted for a liberal candidate over a conservative one; but such a finding tells us only that a relationship exists, not necessarily why it exists. An ethnographer, through participant observation or intensive interviewing, can tell us the understandings blacks have of liberalism and conservatism to explain why they vote as they do. Thus, qualitative analysis is more likely to explain relationships in terms of social meanings, social realities, social norms, and definitions of the situation. Such understandings are not readily quantified (transformed into numbers), and, if they were, they might lose their sense and complexity.

Essentially, then, qualitative analysis is a means of locating patterns and forms of social behavior and explaining verbally why people who engage in such behavior do so. Sociological theories provide the qualitative analyst with concepts such as norms, definition of the situation, roles, and so on, which he can use as a direction in explanation. The content of the concepts in terms of meanings and behavior is provided in the data the researcher has gathered.

The following readings represent participant observation, intensive interviewing, and unobtrusive measures. The first is a participant-observation study of a detective division, in which the authors show that detectives investigate cases (pattern) only if they are seen to be particular kinds of cases (social reality). A causal relationship is established between the patterns and the social reality— a good example of qualitative analysis. In Cressey's discussion of how he formulated a sociological conception of embezzlement and developed and redeveloped hypotheses from intensive interviewing, the process of qualitative analysis and the role of intensive-interview data are well illustrated. Finally, Webb and his associates discuss the creative use of exterior physical signs, expressive movements, and physical location as nonreactive measures.

REFERENCES

CAVAN, SHERRI. 1966. *Liquor License: An Ethnography of Bar Behavior.* Chicago: Aldine.

CICOUREL, AARON. 1964. *Method and Measurement in Sociology.* New York: The Free Press.

DOUGLAS, JACK (ED.) 1972. *Research on Deviance.* New York: Random House.

LOFLAND, JOHN. 1971. *Analyzing Social Settings.* Belmont, Calif: Wadsworth.

SAWYER, H. G. 1961. "The Meaning of Numbers," speech before the American Association of Advertising Agencies.

SCOTT, MARVIN B. 1968. *The Racing Game.* Chicago: Aldine.

SUDNOW, DAVID. 1967. *Passing On: The Social Organization of Dying.* Englewood Cliffs, N.J.: Prentice-Hall.

WEBB, EUGENE, D. T. CAMPBELL, R. D. SCHWARTZ, and L. SECHREST. 1966. *Unobtrusive Measures: Nonreactive Research in the Social Sciences.* Chicago: Rand McNally.

WHYTE, WILLIAM F. 1943, 1955. *Street Corner Society.* Chicago: University of Chicago Press.

ZIMMERMAN, D., and D. L. WIEDER. 1974. "The Diary: Diary Interview Method." In Robert Smith (ed.), *Social Science Methods: A New Introduction.* New York: The Free Press.

8. Participant Observation

DETECTIVE WORK: PATTERNS OF CRIMINAL INVESTIGATIONS
—William B. Sanders and Howard C. Daudistel

SOCIOLOGICAL JURISPRUDENCE IS the study of what actually happens under the auspices of a law (Weber, 1956:11–20). If a law exists along with sanctions for breaking the law, but the law is not generally enforced or obeyed, then from a sociological point of view there is no law in effect. It is moot to argue that a law on the books could be enforced even though it typically is not, for if we are to understand social behavior in relation to the law it is necessary first to understand how the law typically works on a day-to-day basis, not how it conceivably could work given total obedience and enforcement.

To this end, sociologists have focused on various aspects of the criminal justice system. The study of a public defender's office by Sudnow (1965); studies of the police by La Fave (1965), Reiss (1971), Skolnick (1967), Banton (1964), Wilson (1968), and Bittner (1967; 1970); Miller's (1969) study of prosecution, Newman's (1966) study of conviction, and Blumberg's (1967) work on the entire criminal justice system, all point to the day-to-day working of law. These studies have noted to some extent the role of discretion in the application or non-application of the law in legally equivocal and unequivocal situations. At each step in the criminal justice system, from the citizen's decision to lodge a complaint (Reiss, 1971:65–70) or to define the situation as one in

This selection was prepared especially for this volume.

which it is necessary to "call the cops" (Bittner, 1970:95), to the judge's decision as to what sentence a convicted criminal should receive, decisions are made that are not prescribed by statutory law.

The role of discretion provides an area of investigation in law that cannot be accounted for in terms of the law. Wilson (1968), for example, showed that police discretion in the United States varied with departmental policy and community political structure. Departments in communities with partisan political structures were more likely to have "watchman" styles of enforcement, with fewer arrests for almost all types of law violation than departments characterized by "legalistic" styles, which were typically found in communities experiencing a "reform" or "good government" political atmosphere. There is nothing in legal jurisprudence that accounts for such variations in the application of the law. True, the law does provide sanctions for non-enforcement by police, district attorneys, and judges as well as other officials sworn to uphold the law (La Fave, 1965), but since these sanctions are not routinely employed for the typical discretionary acts of the police and others, then such mandates are no different from laws that are typically not enforced. They exist only as potentials and, when applied, only as exceptions.

In addition to their interest in the organizational and political elements entering into decisions to invoke the law, sociologists have been interested in the role of custom in interpretations of situations as legal or illegal (cf. Simmel, 1950:99–104). The influence of custom on discretion has been viewed in terms of prejudice, especially racism, and in terms of broader, more general aspects of customs as well. Reiss (1971) and Black and Reiss (1970) found that black citizens were more likely to demand an arrest in potential arrest situations than were whites; thus they account for the differential arrest rates for blacks and whites, in terms of citizen discretion. Other writers (e.g., Skolnick, 1972; Werthman and Piliavin, 1967; and Piliavin and Briar, 1964) have attributed the differential arrests to ethnic prejudice. La Fave (1965), more than anyone else, has shown that custom provides police with an understanding of what is considered proper and improper in deciding whether or not to make an arrest. For example, as religious customs have changed, so too have the instances when police invoke "blue laws" still on the books.

Another largely ignored aspect of discretion concerns the interpretive practices in formulating accounts of a crime. Sudnow (1965:255) treated the sections of criminal law, not as categories for classifying acts as one type of crime or another, but rather as conceptual schemes used by personnel in the criminal justice system for organizing their everyday activities. Reports of crimes were formulated by the public defenders in terms of normal typifications.* Thus, each case, rather than being treated as unique, was treated as an instance of a typical sort of crime consisting of the circumstances, props, and actors normally making up that type of crime. "Normal" crimes, as opposed to "weird" crimes, "unusual" crimes, or "odd instances of an otherwise normal crime," were crimes that were construed as instances of situations consisting of typical characteristics. For example, normal burglaries were seen to involve kinds of criminals, circumstances, and props that were different from those involved in normal robberies, rapes, and other normal crimes.

Crimes tended to be handled by public defenders and prosecutors on the basis of what sort of normal crime was used as an interpretive scheme for understanding how to proceed. Subseqent decisions were based on typifications that served as interpretive schemes for information pertaining to the case. For example, if a crime involved the use of nylon hosiery, the hosiery in a crime seen to be a normal burglary would be interpreted as having been used by the burglar to cover his hands so as not to leave prints. However, if the crime were formulated to be a typical robbery, the hosiery would be interpreted as having been used as a mask. Similarly, other elements of a crime would be differentially formulated depending on what typification of the crime and criminal the public defender incorporated. Since the initial formulation of a crime serves as an interpretive scheme for subsequent action, it is crucial for understanding how the criminal justice process works to study those whose everyday work involves formulating crimes to be of one normal type or another.

Normal Crimes and Normal Detective Work

Citizen Response Detectives.   A substantive area of the criminal justice system that has not been studied in detail by sociologists

---

* For a full discussion of the concept of "typification," see Schutz (1971).

involves the role of the police detective in the legal process. Skol-nick (1967) examined vice squad detectives and their organization; however, there has been no in-depth study by sociologists of what might be called "citizen response detectives." Members of the vice squad, narcotics details, and intelligence divisions have to "drum up their own business," and their work involves what have been called crimes without victims (Schur, 1965). On the other hand, citizen response detectives* respond to complaints that someone has been victimized and needs the police to find the criminal and bring him to justice.

Formulating Crimes. In order for a reported crime to be inves-tigated by detectives, it first has to be formulated as a type of crime that is normally investigated. Generally, the detectives will simply treat a crime in terms of the penal code type reported by the patrol. For example, if the patrol reports a 415 PC (disturbing the peace), the detectives will formulate the circumstances in the same way, interpreting the particulars of the report in terms of a 415 PC. Sometimes, however, a patrol report will use a penal code (or any other legal code) that does not provide the proper typifica-tion of the circumstances of the case for the detectives. In one case, for example, the patrol officer used the penal code for attempted murder (217 PC) to characterize a family dispute. The major crimes sergeant looked at it and said it was a "glorified domestic," referring to a kind of dispute generally typified as "415 PC Domestic" (a family fight that disturbs the peace). Typifica-tions of family fights do not include attempts by family members to murder one another; therefore, the charge of attempted murder was seen as an improper characterization of the event.†

In this way, a case will be formulated as either a case-to-be-worked or a case-to-be-ignored. Once a complaint is established as a case-to-be-worked, it is formulated as either a typical-case-of-this-sort-of-crime or an unusual-instance-of-this-sort-of-crime. For exam-ple, a crime in which only stereo components were taken is seen as a typical burglary, whereas one in which only pencils and shoe-

---

* For the remainder of this paper, we will use the term "detective" to denote "citizen response detective."

† In a purely statistical sense, the typification of family fights as non-mur-derous is inaccurate, for such disputes are more likely to end in murder than any other single situation.

laces were taken while television sets, radios, and other property commonly taken in burglaries were not is seen as an unusual burglary.

The constituted sense of a crime (i.e., what a crime is formulated to be), moreover, is subject to reformulation in the course of the investigation depending on what leads develop and what information is uncovered. If the leads and information substantiate the initial formulation, it will then tend to crystallize as an interpretive scheme for understanding the events in the case. If, on the other hand, the original formulation cannot account for information uncovered in the case and rival formulations can, either the case will take a new direction or it will cease to be seen as a case-to-be-worked. For example, a case was reported by a girl as a robbery-kidnapping. She told the detectives that she had been forced at gunpoint to drive to an isolated location and give up $1,300 belonging to her employer, which she had been taking to the bank. Several aspects of her account, however, were not consistent with various particulars discovered by the investigators. She had said that the robber wedged himself behind the seat of the vehicle and pointed a gun at her, but packages on the floor behind the seat were not crushed, as they would have been if the robber had been where she said he was. If, on the other hand, the events were interpreted in terms of an embezzlement—i.e., as if the girl had taken the money and made up the story about the robber—such particulars could be accounted for consistently.

METHODOLOGY

In order to convey the method and approach of this study, it will be necessary to explain its context in a larger project engaged in by the researchers. The larger project involved three researchers studying various aspects of the paperwork in a county sheriff's office. Two of the researchers conducted observations and interviews with detectives, and the third did the same with patrol deputies.

Data collection involved participant observation and interviews. Each researcher collected field notes and completed "case reports" (standardized observation schedules for each case on which they accompanied a detective). The field notes were typed and duplicated so that the data collected by one researcher were available to the others. The "case reports" were developed for following cases from their inception, usually with the patrol deputies, through the detective office, to final disposition in the courts. The forms included spaces for recording the type of crime listed by the deputies and the detectives in terms of the California Penal Code, the dispatch code, unused sections of the narrative section of the report forms, an estimate of the adequacy of the report, involvement of the identification (ID) bureau, and twelve items that are typically involved in cases and are relevant to how that case is worked. The patrol researcher would give his form, based on the report taken by the patrol unit, to the detective researchers, who would, if possible, follow the case through the detective division. However, since we were seldom fortunate enough to have a case that was observed by the single patrol researcher assigned to the detective whom the detective researchers were accompanying, the patrol reports themselves were usually used as a source of information. Finally, the researchers made and transcribed tape recordings of interviews with detectives, radio transmissions, and interrogations as well as other recordable events.

For this paper the researchers examined their notes and tapes to find typical instances of reported crimes that were normally handled by the detectives. Data were organized around the hypothesis that criminal acts regarded as instances of typical crimes, such as burglary, rape, etc., would initiate a typical investigative pattern linked to that formulation. Conversely, crimes regarded as unusual instances of a type of crime would be handled in a manner unlike the typical investigations.

Two detective units, the burglary detail and the major-crimes detail, were chosen for the study. Both details typically involved citizen-response types of crimes, yet the nature and circumstances of the crimes for each detail were different enough to show different investigative procedures.

CASE-WORKING PATTERNS

The formal activities of detectives in the law-enforcement agency studied can be seen in terms of a "case-working role." With the exception of detective sergeants and the detective captain, who have administrative duties, detectives are expected to spend their working hours on assigned cases. Normally, the cases are assigned on the basis of a detective's special ability to work a particular type of case, such as arson or bomb threats, a detective's request to work a particular case, or simple caseload availability.

In contrast to patrol officers and special investigation detectives (i.e., narcotics and vice officers), the detectives always received their cases after a victim had made a complaint (except in the case of homicides, of course) and an initial patrol report was filed. Consequently, all the cases received by the burglary and major-crimes details can generally be defined as criminal offenses that have been reported to and officially recorded by patrol officers.

In the organizational context, a case can be seen as an investigation that consists primarily of gathering and processing information, some of which has been assessed and documented by others within the organization. For example, a victim places a call to the sheriff's department and reports that a burglary has taken place. The information provided by the caller is recorded on tape and documented by a watch commander. On the basis of this information, the watch commander requests that a patrol car be sent to the crime scene and contact made with the reporting party. A departmental dispatcher then assigns a patrol officer to the address given by the caller. The patrolman "takes a report" of the burglary to provide the detectives with information on the type of crime, victim's name and address, names and addresses of witnesses or persons who may have knowledge or information, name or description of possible suspects, method of committing crime, and a narrative description of the crime including a list of the items or amount of cash taken if it's a robbery, the extent of harm or nature of act committed upon the victim if it involves attack, and a description of any physical evidence found at the scene.

On occasion, after a call has been made to the department and a patrol unit assigned, the documentation of the crime may not proceed in a chronological fashion from patrol report to detective investigation. Sometimes patrol officers who are dispatched to major burglaries or major crimes such as homicides, robberies, or bombings call on detectives and request them to be present during the initial investigation. On these occasions, even though the detectives may begin their investigation before an official written report has been received from patrol, a formal report is always filed by patrol and eventually reviewed by detectives.

DECISION TO WORK A CASE

At the detective bureau, the detective sergeants take ("pull") those reports that seem to be relevant to their detail. From those pulled, they decide which cases are to be worked and what order of priority they will receive if they are to be worked. If the case is not to be worked, the sergeant decides whether to inactivate it, close it, or "PR" the case.

Working a case means that the sergeant assigns one or more detectives to investigate it in an attempt to find and catch the culprit. In some cases the sergeant was not certain whether a case should be worked and asked one of the detectives to "check it out" so that he could later decide whether time should be spent on investigation. Such cases were treated here as "worked" cases.

Cases thought not to be significant enough to work or in which the victim did not want to prosecute the criminal were closed— that is, simply filed away and ignored. Many cases that were worked ended up closed if the investigation showed that the circumstances did not constitute grounds for action, or if the victim changed his mind and did not want prosecution.

A case that was *inactivated* was neither worked nor closed but filed away waiting for information or leads that would give the detectives something concrete to investigate. Minor cases with no investigative leads were inactivated immediately by the sergeant. Many other cases that were worked ended up being inactivated after the investigation failed to uncover a suspect or evidence that could be used to convict a suspect.

When a case was pulled but not investigated, the victim would sometimes demand that someone should do something. The department in such instances felt that it was good public relations to contact the victim and go through the routine questions they would ask were they working the case. If good leads did develop, the case would be worked, but generally this was simply a means of mollifying the victim. (Cf. Goffman, 1952.) The detectives referred to such contacts as "PR's" (public relations), and to work a case in such a way was to "PR" the victim.

Working Burglaries. The decision to work a burglary is based to a great extent on the amount of loss. Since most burglaries have no leads for the detectives to work, very few burglaries would be investigated if the existence of leads were the only criterion. If, however, a number of small burglaries amounting to relatively little loss are seen to have been committed by the same burglar, any burglary that is believed to have been committed by that burglar will be investigated no matter how small the loss.

Once the decision to work a case has been made by the sergeant, depending on whether the detective assigned to the case sees it as an instance of a typical burglary (juvenile, junkie, professional, inside job, etc.), the case will be worked with the expectation that it will eventually be solved or inactivated. In cases involving no leads but substantial loss, the focus of the investigative work is to determine the exact extent of loss for insurance purposes and to get an accurate description of the property taken, so that if found it can be returned to the owner and used to locate the culprit. In such cases, after the initial investigation and logging of the property, the case is typically inactivated pending further leads.

On the other hand, if the detective formulates the crime as a solvable case, much more work and different patterns of work will ensue. If there are witnesses, usable physical evidence, and possible suspects, the detective has something to follow. Witnesses can be contacted and interviewed, physical evidence can be used to estimate how and when the crime was committed, and possibly may reveal something about the criminal. All this gives the detective something to work with, although it may not be enough for him to clear the case.

The following burglary, although atypical of that crime, illustrates elements in a case that can be worked.

Case 35

A girl was burglarized of $80 in cash and her room was set on fire, destroying her bed and some of the room's furnishings. The burglar's point of entry was believed to be a window which had been broken and then opened. Fingerprints were found on either side of a piece of the broken glass. The detective believed these belonged to the burglar since he felt it unlikely that anyone else would have left fingerprints on both sides; someone looking out the window would have left his prints on only one side. The victim was asked whether anyone she knew might have been responsible, and she gave the detective a list of several names. The prints from the window pane were compared with the prints of those people the victim thought might have been involved and were found to match those of one of the people mentioned. The detective arrested the suspect, and he was subsequently convicted of second-degree burglary.

Because of the availability of a list of possible suspects and the fingerprints, the detective had several leads. With only fingerprints, there would have been little to follow in the case since fingerprints are of little value without a limited list of suspects.* Several thousand fingerprints are on file in the sheriff's office, and the department lacks the devices and the personnel necessary to locate a single print out of the huge number on file. Typically, however, burglaries do not hold such investigative leads which can be followed for identifying and locating the burglar.

Working Major Crimes.   Working a case in major crimes differs from working a burglary case in several respects. First, the cases referred to the major-crimes detail for the most part involve acts against persons, whereas the burglary detail handles crimes against property. "Crimes against persons" in the sheriff's office include everything from disturbing the peace (415 PC)† by loud parties, fights, domestic quarrels, noisy vehicles, and the like to homicide (187 PC) (Daudistel, 1971:19). Other typical crimes referred to the major crimes detail include battery (242 PC), assault with a deadly weapon (245 PC; ADW's), rape (261 PC), robbery (211 PC), kidnapping (207 PC), arson (447a PC), and annoying phone calls (653m PC).‡ What most of these crimes (except annoying phone calls and arson) have in common is that the victim comes face-to-face with the criminal and, except for homicides, can usually identify the suspect.

---

* Most victims believe that if fingerprints are found a case can automatically be solved. Television dramas are greatly responsible for this myth, and burglary detectives are invariably asked by victims why they have not caught the burglar and recovered their property in cases where prints are found.

† Throughout this paper, reference is made to the California Penal Code statutes in order to demonstrate the way in which detectives refer officially and informally to various crimes. For instance, it would be unusual to hear a detective refer to "disturbing the peace"; rather he would refer to a "415." "PC" simply designates "Penal Code" as opposed to "HS" (Health and Safety Code), "VC" (Vehicle Code), and other legal codes.

‡ Any form of annoying phone call, usually threatening and obscene ones, was reported by patrol and detectives as a 653m PC.

These crimes also differ from burglary in that, with the exception of robbery, there is rarely any property involved. Moreover, in robberies the "property" is usually money, and usually an amount that exceeds what is normally carried by a person. Burglaries most commonly involve non-cash property, such as bicycles, stereo equipment, television sets, and similar items that can easily be converted into cash.

Burglaries and major crimes also differ in the cases worked, the way in which they are worked, and the volume of cases worked. Most cases reported as 459 PC (burglary) are worked to some extent, and the burglary detective has a more or less constant flow of cases he works on a day-to-day basis. On the other hand, cases seen as "workable" come to the attention of the major crimes sergeant only sporadically. This is not to say that the crimes are reported sporadically by patrol and pulled by major crimes; rather, the *crimes to be worked* are sporadic. For instance, the following list represents a typical set of crimes pulled by the major crimes sergeant, but none of the crimes reported in this particular set were worked:

1. 415 Disturbing the peace
2. 415 Disturbing the peace
3. Possible 653m—Annoying phone call
4. 245 Assault with a deadly weapon/ 459 Burglary
5. 242 Battery
6. Suspicious vehicle
7. Possible 245, assault with a deadly weapon
8. Missing person (mentally retarded)
9. Attempted suicide 5150 W&I* (mental case)

The two 415's and the battery case were not worked, as is typically the case, since generally by the time the detectives get the reports the trouble has been resolved either by the disputing parties or by the patrolman. Likewise, many annoying phone calls, like the one in this case, involve people who know one another, often

---

* "W&I" refers to the Welfare and Institutions Code. All attempted suicides are classified as 5150's.

divorced or separated couples, and they have settled their differences by the time the report reaches the detective detail. On the other hand, in cases where the victim does not know the caller, there is generally no way to find who made the call and nothing to go on unless the caller has developed an identifiable "MO" (method of operation) known to the detectives. In most 653m cases where the caller is not an acquaintance of the victim, the caller is either unidentifiable or ceases his activities before any leads develop.

On the other hand, the two 245's received were not seen as typical assaults. For example, the one reported with the burglary was part of an ongoing altercation between a family and an unknown youth the family said had been bothering them. A burglary detective had been working the case and, because he believed that no actual burglary or assault was involved, the major crimes sergeant preferred not to waste time on it. The other reported assault involved a car being run off the road by a truck. There was nothing in the report to indicate that the incident was intentional, and there was only a vague description of the truck. Thus, it was not seen to be an unequivocal assault, nor was there a way to begin to locate a suspect.

The final two reports in the sample, missing person and attempted suicide, were pulled by the major crimes sergeant only for information since no investigation was necessary. The "missing person" report involved a mentally retarded child who had wandered away but was later found. By pulling such reports, the detectives have information about a particular individual who may turn up missing again; should this occur, the report pulled can serve as a resource for locating him. Missing persons who are able to stay out of sight and successful suicides are always worked by the major crimes detail. Similarly, the suspicious vehicle report represents an incident that need not be worked but may provide useful information.

It may appear from the foregoing that the major crimes detail finds excuses for doing very little work. This is not so, but it is true that detectives prefer to devote their time and resources to transgressions that are seen as "righteous" (i.e., actual, unequivocal) crimes, and in which the victim wants or needs action to be taken by the detectives. Thus, such crimes as disturbing the peace, making annoying phone calls, and batteries are typically not worked, whereas assaults, rapes, robberies, and other serious crimes against persons typically are worked. Because such crimes occur irregularly, the pace of crimes worked is one of frenzied activity and lulls.

Other indicators of activity can be gleaned from borderline cases-to-be-worked. In the previous example, the reported assaults were not worked, but 245 assaults normally are worked. On the other hand, 242 batteries are not typically worked, for, as we explained earlier, the trouble is usually over by the time the report is received by the detectives. As might be expected, battery cases are more likely to be worked during lulls in activities and assault cases are put aside during busy periods. However, the decision to work a case is determined primarily by whether it is seen as "workable" and by the citizen's eagerness to have the case pursued.

In the above example, it was shown that the 245 assaults that were not worked were not seen to be workable. One was regarded as phony and the other was not clearly an intentional assault. On the other hand, it is important to see why 242 batteries are worked. From observations and interviews, it appears that the discretion to work a battery case lies largely with the victim. Two battery cases worked while the researcher was present illustrate this aspect of what Reiss (1971) calls "citizen discretion."

CASE 57

A delivery boy claimed he was shoved by an elementary school teacher when he attempted to deliver some flowers to the school. The delivery boy came down to the detective bureau and filled out a statement as to what occurred. Even though the boy was not harmed, it appeared to be a clear case of battery. The victim had lost his job over the incident and wanted to bring charges against the teacher.

The detective assigned to the case first contacted the florist where the delivery boy had been employed. There he learned the name of the "teacher" and found that he was actually the school principal. He then contacted the principal and interviewed him as the suspect in the case. The principal denied the charges, claiming that the delivery boy had been rude and was asked to leave, but that he, the principal, had not shoved the boy. The principal filled out a statement and gave the detective the name of a witness to the incident.

Before leaving, the detective asked the principal not to contact the witness until he had had a chance to talk with him. The principal agreed.

It later appeared that the principal *had* contacted the witness since he was waiting at the side of the house when we arrived but went around back and reappeared at the front door when the detective rang the bell. In general he backed up the principal's story, but there were some discrepancies. The principal said the delivery boy came from one part of the building, and the witness said he came from another.

From this investigation, the detective said it was the principal's word against the delivery boy's as far as a judge or jury would be concerned, but he felt that the principal may have been lying. He submitted the report of the information he had gathered to the district attorney and let him make the decision whether or not to file charges. (The final decision rests with the district attorney anyway, but in general detectives will give their opinion as to the culpability of suspects involved.)

Case 63

A man and woman came to the detective bureau to make out a statement. They claimed that the man's former girlfriend had struck his present girlfriend in a bar, where the man worked as a piano player. The detective assigned to work the case said he was not planning to arrest the suspect since the battery appeared to be an "unprosecutable case," but he wanted to talk with the suspect and warn her against any further attacks on her old boyfriend's new girlfriend. He explained that the case appeared to be unprosecutable because the suspect had four children to care for and was on welfare and because the complainants may have fought back, making it a case of mutual combat. He felt that the DA would take into consideration the suspect's circumstances and not take the complaint; therefore, a thorough investigation to prepare the case for trial would be a waste of effort.

In both of these cases, the work done by the detectives was initiated by a citizen's insistence that something be done. Normally, no investigation of such cases would be made without citizen demand.

It is in the cases that are almost always worked and worked extensively that the investigative patterns of the major crimes detail as distinct from those of the burglary detail can be seen most clearly. Most typical of the major crimes worked in some volume during the period of observation were rapes, attempted rapes, and other sex crimes in which a victim complained to the police. (Of course, homicides, robberies, kidnappings, and other serious crimes against persons are always worked by the major crimes detectives, but in the county where the research was conducted such crimes were rare compared to reported rapes.)

In most burglaries, as noted, working the case consists of contacting the victim, getting a list of the property taken, and attempting to find leads that might be useful in identifying the perpetrators. Typically, the burglarized victim has little information, and the crime scene yields no leads. Thus, working a burglary involves comparatively little time. However, a rape case normally involves extensive work and time, for leads are available through the victim. For example, the following case took the investigating detective over a month to clear, and while he was involved with this case he worked no others.

CASE 48

A girl was forcibly taken from her apartment and raped by 15 to 20 members of a motorcycle gang. She was forced to perform fellatio on her assailants and anally raped as well. The suspects were charged with 207 PC (kidnapping), 261 PC (rape), 288a PC (oral copulation), and 286 PC (sodomy). In the investigation twenty-eight different forms were used, including eighteen follow-up reports and numerous teletypes used in identifying and locating the suspects. Several of the gang members were arrested, but because of a mistake in the DA's office only the kidnapping charge was filed.

In another rape case, the detective spent sixteen days working on identifying and locating the suspect.

CASE 50

A girl walking on a beach was raped at knifepoint by the suspect. The suspect then forced the girl to drive him to another location in a populated area where the girl escaped. The suspect followed the girl and was seen by several witnesses. The detective working the case interviewed the witnesses who were able to describe the suspect. Going through the field interrogation files, the detective was able to get a name for a person who fit the description given by the victim and witnesses. Since the suspect had prior convictions, the detective was able to get a mug shot which was identified by the victim and witnesses. With the suspect identified, the detective was able to locate him through relatives. The suspect was finally arrested when he came to pick up his pay check from his former employer.

This case involved four follow-up reports, a complaint report, and an arrest report by the detectives working the case. A typical burglary, on the other hand, usually involves only a single follow-up report, which explains that the case has been inactivated because of a lack of investigative leads. This is not to say that burglary detectives do not have cases that involve weeks of investigative work and numerous reports, but because of the perceived circumstances of typical burglaries (i.e., how detectives view what is involved in most burglaries), there are no leads to work with or follow up. Given the necessary leads, burglary cases are worked with the same intensity as major crimes, but major crimes are typically worked and involve a good deal of time whereas this is not typical of burglaries.

A final type of major crime that is worked involves a suspect who is caught immediately and with little question as to his guilt. The following case represents this type of situation.

Case 59

A man entered a girl's apartment claiming that he was looking for someone who lived there. She told him that the person he was looking for did not live there and asked the man to leave. Instead of leaving, the man attacked and raped her. He then fell asleep. When she was sure the suspect was sound asleep, the victim called the sheriff's office. When the deputies arrived at the scene of the crime, the suspect was still asleep in the victim's bed and was arrested there.

Unlike most rapes, this one involved very little investigative work; all the detective needed was a statement by the victim, and all he had to do was to prepare a single follow-up report for the DA. However, even when there is a suspect in custody and there is little doubt concerning his guilt, the case may involve massive investigative and paper work. For example, the following case involved numerous follow-up reports, interviews, interrogations, and examination of physical evidence even though the suspect immediately turned himself over to the sheriff's office.

Case 68

A man called the sheriff's office claiming he had shot two men. The man had invited two foreign diplomats to Mountainbeach, where he had promised to give them a painting stolen from one of their former monarchs and a bank note signed by famous revolutionaries. In return, they had promised to give him a letter of commendation from their government. When the diplomats arrived, an argument ensued and both diplomats were shot and killed.

The FBI, the U.S. Attorney General, and even the President became interested in the case because of the status of the victims. A nationally known defense lawyer took up the cause of the defendant, and what would otherwise have been a "walkthrough" (i.e., a homicide where the suspect immediately admits his guilt and pleads guilty in court) developed into a *cause célèbre*.

The case was seen to have international implications, and because of this, rather than the objective elements of the case, a great deal of investigative work had to be done.

In conclusion, it appears that whether a case is worked or not depends primarily on its being formulated as "workable" (i.e., the existence of leads, the amount of loss or harm), except in situations where the victim demands that something be done for a case that is not taken to be workable or where the work load of the detectives preclude their working a borderline case they normally would take. Because the cases-to-be-worked by the major crimes detail are more likely to have workable leads, they were more likely than burglaries to be worked further and to be solved. Conversely, because of the lack of investigative leads in typical burglary cases, a greater proportion of inactivated cases and fewer follow-up reports per case are found in the burglary file.

References

Banton, Michael. 1964. *The Policeman in the Community*. New York: Basic Books.

Bittner, Egon. 1967. "The Police on Skid Row: A Study in Peace-Keeping," *American Sociological Review*, 32, October.

————. 1970. *The Functions of the Police in Modern Society*. Chevy Chase: National Institute of Mental Health.

Black, Donald J., and Albert J. Reiss, Jr. 1970. "Police Control of Juveniles." *American Sociological Review*, 35 (February).

BLUMBERG, ABRAHAM. 1967. *Criminal Justice*. Chicago: Quadrangle Books.

DAUDISTEL, HOWARD. 1971. *Cop Talk: An Investigation of the Police Radio Code*, unpublished M.A. thesis. Santa Barbara: University of California.

GOFFMAN, ERVING. 1951. "On Cooling the Mark Out: Some Aspects of Adaptation to Failure," *Psychiatry*, 15 (November), pp. 451–63.

LA FAVE, WAYNE. 1965. *Arrest: The Decision to Charge a Suspect with a Crime*. Boston: Little, Brown and Company.

MILLER, FRANK W. 1969. *Prosecution: The Decision to Charge a Suspect With a Crime*. Boston: Little, Brown and Company.

NEWMAN, DONALD J. 1966. *Conviction: The Determination of Guilt or Innocence Without Trial*. Boston: Little, Brown and Company.

PILIAVIN, IRVING, and SCOTT BRIAR. 1964. "Police Encounters with Juveniles," *American Sociological Review*, 70 (September).

REISS, ALBERT J., JR. 1971. *The Police and the Public*. New Haven: Yale University Press.

SCHUR, EDWIN M. 1965. *Crimes Without Victims*. Englewood Cliffs, N.J.: Prentice-Hall.

SCHUTZ, ALFRED. 1971. *Collected Papers: The Problem of Social Reality*. Edited and introduced by Maurice Natanson. The Hague: Martinus Nijhoff.

SIMMEL, GEORG. 1950. *The Sociology of Georg Simmel*. Edited by Kurt H. Wolff. New York: The Free Press.

SKOLNICK, JEROME H. 1967. *Justice Without Trial: Law Enforcement in Democratic Society*. New York: John Wiley & Sons.

————. 1972. "The Police and the Urban Ghetto." In Charles E. Reasons and Jack L. Kuykendall, *Race Crime and Justice*, 236–58. Pacific Palisades: Goodyear.

SUDNOW, DAVID. 1965. "Normal Crimes: Sociological Features of the Penal Code in a Public Defender Office," *Social Problems*, 12 (Winter), pp. 255–76.

WEBER, MAX. 1956. *Max Weber Law and Economy*. Edited by Max Rheinstein. Cambridge, Mass.: Harvard University Press.

WERTHMAN, CARL, and IRVING PILIAVIN. 1967. "Gang Members and the Police." In David J. Bordua, *The Police: Six Sociological Essays*. New York: John Wiley & Sons.

WILSON, JAMES Q. 1968. *Varieties of Police Behavior*. Cambridge: Harvard University Press.

EXERCISES

The following set of exercises is designed to introduce the student to some of the practical problems of participant observation. The first exercise offers experience in the initial problems of participant observation research, and the following two are observation projects that cover a spectrum of techniques and problems in this method.

EXERCISE 1

The purpose of this exercise is to develop skills and understanding in gaining access to settings, organizations, and cultures and to find how observations can be recorded under different situations. To do this, take a setting, an organization, and a culture (including subcultures) that you think might be interesting to study and find out what is necessary to gain access. The setting and organization may be public or private domains: for example, a museum would be a public setting, while a living room would be a private setting; your local government would be a public organization, and the IBM corporation would be a private one. The cultures or subcultures may be deviant or nondeviant; heroin users would constitute a deviant subculture, and ski enthusiasts would constitute a nondeviant subculture. Some subcultures, especially nondeviant ones, have formal organizations, and access to the subculture may be through such organizations; therefore, explain how access is gained to the organization, and how this might lead to access to the subculture.

Public, nondeviant situations are generally much easier to gain access to than are private, deviant situations.

Once you have explained how access is gained in each of the three situations, explain how you would collect and record your observations. Could notes be taken while observations are being made, or would the researcher have to make notes later? Would the researcher be known or unknown, and how would he account for his presence if unknown? Would the researcher have access to several different situations or only a few? At what times could the researcher be present? Once these questions are answered, you should be able to give instructions to a researcher on how to gain access and collect all the data he needs.

EXERCISE 2

The purpose of this exercise is to develop skills in recognizing social patterns of behavior. As was pointed out in the introduction, patterns are behaviors that are typical, persistent, trans-situational, and transpersonal. To begin to recognize social patterns, it is helpful to observe situations when there is a dramatic change in behavior patterns. For example, the interaction in a hospital emergency ward changes when an emergency case arrives, or in a firehouse when the firemen mobilize for a fire. There are other situations in settings, organizations, and cultures when one routine behavior pattern changes to another. In these situations, the two different social patterns, seen in juxtaposition, highlight one another and are therefore more easily observed.

To find such situations, it will be necessary to use your imagination and think of where in your own experience such abrupt changes occur. Two questions will be helpful in locating such situations. First, what social behavior is organized to handle changing circumstances routinely? Secondly, what time changes are there that entail changes in behavior? Behavior at bus stops, for example, is organized to prepare for the arrival of the bus; when the bus arrives, the circumstances have changed, and those waiting behave differently from the way they did before. The behavior of spectators at a horse race, mentioned earlier, is another example. On the other hand, time orders changes in behavior. Before a coffee break, office workers engage in one type of behavioral pattern that can be seen to change as the time for the office break arrives.

EXERCISE 3

This exercise has a dual purpose. On the one hand, it is designed to find relationships between behavioral settings and social-behavioral patterns using participant observation. On the other hand, it is intended to demonstrate how more than a single method can be usefully employed in doing research.

For predicting social behavior, few indicators are better than social settings. It is obvious that different behavior will be found in churches from what will be found in bars, and it is not difficult to predict the forms of behavior one will observe. Group prayer in churches, for instance, is setting-specific to churches, temples, and synagogues. On the other hand, some behavior is independent of a particular setting and can be found in numerous settings, such as face-to-face conversations.

For this exercise, observe some social setting and describe a setting-specific behavior. If feasible, students should be divided into groups of five with each student in the group observing a different setting. Once a behavior pattern has been identified as setting-specific, it should be described in detail, so that the description could be used to replicate the behavior. Then, each student should give the description of his setting-specific behavior to another student, to be used as an experimental variable in a field experiment. The students will then introduce the behavior from another setting into the setting they originally observed. If there are negative sanctions for the behavior, this will serve as evidence that the behavior is setting-specific for the setting in which it was originally observed. If not, then the behavior can be taken to be general to more than a single setting.

Some settings you might consider are parks, amusement arcades, restaurants, waiting rooms, and other places where a lot of people gather. Behaviors to look for include smoking, talking, using drugs, laughing, drinking, eating, and the specific absence of these and other activities.

A word of caution is in order, however. Some behavior that is quite normal in one setting can be seen as intolerable in another, and the consequences for such behavior may be quite dramatic. For instance, if one member of a group observed a nudist colony and another member tested the specificity of nudist-colony behavior in a courtroom, the experimenter might land in jail. It is important to use discretion in this exercise. If you believe that a certain behavior would have dangerous consequences in another situation, instead of actually introducing the behavior, interview participants of the setting and ask what their reactions would be.

ADDITIONAL READING SUGGESTIONS

GOFFMAN, ERVING. 1963. *Behavior in Public Places*. New York: The Free Press. Offers a conceptual framework for analyzing public interaction. Useful for analyzing public social settings and organizations.

LOFLAND, JOHN. 1971. *Analyzing Social Settings*. Belmont, Calif.: Wadsworth. An excellent resource for setting up and analyzing participant-observation research as well as research using intensive interviewing. Lofland designed the book to be used while the research is in progress. It serves as a useful guide in doing ethnographies.

ZIMMERMAN, DON H., and D. LAWRENCE WIEDER. 1974. "The Diary: Diary Interview Method." In Robert Smith (ed.), *Social Science Methods: A New Introduction*. New York: The Free Press. Discusses research in a drug subculture, using diaries kept by subjects as a source of data. Besides providing a useful new tool for ethnographic research, it includes an outstanding discussion of how the authors located social patterns.

9. Intensive Interviews

DEVELOPMENT OF A GENERALIZATION EXPLAINING VIOLATION OF FINANCIAL TRUST
—Donald R. Cressey

ALMOST ALL PUBLISHED MATE-rials pertinent to the current research are studies of "embezzlement," and this legal concept was at first used to define the behavior under scrutiny here.* Upon contact with only a few cases, however, it was discovered that the legal category did not describe a homogeneous class of criminal behavior. Persons whose behavior was not adequately described by the definition of embezzlement were found to have been imprisoned for that offense, and persons whose behavior was adequately described by the definition were confined for some other offense. From the legal viewpoint, the use of the word "embezzlement" to denote the behavior of one who has been convicted of forgery or some other offense is obviously erroneous. Also, generalization about a kind of "embezzlement" different from that described by the legal defini-

* "The fraudulent appropriation to his own use or benefit of property or money entrusted to him by another, on the part of a clerk, agent, trustee, public officer or other person acting in a fiduciary capacity." Black's Law Dictionary (1933:633).

From Other People's Money: A Study in the Social Psychology of Embezzlement, by Donald R. Cressey, © 1957, 1971 by Wadsworth Publishing Company, Inc., Belmont, California 94002. Reprinted by permission of the publisher.

tion would be of little scientific value, since another investigator would be unable to search for negative cases.*

To avoid these legal and scientific difficulties, the legal concept "embezzlement" was abandoned, and in its place two criteria for inclusion of any particular case in the investigation were established. First, the person must have accepted a position of trust in good faith. This is almost identical with the requirement of the legal definition that the "felonious intent" in embezzlement must be formulated *after* the time of taking possession. All legal definitions are in agreement in this respect. Second, the person must have violated that trust by committing a crime. These criteria permit the inclusion of almost all persons convicted of embezzlement and larceny by bailee and, in addition, a proportion of those convicted of confidence game, forgery, and other offenses. Some of the offenses in each category are violations of positions of trust which were accepted in good faith. The phenomenon under investigation was therefore defined as "criminal violation of financial trust." The use of this new concept had the effect of providing a rigorous definition of the behavior under investigation, so that a generalization about all instances of the behavior could be attempted, but it did not do violence to the legal definition of "embezzlement" or of the other crimes.

To illustrate the inadequacy of the use of legal concepts, as such, in scientific generalization about embezzlement we need only refer

---

* The literature on "embezzlement" is replete with examples of the vague use of the concept in this way, and as a result there has been practically no progress toward the cumulative development of a theoretical explanation of the type of behavior that embezzlement entails, and even the factual conclusions of empirical studies are not immediately comparable in all aspects. Bonding companies, for instance, ordinarily use the term to denote the behavior of all fidelity and surety bond defaulters (United States Fidelity and Guaranty Company, 1937, 1950; and Peterson, 1947). It also has been used to denote the criminal behavior of all persons employed in banks (Pratt, 1947; 1948). In one instance, the concept has been used in such a way that it included swindlers as well as embezzlers (Riemer, 1941), The varied usage of the term is due to oversight on the part of some investigators, but it is also due in part to the existence of a variety of legal definitions among the states and foreign countries. For example, in Swedish law, "embezzlement" includes some of the offenses that the laws of some of our states define as confidence game or obtaining money under false pretenses, and in some states there is no embezzlement, that type of offense being included in a broad definition of "larceny."

to the varied usage of legal terms by the state of Illinois in sentencing men to its penitentiaries. First, this state uses "obtaining money by means of confidence game" to cover a multitude of offenses including, in order of frequency used for commitment, the issuing of a fraudulent check, obtaining money or property by some other trick in which advantage is taken of the confidence which the offender has established in the victim, and the criminal conversion of money or property accepted in good faith while acting in a fiduciary capacity. The last type of behavior is fundamentally different, sociologically, from that in which a man sells non-existent goods to a victim or issues a check on a non-existent account, and it is obviously much closer to embezzlement than it is to classical confidence game. However, in such cases it frequently is difficult for a defendant to prove that "criminal intent" was absent at the time the money or property was accepted and that instead it was present only after the property had come into his legal possession. Often the defendant is not interested in producing such proof.

Second, the definition of forgery is in Illinois more precise than that of confidence game, but again some forgeries are more closely related to embezzlement than they are to other forgeries. Those forgeries committed in situations where the criminal is trusted (i.e., a forged check is accepted by a victim) are no more homogeneous sociologically than crimes called "confidence game" are homogeneous because the person is similarly trusted. In many instances, one forges as a part of his embezzlement, so that the prosecuting attorney has, in effect, the choice of prosecuting him for either or both crimes. The behavior of a bank teller who, for example, forges a customer's name on a withdrawal slip made out in the amount of $100 and then pockets the money is logically identical, using the concept "criminal violation of financial trust," to embezzlement by a teller who simply indicates that a $100 withdrawal has been made when in fact it has not been made.

Third, larceny by bailee and embezzlement are legally distinguishable in Illinois (this is not true in all states), but the legal distinction is relevant for scientific purposes only in the way that the legal distinction between forgery and embezzlement is relevant. The legal differentiation hinges on the nature of the trust relationship—whether of trustor-trustee or of bailor-bailee—but such differentiation is unnecessary if the trust-violation concept is used instead of the legal categories. Again, the matter of legal proof presents perplexing problems, since it is difficult to prove in court, for example, whether one who rented an automobile and absconded with it actually intended to abscond with it at the time he rented it (confidence game) or whether he rented it in good faith and then later decided to abscond with it (larceny by bailee).

Fourth, not even the relatively precise definition of embezzlement is used consistently in the state. We encountered four different cases in which persons convicted of embezzlement had obviously intended to "beat" their victims at the time they accepted the position of trust. In one such case, which demonstrates the legal importance of proving the presence of criminal intent at different periods, a man was convicted of embezzlement after selling a truckload of merchandise belonging to his employer. He confessed to the interviewer that this was the seventh or eighth time he had obtained a fictitious driver's license and applied for a truck-driving job with the intention of absconding with merchandise. Had the state been able to prove this, it probably would have convicted him of confidence game. The case was not used in the research, since it was not subsumed under the sociological concept.

The main source of direct information in regard to the behavior under scrutiny, now called "the criminal violation of financial trust," was interview material obtained in informal contacts with all prisoners whose behavior met the criteria and who were confined at the Illinois State Penitentiary at Joliet (April–September, 1949), the California Institution for Men at Chino (October–May, 1950–51), and the United States Penitentiary at Terre Haute, Indiana (June–August, 1951). In each institution the names of all inmates confined for offenses such as embezzlement, larceny by bailee, confidence game, forgery, uttering fictitious checks, conspiracy, grand theft (California), theft of government property, falsification of a bill of lading used in interstate shipment, and theft of goods in interstate shipment was obtained. The personal file of each of 503 inmates was examined with the aim of screening out those cases which obviously did not meet the criteria. Official documents such as the "State's Attorney's Report," "The Attorney General's Report," pre-sentence investigation reports, the prosecuting agency's report, and official commitment papers were heavily relied upon, but other documents, such as letters from former employers and from relatives and friends, newspaper clippings, and the prisoner's statement upon admission to the institution also were consulted. These documents revealed, as expected, that many cases did not meet the first criterion—acceptance of a position of trust in good faith—and these cases were not considered further. Whenever there was doubt, however, the case was kept in the list of eligible cases and later the subject was interviewed.

All persons whose cases were not eliminated in this screening process were then interviewed briefly. The main purpose of these interviews was to introduce the subjects to the investigator. They were assured that he was in no way connected with a law-enforcement agency or with the security of the institution. These interviews were of from one-half hour to one and one-half hours duration, depending entirely upon the subject's willingness to talk without being questioned and with a minimum of encouragement and prompting. If analysis of the official and personal documents had established doubt as to whether a subject's case met the criteria, his history in the position of trust was reviewed in regard to the circumstances under which the position was accepted, the term of incumbency before violation, and the circumstances of the violation. Thus, if one answers a "blind" newspaper advertisement for an employee and through it obtains a position, or if he more or less "falls" into a position, it usually may be presumed that he accepted the position of trust in good faith. On the other hand, if he accepts a position of trust under an assumed name there is reason to be suspicious of his intentions. Similarly, one who worked honestly as an accountant for a firm for ten years before he embezzled usually can be presumed to have accepted the position in good faith, and one who absconded with the available funds on the first day of his employment ordinarily can be presumed not to have accepted the position in good faith. Finally, there is a high probability that one who reports his dishonest behavior to his employer or to law enforcement officers accepted the position in good faith. Statements concerning the circumstances surrounding the trust violation could ordinarily be found in official documents, and the subject could be interviewed in respect to the other two aspects of his history without much direct reference to his offense.

In the interviews the subjects were never asked the question, "Did you accept your position of trust in good faith?" Instead, the interviewer prompted each subject to talk about the circumstances surrounding acceptance of the position of trust and the term of incumbency before violation, then waited for the subject to give the desired information spontaneously. The subjects did not know what the criteria were, and it was not until later that they learned that trust violators were the subject of the study. When he reported for the initial interview one subject believed that only Jewish prisoners were being studied. Thus, it was impossible for an inmate to construct logical lies in order to deceive the investigator about whether or not his case met the criteria. Ordinarily, evidence of acceptance in good faith came out in the first interview in the form of statements such as the following: "I had no idea I was going to do this until the day it happened." "For two years I have been trying to understand why I did this after being honest all my life." "I never at any time had any intentions of beating that man." "He wouldn't give me what he'd promised so I just decided to pay myself." Evidence of acceptance in bad faith was presented as follows: "I'm the biggest Con Man in Chicago." "I thought this looked like a pretty good score, so I took it." "My case wasn't like embezzlement because I knew when I took their money that I was going to use it for myself."

The 73 inmates at Joliet, the 21 at Chino and the 39 at Terre Haute whose cases met the criteria were interviewed frequently and at length. Not all were seen the same number of times, and in general the interviews with those seen a small number of times were longer than those with the men interviewed more frequently. Most of the interviews were conducted in a special interviewing room, but a few were conducted at the inmate's place of employment in the institution. In some cases verbatim notes could be written during the interviews without disturbing the subject, but in other cases it seemed appropriate to make only outline notes, and in some cases no notes could be taken at all. In the last two instances the content of the interview was written down in the subject's own words as soon as he left the room. At Chino a few cases were recorded on tape.

The length and frequency of interviews with individual subjects depended to a large extent upon the subject himself. Those subjects who seemed reluctant to talk freely were seen more frequently than those with whom a friendly and confidential relationship was established early in the process, but those who were unable to talk freely and spontaneously about the details of their cases and backgrounds, even if they so desired, were not interviewed as frequently as those who were able to do so. That is, "good" subjects were interviewed more often and more extensively than "poor" subjects —those whose intelligence, educational background, or vocabulary restricted the communication of their experiences. Those who described their behavior fluently became crucial cases, their testimony causing the abandonment of the hypothesis which had guided the research up to the time they were encountered. In sessions in which the interviewer asked indirect questions and the subject gave short, restricted answers, the new hypotheses were then checked against the less fluent cases.

Hypotheses in regard to the problem of systematic causation were formulated progressively in much the same way that the behavior being studied was clarified and redefined to include more than is denoted by the legal term "embezzlement." When a hypothesis was formulated, a search for negative cases was conducted, and when such cases were found the hypothesis was reformulated in the light of them. Consequently, after the final generalization was formulated much of the interview material became obsolete. . . . An average of about fifteen hours was spent with each subject. . . .

The first hypothesis about which information was sought in the interviews was that positions of financial trust are violated when the incumbent has learned in connection with the business or profession in which he is employed that some forms of trust violation are merely technical violations and are not really "illegal" or "wrong," and, on the negative side, that they are not violated if this kind of definition of behavior has not been learned. This hypothesis was suggested by Sutherland in his writings on white collar crime (Sutherland, 1949), but it was abandoned almost immediately. Some of the first violators interviewed expressed the idea that they knew the behavior to be illegal and wrong at all times and that they had merely "kidded themselves" into thinking that it was not illegal. Others reported that they knew of no one in their business or profession who was carrying on practices similar to theirs and some of them defined their offenses as theft, rather than trust violation.

In view of these negative cases, a second hypothesis, which included some of the popular notions regarding the importance to trust violation of gambling and family emergencies, as well as the potential trust violators' attitudes toward them, was formulated. This hypothesis was in part based on Riemer's observation that the "opportunities" inherent in trust positions form "temptations" if the incumbents develop anti-social attitudes which make possible an abandonment of the folkways of business behavior (Riemer, 1941). The formulation was that positions of trust are violated when the incumbent defines a need for extra funds or extended use of property as an "emergency" which cannot be met by legal means, and that if such an emergency does not take place trust violation will not occur. This hypothesis proved fruitful, but like the first one it had to be revised when persons were found who claimed that while an emergency had been present at the time they violated the trust, other, perhaps even more extreme emergencies, had been present in earlier periods when they did not violate it. Others reported that there had been no financial "emergency" in their cases, and a few "explained" their behavior in terms of antagonistic attitudes toward the employer, feelings of being abused, underpaid, or discriminated against in some other way.

The next revision was based on the second hypothesis but it shifted the emphasis from emergency to psychological isolation, stating that persons become trust violators when they conceive of themselves as having incurred financial obligations which are considered as non-socially sanctionable and which, consequently, must be satisfied by a private or secret means. Negatively, if such non-shareable obligations are not present, trust violation will not occur. A similar hypothesis has been suggested by LaPiere and Farnsworth who cite Sutherland as having shown that in cases of white collar crime the person is frequently confronted "with the alternative of committing a crime or losing something he values above his integrity" (LaPiere and Farnsworth, 1949:344). But the specific hypothesis here was unknowingly suggested by a prisoner who stated that he believed that no embezzlement would ever occur if the trusted person always told his wife and family about his financial problems, no matter what the consequences. It directed attention to the fact that not all emergencies, even if they are created by prior "immoral" behavior on the part of the trusted person, are important to trust violation. However, when the cases were re-examined to determine whether the behavior in question could be explained by this hypothesis it was found that in a few of them there was nothing which could be considered as financial *obligation*, that is, as a debt which had been incurred in the past and for which the person at the present time felt responsible. Also, in some cases there had been non-sanctionable obligations at a prior time, and these obligations had not been alleviated by means of trust violation. It became increasingly apparent at this point that the origin of trust violation could not be attributed to a single event, but that its explanation could be made only in terms of a series or conjuncture of events, a process.

Again the hypothesis was re-formulated, emphasizing this time not financial *obligations* which were considered as non-socially sanctionable, and hence as non-sharable, but non-sharable *problems* of that nature. That is, by using the more general "problem" concept it was emphasized that the subject could be in financial difficulty not only because of an acknowledged responsibility for past debts, but because of present discordance between his income and expenditures as well. This hypothesis also pointed up the idea that not only was a non-sharable problem necessary, but also that the person had to, first, be aware of the fact that the problem could to some extent be solved by means of trust violation and, second, possess the technical skill necessary for such violation. Negative cases appeared, however, in instances where men reported that what they considered a non-sharable problem had been present for some period of time and that they had known for some time before the trust violation took place that the problem could be solved by violating their position of trust by using a particular skill. Some stated that they did not violate the trust at the earlier period because the situation was not in sharp enough focus to "break down their ideas of right and wrong."

Such statements suggested the final revision, which took the following form: Trusted persons become trust violators when they conceive of themselves as having a financial problem which is non-sharable, are aware that this problem can be secretly resolved by violation of the position of financial trust, and are able to apply to their own conduct in that situation verbalizations which enable them to adjust their conceptions of themselves as trusted persons with their conceptions of themselves as users of the entrusted funds or property.

This hypothesis proved to be far superior to the others, and no evidence necessitating its rejection has been found as yet. It was developed in the initial phase of the study, at the Illinois State Penitentiary, and was, consequently, based on all cases of trust violation confined in one state institution. A search of the cases reported in the literature, and examination of about two hundred cases collected by E. H. Sutherland in the 1930's likewise showed no negative cases. While many of the reports in the literature and in the Sutherland materials did not contain crucial information which would either affirm or contradict the hypothesis, those which did contain pertinent information affirmed it.

Similarly, in the second phase of the study at the state institution at Chino, California, no negative cases were found, and the final phase, at the United States Penitentiary at Terre Haute, Indiana, was explicitly undertaken so that a search for negative cases could be made among Federal bank embezzlement and post office embezzlement cases. In all of the cases interviewed the process was found to be present, and when cases were examined with a view to answering the question: "Why did these men not violate their trust in an earlier period?" it was seen that in earlier periods one or more of the events in the process had not been present. None of the interviewees were informed about the hypothesis, and the fact that any of the cases might have contradicted it but that none did so may be considered as evidence of validity. In a sense, a prediction for unknown cases of trust violation at Chino and Terre Haute was made on the basis of experience with trust violation in Illinois, and this prediction was borne out in all instances.

The presence of a non-sharable financial problem will not in itself guarantee that the behavior in question will follow. The entire process must be present. While most socialized persons have problems which they consider non-sharable, private, and personal, not all of those persons violate positions of trust which they might hold. A trusted person, for example, who feels that the investment which has resulted in his insolvency was so stupid that he must keep it secret in order to avoid ridicule and disgrace could conceivably commit suicide, become a philosopher of the sort that renounces all worldly things, or use one of countless means to conceal or relieve his distress (cf. Hall, 1947:403). Similarly, one in somewhat the same position could conceivably be sharply aware of the fact that his disgrace could be avoided if he violated his trust position, yet he would not necessarily violate that position. He must first apply to the situation a verbalization which enables him to violate the trust and, at the same time, to look upon himself as a non-violator.

The final hypothesis in its complete form made it possible to account for some of the features of trust violation and for some individual cases of that behavior which could not be accounted for by other hypotheses. However, the fact that it was revised several times probably means that future revision will be necessary, if negative cases are found. The location by another investigator of persons who have violated positions of trust which were accepted in good faith, but in whose behavior the process was not present, will call for either a new revision of the hypothesis or a re-definition of the behavior included in the scope of the present hypothesis.

References

Black's Law Dictionary. 1933. St. Paul: West.

HALL, JEROME. 1947. *Principles of Criminal Law*. Indianapolis: Bobbs-Merrill.

LA PIERE, R. T., and P. R. FARNSWORTH. 1949. *Social Psychology*. New York: McGraw-Hill.

PETERSON, VIRGIL. 1947. "Why Honest People Steal," *Journal of Criminal Law and Criminology*, 38 (July–August), pp. 94–103.

PRATT, L. A. 1947. *Bank Frauds: Their Detection and Prevention*. New York: Ronald Press.

———. 1948. "I Catch Bank Embezzlers," *Collier's*, 122 (November 20), pp. 51 ff.

RIEMER, SVEND. 1941. "Embezzlement: Pathological Basis," *Journal of Criminal Law and Criminology*, 32 (November–December), pp. 411–23.

SUTHERLAND, E. H. 1949. *White Collar Crime*. New York: Dryden.

United States Fidelity and Guaranty Company. 1937. *1001 Embezzlers*. Baltimore: Author.

———. 1950. *1001 Embezzlers: Post War*. Baltimore: Author.

EXERCISES

This set of exercises explores the many uses of the interview. Without language, society would not exist as we now know it. More than anything else, language sets man apart from the lower animals. The interview uses language as the medium for discovering not only another's experiences, attitudes, and values but also his perception of reality. Moreover, the interview can be used with just about every other method in one fashion or another. Skills in interviewing are therefore the most important of those the sociologist must learn.

EXERCISE 1

One of the uses of the interview is in combination with participant observation. Often a researcher will observe behavior that he does not understand and will simply inquire why the actors do what they do. In this way, he is able to find the subjective meaning or the social meaning of the act. Take, for example, the observable action of people stopping at stoplights when no cars are approaching the intersection. To an uninformed observer, such behavior may seem strange; the act is observable, but its social meaning is not, and unless he asks why people behave that way, he may draw incorrect conclusions. The informal interview is very useful for finding the meanings of such behavior.

For this exercise, attend a sports event that is foreign to you. While you're watching the event, ask the people around you why the players are doing what they do. As soon as you understand why the game is played in the manner it is, you will have enough data. If you are familiar with all sports, both foreign and domestic, then find a setting where the people act in a way you do not fully understand and, using the informal interview, find out what meaning their acts have for them.

EXERCISE 2

A form of interviewing called "snowballing" entails asking one person a question that will lead to another person and so on until the researcher has the answer to his question. For example, a group of students in a large city wanted the city to repair a road leading to their school, where there had been several accidents. They began by calling one agency, which referred them to another agency, which in turn referred them to still another agency. This went on for days until they finally found out who could do the necessary work. By recording each call, they were able to create a "map" of the city bureaucracy and the process of the "runaround." Thus, the snowball interview was used successfully to solve a social problem as well as to describe an all too typical bureaucratic process. By doing the same thing, you will be able to find how your city government responds to citizens' legitimate complaints as well as gain skill in interviewing.

EXERCISE 3

One problem in interviewing is knowing what the respondent is talking about. Many groups use a special language or jargon to communicate with other members. The language might be informal, such as that employed by drug users, surfers, or jazz musicians; or it may be a formal language, such as the code used by the police in their communications. Simply choose a group of interest and interview one or more members concerning the language peculiar to that group. From these interviews, construct a glossary of terms and phrases. In this way, you will not only build up a valuable resource for interviewing the group in later research, but you will also have a set of indicators that a person is or is not a member of this group.

EXERCISE 4

The purpose of this exercise is to find why people join the organizations they do. It would probably expedite the data gathering and avoid redundancy if this exercise were carried out as a class project, since the various groups and organizations in your school will be used as the source of data.

Design an interview schedule that will allow you to find under what conditions an individual came into contact with a given group (for example, was he recruited by a group member or did he seek out the group on his own?), whether the individual joined the group for sociability or because of special properties of the group or both, and whether his reasons for remaining in the group are the same as those he had for joining it. Once the data are collected from a sample of groups and organizations in your school, analyze them in terms of the type of group and type of reason for joining. For example, if the organization's function is a service one, you might find that members joined expecting little sociability; however, they may have met people they enjoyed doing things with in the group and remained in it for sociability. Below is an outline of a form that can be used in such an analysis:

	Reason for Joining			Reason for Remaining		
Group	Group Function	Sociability	Both	Group Function	Sociability	Both

ADDITIONAL READING SUGGESTIONS

BECKER, HOWARD. 1956. "Interviewing Medical Students," *American Journal of Sociology*, 62 (September), pp. 199–201. Explains the problems encountered in interviewing medical students and offers practical advice applicable to other research areas.

CHAMBLISS, WILLIAM. 1972. *Box Man*. New York: Harper and Row. An example of research based almost totally on an intensive interview. Chambliss taped an interview with a professional thief, and most of the book consists of the thief's narrative.

CICOUREL, AARON. 1964. *Methods and Measurement in Sociology*, Chap. 3. New York: The Free Press. Discusses theoretical problems and underlying assumptions in the use of interviews. Especially useful in the discussion of the role of language in interviews.

DOUGLAS, JACK (ed.). 1972. *Research on Deviance*. New York: Random House. This collection represents writings of researchers who have gathered ethnographic data. Even though most of the collection focuses on problems in observation, much of the information is useful for interviewing groups that are in one way or another less accessible to the researcher than non-deviant groups.

10. Unobtrusive Measures

PHYSICAL EVIDENCE
—Eugene J. Webb, Donald T. Campbell, Richard D. Schwartz, and Lee Sechrest

EXTERIOR PHYSICAL SIGNS

MOST OF THE EXTERIOR PHYSICAL signs discussed are durable ones that have been inferred to be expressive of current or past behavior. A smaller number are portable and shorter-lived. The bullfighter's beard is a case in point. Conrad (1958) reports that the bullfighter's beard is longer on the day of the fight than on any other day. There are supporting comments among matadors about this phenomenon, yet can one measure the torero's anxiety by noting the length of his beard? The physical task is rather difficult, but not impossible in this day of sophisticated instrumentation. As in all these uncontrolled measures, one must draw inferences about the criterion behavior. Maybe it wasn't the anxiety at all. Perhaps the bullfighter stands farther away from the razor on the morning of the fight, or he may not have shaved that morning at all (like baseball pitchers and boxers). And then there is the possible intersubject contaminant that the more affluent matadors are likely to be shaved, while the less prosperous shave themselves.

A less questionable measure is tattoos. Burma (1959) reports on the observation of tattoos among some nine hundred inmates of three different institutions. The research measure was the propor-

From *Unobtrusive Measures: Nonreactive Research in the Social Sciences*, © 1966 by Rand McNally and Company, Chicago, pp. 115–127.

tion of inmates with tattoos: "significantly more delinquents than nondelinquents tattoo themselves." Of course, one could hardly reverse the findings and hold that tattooing can be employed as a single measure of delinquency. Returning to the bull ring for a moment, "There are many ordinary bullfighters, but ordinary people do not fight bulls" (Lea, 1949:40).

More formal classification cues are tribal markings and scars. Doob (1961:83) reports on a walk he and an African companion took through a Nigerian market.

> I casually pointed to a dozen men, one after the other, who had facial scars. My African friend in all instances named a society; then he and I politely verified the claim by speaking to the person and asking him to tell us the name of his tribe. In eleven instances out of twelve, he was correct. Certainly, however, he may have been responding simultaneously to other cues in the person's appearance, such as his clothing or his skin color.

In a report whose authors choose to remain anonymous (Anonymoi, 1953–60), it was discovered that there is a strong association between the methodological disposition of psychologists and the length of their hair. The authors observed the hair length of psychologists attending professional meetings and coded the meetings by the probable appeal to those of different methodological inclinations. Thus, in one example, the length of hair was compared between those who attended an experimental set of papers and those who attended a series on ego-identity formation. The results are clear cut. The "tough-minded" psychologists have shorter-cut hair than the long-haired psychologists. Symptomatic interpretations, psychoanalytic inquiries as to what is cut about the clean-cut young man, are not the only possibilities. The causal ambiguity of the correlation was clarified when the "dehydration hypothesis" (i.e., that lack of insulation caused the hard-headedness) was rejected by the "bald-head control," i.e., examining the distribution of baldheaded persons (who by the dehydration hypothesis should be most hardheaded of all).

Clothes are an obvious indicator, and A. M. Rosenthal (1962:20), wrote of "the wide variance between private manners and public behavior" of the Japanese:

> Professor Enright [British lecturer in Japan] and just about every

other foreigner who ever visited Japan have noted with varying degrees of astonishment that there is a direct relationship between the politeness of a Japanese and whether or not he is wearing shoes.

It is quite likely that this relationship reflects the selective distribution of shoes in the Japanese society more than any causal element, an example of a population restriction. The economically marginal members of the Japanese population should, one would think, be more overt in expressing hostility to foreign visitors than those who are economically stable—and possession of shoes is more probably linked to affluence than it is to xenophobia.

Shoe styles, not their presence, have been used as the unit of discrimination in the United States society where almost everybody does wear shoes. Gearing (1952), in a study of subculture awareness in south Chicago, observed shoe styles, finding features of the shoe to correspond with certain patterns of living. In general, the flashier shoe more often belonged to the more culture-bound individual. Similar concern with feet was shown by the OSS Assessment Staff (1948) when, because standard uniforms reduced the number of indicators, they paid special attention to shoes and socks as a prime indication "of taste and status."

Despite the general consensus on clothing as an indicator of status, little controlled work has been done on the subject. Flugel (1930) wrote a discursive book on clothing in general, and Webb (1957) reported on class differences in attitudes toward clothes and clothing stores. Another investigation shows many differences between clothing worn by independent and fraternity-affiliated college males. Within the fraternity groups, better grades are made by the more neatly dressed (Sechrest, 1965b).

Kane (1958; 1959; 1962) observed the clothing worn by outpatients to their interviews. He has considered pattern, color, texture, and amount of clothing, relating these characteristics to various moods, traits, and personality changes. In a more reactive study, Green and Knapp (1959) associated preferences for different types of tartans with need achievement; it would be of interest to see if this preference pattern were supported in clothing purchased or worn.

A southern chief of detectives has discussed using clothing clues as predictor variables. In a series of suggestions to police officers, he noted the importance of dress details. When Negroes are planning a mass jail-in, "The women will wear dungarees as they enter the meeting places" (Anonymous, 1965).

Jewelry and other ornamental objects can also be clues. Freud gave his inner circle of six, after World War I, rings matching his own. On another intellectual plane, observers have noted that in some societies one can find illiterates who buy only the top of a pen and then clip it to clothing as a suggestion of their writing prowess. One could observe the frequency of such purchases in local stores, or less arduously, examine sales records over time from the manufacturer, considering the ratio of tops to bottoms for different countries or regions. The observation method would have an advantage in that one could make coincidental observations on the appearance of those purchasing the tops alone, or isolate a sample for interviewing. The archival record of top and bottom shipments is infinitely more efficient, but more circumscribed in the content available for study.

As part of their study of the social status of legislators and their voting, MacRae and MacRae (1961) observed the houses lived in by legislators and rated them along the lines suggested by Warner (Warner, Meeker, and Eells, 1949). This house rating was part of the over-all social-class index produced for each legislator.

Observation of any type of possession can be employed as an index if the investigator knows that there is a clear relationship between possession (ownership) of the object and a second variable. Calluses, for example, can serve as an observable indicator of certain classes of activity. Different sports make selective demands on tissue, for example, and the calluses that result are reliable indicators of whether one is a squash player or a golfer. Some occupations may also be determined by similar physical clues.

With these measures used alone, validity is often tenuous. Phillips (1962) is unusual in giving multiple indicators of the changes in Miami resulting from the influx of a hundred thousand Cubans. Two years following the Castro revolution, he observed:

Bilingual streets signs (No Jaywalking; Cruce por la Zona para Peatones)
"A visitor hears almost as much Spanish as English."
Signs in windows saying "Se Habla Español"

Stores with names like "Mi Botanica" and "Carniceria Latina"
Latin-American foods on restaurant menus
Supermarkets selling yucca, malanga, and platanos
The manufacture of a Cuban type of cigarette
Radio broadcasts in Spanish
Spanish-language editorials in the English-language newspapers
Services held in Spanish by 40 Miami churches

Perhaps Phillips was overstating his case, but the marshalling of so much, and so diverse, observational evidence is persuasive. For a prime source in such studies of the unique character of cities, and their changes, there is that eminent guide, the classified telephone directory. It can yield a wide range of broad content information on the economy, interests, and characteristics of a city and its people. Isolating the major United States cities, which ones have the highest numbers of palmists per thousand population?

EXPRESSIVE MOVEMENT

The more plastic variables of body movement historically have interested many observers. Charles Darwin's (1872) work on the expression of emotions continues to be the landmark commentary. His exposition of the measurement of frowning, the uncovering of teeth, erection of the hair, and the like remains provocative reading. The more recent studies on expressive movement and personality measurement are reviewed by Wolff and Precker (1951:457–97). Of particular interest in their chapter is the emphasis on consistency among different types of expressive movement. They review the relation between personality and the following measures: facial expression, literary style, artistic style, style of speech, gait, painting and drawing, and handwriting. Not all of these studies are nonreactive, since the central criterion for this is that the subject is not aware of being measured.

Examples of using expressive movement as a response to a particular stimulus—i.e., stimulus-linked rather than subject-linked—are provided in the work of Maurice Krout (1933; 1937; 1951; 1954a; 1954b). Although this work was done in a laboratory setting, it was under façade conditions. That is, subjects were unaware of the true purpose of the research, considering the experiment a purely verbal task. There is a good possibility for application of

Krout's (1954a) approach in less reactive settings. He elicited autistic gestures through verbal-conflict situations, and his analysis deals primarily with digital-manual responses. An example of his findings is the correlation between an attitude of fear and the gesture of placing hand to nose. Darwin (1872) mentioned pupil dilation as a possible fear indicator.

Kinesics as a subject of study is relevant here, although as yet large amounts of data are not available. Birdwhistell (1960:54–64; 1963:123–40) has defined kinesics as being concerned with the communicational aspects of learned, patterned, body-motion behavior. This system of nonverbal communication is felt to be inextricably linked with the verbal, and the aim of such study is to achieve a quantification of the former which can be related to the latter. Some "motion qualifiers" have been identified, such as intensity, range, and velocity. Ruesch and Kees (1956) have presented a combination text-picture treatment in their book, *Nonverbal Communication*. An example of the impressionistic style of observation is provided by Murphy and Murphy (1962:12), who reported on the differences in facial expressions between young and old Russians: "While faces of old people often seemed resigned, tired and sad, generally the children seemed lively, friendly, confident and full of vitality."

Something of the detail possible in such studies is shown in Wolff's (1948; 1951) work on hands. In the first study, Wolff observed the gestures of mental patients at meals and at work, concluding, "I found sufficient evidence that correlations exist (1) between emotional make-up and gesture, (2) between the degree of integration and gesture" (1948:166). The second study was anthropometric, and Wolff compared features of the handprints of schizophrenics, mental defectives, and normals. The hands were divided into three major types: (1) elementary, simple and regressive; (2) motor, fleshy and bony; and (3) small and large. On the basis of an individual's hand type, measurements, nails, crease lines, and type of skin, she delineates the main characteristics of their personality, intelligence, vitality, and temperament.

Without necessarily endorsing her conclusions, we report the finding of a confused crease-line pattern peculiar to the extreme of mental deficiency. Other structural characteristics such as concave primary nails, "appeared to a greater or lesser degree in the hands of mental defectives . . . but were completely absent in the hands of the control cases" (Wolff, 1951:105).

A journalistic account of the expressive behavior of hands has been given by Gould (1951:1). Here is his description of Frank Costello's appearance before the Kefauver crime hearings:

> As he [Costello] sparred with Rudolph Halley, the committee's counsel, the movement of his fingers told their own emotional story. When the questions got rough, Costello crumpled a handkerchief in his hands. Or he rubbed his palms together. Or he interlaced his fingers. Or he grasped a half-filled glass of water. Or he beat a silent tattoo on the table top. Or he rolled a little ball of paper between his thumb and index finger. Or he stroked the side piece of his glasses lying on the table. His was video's first ballet of the hands.*

It is of interest that conversations of male students with females have been found to be more frequently punctuated by quick, jerky, "nervous" gestures than are conversations between two males (Sechrest, 1965b).

Schubert (1959) has suggested that overt personal behavior could be used in the study of judicial behavior. In presenting a psychometric model of the Supreme Court, he suggests that the speech, grimaces, and gestures of the judges when hearing oral arguments and when opinions are being delivered are rich sources of data for students of the Court.

On the other side of the legal fence, witnesses in Hindu courts are reported to give indications of the truth of their statements by the movement of their toes (Krout, 1951). The eminent American legal scholar J. H. Wigmore, in works on judicial proof and evidence (1935; 1937), speaks of the importance of peripheral expressive movements as clues to the validity of testimony.

That these cues can vary across societies is demonstrated by Sechrest and Flores. They showed that "leg jiggling" is more frequent among Filipino than American males, and held that jiggling is a "nervous" behavior. As evidence of this, they found jiggling more frequent in coffee lounges than in cocktail lounges.

The superstitious behavior of baseball players is a possible area of study. Knocking dust off cleats, amount of preliminary bat swinging, tossing dust into the air, going to the resin bag, and

---

* © 1951 by the New York Times Company. Reprinted by permission.

wiping hands on shirts may be interpreted as expressive actions. One hypothesis is that the extent of such superstitious behavior is related to whether or not the player is in a slump or in the middle of a good streak. This study could be extended to other sports in which the central characters are relatively isolated and visible. It should be easier for golfers and basketball players, but more difficult for football players.

From a practical point of view, of course, coaches and scouts have long studied the overt behavior of opponents for clues to forthcoming actions. (It is known, for example, that most football teams are "right sided" and run a disproportionate number of plays to the right [Griffin, 1964].) Does the fullback indicate the direction of the play by which hand he puts on the ground? Does the linebacker rest on his heels if he is going to fall back on pass defense? Does the quarterback always look in the direction in which he is going to pass, or does he sometimes look the other way, knowing that the defense is focusing on his eyes?

A police officer reported eye movement as a "pickup" clue. A driver who repeatedly glances from side to side, then into the rear-view mirror, then again from side to side may be abnormally cautious and perfectly blameless. But he may also be abnormally furtive and guilty of a crime. Another officer, in commenting on auto thefts, said, "We . . . look for clean cars with dirty license plates and dirty cars with clean plates," explaining that thieves frequently switch plates (Reddy, 1965).

In a validation study of self-reported levels of newspaper readership, eye movement was observed when people were reading newspapers in trains, buses, library reading rooms, and the street (Advertising Service Guild, 1949). A number of interesting eye movement and direction studies have been conducted in controlled laboratory settings. Discussion of them is contained in the following chapter on observational hardware.

PHYSICAL LOCATION

The physical position of animals has been a favored measure of laboratory scientists, as well as of those in the field. Imanishi (1960), for example, described the social structure of Japanese macaques by reporting on their physical grouping patterns. The dominant macaques sit in the center of a series of concentric rings.

For people, there are the familiar newspaper accounts of who stood next to whom in Red Square reviewing the May Day parade. The proximity of a politician to the leader is a direct clue of his status in the power hierarchy. His physical position is interpreted as symptomatic of other behavior which gave him the status position befitting someone four men away from the Premier, and descriptive of that current status position. In this more casual journalistic report of observations, one often finds time-series analysis: Mr. B. has been demoted to the end of the dais, and Mr. L. has moved up close to the middle.

The clustering of Negroes and whites was used by Campbell, Kruskal, and Wallace (1965) in their study of seating aggregation as an index of attitude. Where seating in a classroom is voluntary, the degree to which the Negroes and whites present sit by themselves versus mixing randomly may be taken as a presumptive index of the degree to which acquaintance, friendship, and preference are strongly colored by race, as opposed to being distributed without regard to racial considerations. Classes in four schools were studied, and significant aggregation by race was found, varying in degree between schools. Aggregation by age, sex, and race has also been reported for elevated trains and lunch counters (Sechrest, 1965b).

Feshbach and Feshbach (1963:499) report on another type of clustering. At a Halloween party, they induced fear in a group of boys, aged nine to twelve, by telling them ghost stories. The boys were then called out of the room and were administered questionnaires. The induction of the fear state was natural, but their dependent-variable measures were potentially reactive. What is of interest to us is a parenthetical statement made by the authors. After describing the ghost-story-telling situation, the Feshbachs offer evidence for the successful induction of fear: "Although the diameter of the circle was about eleven feet at the beginning of the story telling, by the time the last ghost story was completed, it had been spontaneously reduced to approximately three feet."

Gratiot-Alphandery (1951a; 1951b) and Herbinière-Lebert (1951) have both made observations of children's seating during informal film showings. How children from different age groups clustered was a measure used in work on developmental changes.

Sommer (1961) employed the position of chairs in a descriptive way, looking at "the distance for comfortable conversation." Normal subjects were used, but observations were made after the subjects had been on a tour of a large mental hospital. Distances among chairs in a lounge were systematically varied, and the people were brought into the lounge after the tour. They entered by pairs, and each pair was asked to go to a designated area and sit down. A simple record was made of the chairs selected.

The issue here is what one generalizes to. Just as the Feshbachs' subjects drew together during the narration of ghost stories, it would not be unrealistic to expect that normal adults coming from a tour of a mental hospital might also draw closer together than would be the case if they had not been on the tour. Their seating distance before the tour would be an interesting control. Do they huddle more, anticipating worse than will be seen, or less?

Sommer (1959; 1960; 1962) has conducted other studies of social distance and positioning, and in the 1959 study mentions a "waltz technique" to measure psychological distance. He learned that as he approached people, they would back away; when he moved backward during a conversation, the other person moved forward. The physical distance between two conversationalists also varies systematically by the nationality of the talkers, and there are substantial differences in distance between two Englishmen talking together and two Frenchmen in conversation. In a cross-cultural study, this would be a response-set characteristic to be accounted for.

Sommer's work inspired a study in Germany (Kaminski and Osterkamp, 1962), but unfortunately it is not a replication of Sommer's design. A paper-and-pencil test was substituted for the actual physical behavior, and 48 students were tested in three mock situations: classroom, U-shaped table, and park benches. Sechrest, Flores, and Arellano (1965) studied social distance in a Filipino sample and found considerably greater distance in opposite-sex pairs as compared with same-sex pairs. Other tests include measuring the distance subjects placed photographs away from themselves (Smith, 1958; Beloff and Beloff, 1961) and Werner and Wapner's (1953) research on measuring the amount of distance walked under conditions of danger.

Sommer (1960) noted how the physical location of group members influenced interactions. Most communication took place among neighbors, but the corner was the locus of most interaction. Whyte (1956) observed that air conditioners were dispersed in a nonrandom way in a Chicago suburban community, and Howells and Becker (1962) demonstrated that those who sat facing several others during a discussion received more leadership nominations than did those who sat side by side.

Leipold's (1963) dissertation carried the work further, paying special attention to the individual response-set variable of "personal space," the physical distance an organism customarily places between itself and other organisms. Leipold gathered personality-classification data on a group of 90 psychology students, divided them into two groups on the basis of introversion-extraversion, and administered stress, praise, or neutral conditions to a third of each group. He evaluated the effect of the conditions, and the tie to introversion-extraversion, by noting which of several available seats were taken by the subjects when they came in for a subsequent interview. The seats varied in the distance from the investigator. In one of his findings, he reports that introverted and high-anxious students, defined by questionnaire responses, kept a greater physical distance from the investigator (choosing a farther chair) than did extraverted and low-anxious students. Stress conditions also resulted in greater distance.

That random assignment doesn't always work is shown in Grusky's (1959) work on organizational goals and informal leaders —research conducted in an experimental prison camp. He learned that informal leaders, despite a policy of random bed assignments, were more likely to attain the bottom bunk. Grusky also considered such archival measures as number of escapes, general transfers, and transfers for poor adjustment. On all of these measures, leaders differed significantly from nonleaders. It must be remembered that this was an experimental prison camp, and the artificiality of the research situation presents the risk that a "Hawthorne effect" may be present. What would be valuable would be another study of regular prison behavior to see if these findings hold in a nonexperimental setting.

On still another plane, the august chambers of the United Nations in New York, Alger (1968) observed representatives at the General Assembly. Sitting with a press card in the gallery, he recorded 3,322 interactions among representatives at sessions of the

Administrative and Budgetary Committee. Each interaction was coded for location, initiator, presence or exchange of documents, apparent humor, duration, and so on. His interest was in defining the clusters of nations who typically interacted in the committee.

Using the same approach, it might be possible to get partial evidence on which nations are perceived as critical and uncertain during debate on a proposed piece of UN action. Could one define the marginal, "swing" countries by noting which ones were visited by both Western and Bloc countries during the course of the debate? Weak evidence, to be sure, for there is the heavy problem of spatial restriction. One can only observe in public places, and even expanding the investigation tó lobbies, lounges, and other public meeting areas may exclude the locus of the truly critical interactions. This bias might be selective, for if an issue suddenly appeared without warning, the public areas might be a more solid sampling base than they would be for issues which had long been anticipated and which could be lobbied in private. That the outside observer must have a broad understanding of the phenomenon and parties he is observing is indicated in Alger's study. He comments on the high level of interaction with the Irish delegate, which was not a reflection of the political power of Ireland, but instead the result of the easy affability of the man. This affability might truly influence the power position of his country, and hence be an important datum in that sense, but it is more likely to confound comparisons if it is used as evidence on a nation.

Barch, Trumbo, and Nangle (1957) used the behavior of automobiles in their observational study of conformity to legal requirements. We are not sure if this is more properly coded under "expressive movement," but the "physical position" category seems more appropriate. They were interested in the degree to which turn-signalling was related to the turn-signalling behavior of a preceding car. For four weeks, they recorded this information:

1. Presence or absence of a turn signal
2. Direction of turn
3. Presence of another motor vehicle 100 feet or less behind the turning motor vehicle when it begins to turn
4. Sex of drivers.

Observers stood near the side of the road and were not easily visible to the motorists. There was the interesting finding that conforming behavior, as defined by signalling or not, varied with the direction of the turn. Moreover, a sex difference was noted. There was a strong positive correlation if model and follower were females, and also a high correlation if left turns were signalled. But on right turns, the correlation was low and positive. Why there is a high correlation for left turns and a low one for right turns is equivocal. The data, like so many simple observational data, don't offer the "why," but simply establish a relationship.

Several of the above findings have been verified and perturbingly elaborated by a finding that signalling is more erratic in bad weather and by drivers of expensive autos (Sechrest, 1965b). Blomgren, Scheuneman, and Wilkins (1963) also used turn signals as a dependent variable in a before-after study of the effect of a signalling safety poster. Exposure to the sign increased signalling about 6 per cent.

References

Advertising Service Guild. 1949. *The Press and Its Readers.* London: Art & Technics.

ALGER, C. F. 1968. "Interaction in a Committee of the United Nations General Assembly." In J. D. Singer (ed.), *Quantitative International Politics (International Yearbook of Political Behavior Research).* 6 vols. New York: The Free Press.

ANONYMOI. 1953–60. "Hair Style as a Function of Hard-Headedness vs. Long-Hairedness in Psychological Research: A Study in the Personology of Science," unpublished manuscript. Evanston, Ill.: Northwestern University; Chicago: University of Chicago.

ANONYMOUS. 1965. "Civil Rights: By the Book," *Newsweek,* Vol. 65, No. 37 (March 1).

BARCH, A. M., D. TRUMBO, and J. NANGLE. 1957. "Social Setting and Conformity to a Legal Requirement," *Journal of Abnormal and Social Psychology,* 55, pp. 396–98.

BELOFF, J., and H. BELOFF. 1961. "The Influence of Valence on Distance Judgments of Human Faces," *Journal of Abnormal and Social Psychology,* 62, pp. 720–22.

BIRDWHISTELL, R. 1960. "Kinesics and Communication." In E. Carpenter (ed.), *Exploration in Communication.* Boston: Beacon Hill.

————. 1963. "The Kinesic Level in the Investigations of Emotions." In P. Knapp (ed.), *The Expression of Emotions in Man.* New York: International Universities Press.

BLOMGREN, G. W., T. W. SCHEUNEMAN, and J. L. WILKINS. 1963. "Effects of Exposure to a Safety Poster on the Frequency of Turn Signalling," *Traffic Safety*, 7, pp. 15–22.

BURMA, J. H. 1959. "Self-Tattooing Among Delinquents: A Research Note," *Sociology and Social Research*, 43, pp. 341–45.

CAMPBELL, D. T., W. H. KRUSKAL, and W. P. WALLACE. 1966. "Seating Aggregation as an Index of Attitude," *Sociometry*, 29, pp. 1–15.

CONRAD, B. 1958. *The Death of Manolete*. Cambridge: Houghton Mifflin.

DARWIN, C. 1872. *The Expression of the Emotions in Man and Animals*. London: Murray.

DOOB, L. W. 1961. *Communication in Africa*. New Haven: Yale University Press.

FESHBACH, S., and N. FESHBACH. 1936. "Influence of the Stimulus Object Upon the Complementary and Supplementary Projection of Fear," *Journal of Abnormal and Social Psychology*, 66, pp. 498–502.

FLUGEL, J. C. 1930. *Psychology of Clothes*. London: Hogarth.

GEARING, F. 1952. "The Response to a Cultural Precept Among Migrants From Bronzeville to Hyde Park," unpublished M.A. thesis. Chicago: University of Chicago.

GOULD, J. 1951. "Costello TV's First Headless Star; Only His Hands Entertain Audience," *New York Times*, March 1.

GRATIOT-ALPHANDERY, H. 1951a. "L'Enfant et le film," *Revue Internationale de Filmologie*, 2, pp. 171–72.

————. 1951b. "Jeunes spectateurs," *Revue Internationale de Filmologie*, 2, pp. 257–63.

GREEN, H. B., and R. H. KNAPP. 1959. "Time Judgment, Aesthetic Preference, and Need for Achievement," *Journal of Abnormal and Social Psychology*, 58, pp. 140–42.

GRIFFIN, J. R. 1964. "Coia 'Catch,' Kicking Draw Much Criticism," *Chicago Sun-Times*, October 27, p. 76.

GRUSKY, O. 1959. "Organizational Goals and the Behavior of Informal Leaders," *American Journal of Sociology*, 65, pp. 59–67.

HERBINIÈRE-LEBERT, S. 1951. "Pourquoi et comment nous avons fait 'Mains Blanches': premières experiences avec un film éducatif réalisé spécialement pours les mins de sept ans," *Revue Internationale de Filmologie*, 2, pp. 247–55.

HOWELLS, L. T., and S. W. BECKER. 1962. "Seating Arrangement and Leadership Emergence," *Journal of Abnormal and Social Psychology*, 64, pp. 148–50.

IMANISHI, K. 1960. "Social Organization of Subhuman Primates in Their Natural Habitat," *Current Anthropology*, I, pp. 393–407.

KAMINSKI, G., and U. OSTERKAMP. 1962. "Untersuchungen über die Topologie sozialer Handlungsfelder," *Zeitschrift für experimentelle und angewandte Psychologie*, 9, pp. 417–51.

KANE, F. 1958. "Clothing Worn by Out-Patients to Interviews," *Psychiatric Communications*, Vol. 1, No. 2.

————. 1959. "Clothing Worn by an Out-Patient: A Case Study," *Psychiatric Communications*, 2:2.

————. 1962. "The Meaning of the Form of Clothing," *Psychiatric Communications*, 5:1.

KROUT, M. H. 1933. *Major Aspects of Personality*. Chicago: College Press.

————. 1937. "Further Studies on the Relation of Personality and Gestures: A Nosological Analysis of Austistic Gestures," *Journal of Experimental Psychology*, 20, pp. 279–87.

————. 1951. "Gestures and Attitudes: An Experimental Study of the Verbal Equivalents and Other Characteristics of a Selected Group of Manual Austistic Gestures," unpublished doctoral dissertation. Chicago: University of Chicago.

Lea, T. 1949. *The Brave Bulls*. Boston: Little, Brown.

Leipold, W. D. 1963. "Psychological Distance in a Dyadic Interview as a Function of Introversion-Extraversion, Anxiety, Social Desirability and Stress," unpublished doctoral dissertation. Grand Forks: University of North Dakota.

MacRae, D., and E. MacRae. 1961. "Legislators' Social Status and Their Votes," *American Journal of Sociology*, 66, pp. 559–603.

Murphy, G., and L. Murphy. 1962. "Soviet Life and Soviet Psychology." In R. A. Bauer (ed.), *Some Views on Soviet Psychology*. Washington, D. C.: American Psychological Association.

OSS Assessment Staff. 1948. *Assessment of Men*. New York: Rinehart.

Phillips, R. H. 1962. "Miami Goes Latin Under Cuban Tide," *New York Times*, March 18.

Reddy J. 1965. "Heady Thieves Find Wheeling Their Waterloo," *Chicago Sun-Times*, February 28.

Rosenthal, A. M. 1962. "Japan, Famous for Politeness, Has a Less Courteous Side, Too," *New York Times*, February 25.

Ruesch, J., and W. Kees. 1956. *Nonverbal Communication: Notes on the Visual Perception of Human Relations*. Berkeley: University of California Press.

Schubert, G. 1959. *Quantitative Analysis of Judicial Behavior*. Glencoe, Ill.: The Free Press.

Sechrest, L. 1965. "Situational Sampling and Contrived Situations in the Assessment of Behavior," unpublished manuscript. Evanston, Ill.: Northwestern University.

Sechrest, L., and L. Flores. (In Press.) "The Occurrence of a Nervous Mannerism in Two Cultures," *Journal of Nervous and Mental Disease*.

Sechrest, L., L. Flores, and L. Arellano. 1965. "Social Distance and Language in Bilingual Subjects," unpublished manuscript. Evanston, Ill.: Northwestern University.

Smith, H. T. 1958. "A Comparison of Interview and Observation Methods of Mother Behavior," *Journal of Abnormal and Social Psychology*, 57, pp. 278–82.

Sommer, R. 1959. "Studies in Personal Space," *Sociometry*, 22, pp. 247–60.

————. 1960. "Personal Space," *Canadian Architect*, pp. 76–80.

————. 1961. "Leadership and Group Geography," *Sociometry*, 24, pp. 99–100.

————. 1962. "The Distance for Comfortable Conversations: Further Study," *Sociometry*, 25, pp. 111–16.

Warner, W. L., M. Meeker, and K. Eells. 1959. *Social Class in America*. Chicago: Science Research Associates.

Webb, E. J. 1957. *Men's Clothing Study*. Chicago: Chicago Tribune.

Werner, H., and S. Wapner. 1953. "Changes in Psychological Distance Under Conditions of Danger," *Journal of Personality*, 24, pp. 153–67.

Whyte, W. H. 1956. *The Organization Man*. New York: Simon and Schuster.

WIGMORE, J. H. 1935. A Student's Textbook of the Law of Evidence. Brooklyn: Foundation Press.

_____. 1937. The Science of Judicial Proof as Given by Logic, Psychology, and General Experience and Illustrated in Judicial Trials. 3d ed. Boston: Little, Brown.

WOLFF, C. 1948. A Psychology of Gesture. London: Methuen.

_____. 1951. The Hand in Psychological Diagnosis. London: Methuen.

WOLFF, W., and J. A. PRECKER. 1951. "Expressive Movement and the Methods of Experimental Depth Psychology." In H. H. Anderson and G. L. Anderson (eds.); An Introduction to Projection Techniques. N.J.: Prentice-Hall.

EXERCISES   Each of the following exercises involves either the use or the discovery of an unobtrusive measure or descriptive sign. The significance of such measures is that they are *nonreactive* and *given off*—that is, they are not affected by the researcher's presence, nor are they for the benefit of the researcher. For example, interviews, experiments, and participant observation all have potentially reactive effects on subjects. If a respondent believes that an interview may be used against him in any way, he may tell the interviewer only those things he feels will favorably impress the researcher. Hence, his responses are a *reaction* to the method of gathering information.

On the other hand, unobtrusive measures are signs that indicate a type of behavior or a behavior pattern, but are not meant to do so. For example, Sherlock Holmes told Dr. Watson that he had made a wise decision choosing a certain office for his practice, since the steps to that office were more worn than were the steps to his competitor's across the hall. Similarly, traffic patterns of pedestrians can be determined by the shortcuts that are made across lawns. The following exercises are designed to sensitize you to such measures and signs.

Exercise 1

Various occupations entail various uniforms, tools, and tasks that indicate the occupational role. Make a list of occupations in terms of various physical signs by which the occupation can be recognized. Besides the more obvious physical signs, try to find some more subtle signs as well. For instance, occupations entailing physical work with the hands will result in the workers' having larger fingers than workers in occupations requiring little physical work with the hands. Auto mechanics frequently cut their hands in their work and are likely to have numerous cuts and scars on them. Miners, who also work with their hands, can be distinguished from construction workers in that construction workers are more likely to be tanned. Classify the occupational signs as *clothing, tools* and *artifacts,* or *task signs* left on the body from the work.

EXERCISE 2

A measure of ethnic integration is the clustering of ethnic-specific stores dealing in goods and services preferred by, or characteristic of, various ethnic groups. If, for example, in one section of town many of the signs in store windows are written in Spanish, it can be assumed that the area is a segregated section of Spanish-speaking peoples such as former Mexicans or Puerto Ricans. The extent to which such signs, goods, and services are diffuse is an indication of integration, while clustering is a sign of segregation.

To find the extent of integration or segregation in your community or neighborhood, take a map and a set of colored pins and put a pin on the map for each ethnic sign you can find. Use a different color for each ethnic group. Some indicators will be fairly blatant, such as foreign-language signs, while other indicators will be fairly subtle, such as specific foods or services characteristic of an ethnic group. When you finish, you will find, if the different colors on your map are mixed together, that the area is integrated; if they are clustered, you will have found segregation.

EXERCISE 3

Signs of superstitions can be found in various gestures. For example, when some people spill salt, they will throw some of the spilt salt over their shoulder to ward off bad luck; some will knock on wood so that what is considered a good state of affairs will remain so. To find out what the various indicators of superstition are, interview people from various backgrounds and ask them whether they know of any gestures to bring good luck or ward off bad luck. Compile a list in terms of general superstitions as well as a list of gestures that are specific to certain groups or occupations. In this way, you will have developed a list of indicators that point to superstition as well as a set that can point to membership in various groups or occupations.

EXERCISE 4

People's relationships with one another can be determined by their spatial proximity. To get a sense of the distances people keep when together or separated, go to a public park and observe groupings. Note, for example, that, if two groups are next to one another, the distance between the groups is greater than the distance kept between members of the same group. This can be seen even more clearly if you observe couples sitting together. Compared with the distance the couples keep between themselves, the distance between one couple and the next is great. Try to make these observations on a day when the park will be crowded. On such days, the groups will have to sit closer, and you can determine the minimal amount of space they keep between one another. It will not be necessary to take precise measurements; attempt, rather, to estimate the differences in distance that strangers keep and acquaintances keep. In this way, you will become sensitive to distances as an indicator of social relationships.

ADDITIONAL READING SUGGESTIONS

FAST, J. 1970. *Body Language*. New York: Pocket Books. Explains various body gestures as forms of communication. Many of the interpretations may be questionable, but Fast does provide a highly readable resource on expressive movements.

HALL, EDWARD T. 1959. *The Silent Language*. Greenwich, Conn.. Fawcett. A detailed discussion of the various understandings of space, time, and other dimensions that different cultures hold. Provides numerous unobtrusive measures of cultural identity.

PETSCHEK, WILLA. 1970. "An Unblinking Look at the New York Private Eye," *New York*, 3 (November 23). Discusses numerous unobtrusive measures employed by private eyes. Several would have to be put in a more ethical context for sociological use, but the detectives have developed ingenious devices to measure various social conditions.

WEBB, EUGENE, DONALD T. CAMPBELL, RICHARD D. SCHWARTZ, and LEE SECHREST. 1966. *Unobtrusive Measures: Nonreactive Research in the Social Sciences*. Chicago: Rand McNally. The most comprehensive work on nonreactive measures and indicators for sociological research. In addition, it provides a detailed discussion of how and why multiple measures, especially nonreactive ones, can be employed in social science research.

V: CONTENT ANALYSIS

IN INVESTIGATING APPARENT SUICIDES, DETECTIVES CAREFULLY ANA-
lyze the suicide note, if any, to determine whether the dead person
himself wrote it. For example, if the corpse was a well-educated
person and the suicide note found pinned to his shirt contains
several misspellings and mistakes in grammar, the detectives would
begin investigating the possibility of murder. In the Zodiac case,
the murderer sent several letters to the police, and the contents of
the letters were analyzed for references that would help to identify
the killer. For example, the Zodiac made references to exotic religious beliefs in some of his letters. These references were used as
clues to place the Zodiac in certain parts of the world where such
beliefs were practiced or to groups in the United States that held
these beliefs. From letters, notes, and other written or transcribed
documents, detectives are able to infer a great deal of information.

For the sociologist, content analysis has been used in describing
cultural elements of societies. Such descriptions, in turn, are used
for comparative analysis (Warwick and Osherson, 1973). Content
analysis has also been found to be extremely useful in analyzing
social change. Culture is reflected in the beliefs, sentiments, and
moral themes of a society, and these cultural elements are reflected
in various social writings, whether it be cave drawings or the daily
newspaper. In the same context, as societies change, so, too, do the
form and content of what people in those societies write. By comparing the different writings of a society over a period of time, the
researcher is able to see changes in social behavior. For example,
by looking at old magazines over a relatively brief period, it is pos-

sible to see changes in fashions, interests, technology, and politics. Abrupt changes in a society become apparent in examining various media before and after major events. For example, the Cuban press can be seen to have changed greatly after 1960, when Fidel Castro came into power, reflecting the sweeping changes made under his regime. Such a change is usefully compared to the more subtle changes, or to the lack of change, after an American Presidential election.

The term "content analysis" appears to denote merely a form of analysis, but actually it covers a number of methods of gathering data and several modes of analysis (Cicourel, 1964). For example, a researcher may count the number of favorable and unfavorable political editorials in a nation's newspapers as an indication of that nation's political policy regarding freedom of the press (Simon, 1969:279). Counting editorial comments and coding them as favorable or unfavorable constitute a method of gathering data. Here we shall discuss two forms of content analysis.

WRITTEN DOCUMENT ANALYSIS

Many of the patterns characteristic of society are found in written documents left by societal members. The span of such documents ranges from highly personal ones such as diaries to wholly public ones such as the daily newspaper. Depending on what the researcher wants to know, he can employ different dimensions and different types of documents, but his analysis itself generally follows typical steps. Generally the researcher will look for certain forms or categories in the documents he is examining and try to discover common patterns. In the Jerry Jacobs' study of suicide notes, for example, he found that there were certain typical forms of notes, and even though the contents of the 112 different notes examined were not the same, the notes could be characterized in terms of a few categories. Thus, instead of having 112 different forms of accounts for why people killed themselves, Jacobs was able to show certain specific patterns that document the common thread running through all of them. On the other hand, the researcher may begin with a definite dimension in mind and compare that dimension only in terms of some aspect of interest. For example, he may want to examine popular stories about crimes as they relate to a punishment and treatment dichotomy. Such examination may be used to make inferences about public sentiment toward capital punishment.

The analysis of written documents may be either quantitative or qualitative depending on the problem the researcher has or the type of documents he must deal with. In comparing newspaper editorials, he might want to develop a set of criteria designated as "conservative" and another as "liberal." By counting the number of times conservative or liberal themes are a part of the newspaper's editorials, he can statistically compare newspapers as more or less conservative. Or the researcher can employ a qualitative approach, verbally explaining and comparing different types of editorials as to how they constitute subtle forms of liberal or conservative philosophy. As always, the analytic tool depends on what the researcher is attempting to explain and the nature of the data; and content analysis can take on analytic forms similar to survey research, ethnographic, or just about any other kind of standard research analysis.

CONVERSATIONAL ANALYSIS*

Conversational analysis is a new form of analysis in sociolinguistics. It may be considered a form of ethnographic or interactional analysis, but, because of the work done with written transcripts of conversations, it will be treated here as a form of content analysis. The essential purpose of conversational analysis is to determine the structure of conversations and the effect of the structure on the talk in conversation (Sacks, 1972). Most of the work done to date has focused on the sequential structure of conversations and has been based on data in the form of conversation transcriptions.

Conversational analysis relies on transcripts of recorded conversations. These transcripts are useful for analysis, since they "fix," or "freeze," the interaction. The analyst can go over the transcripts at his leisure to search for sequential structure and forms in the interaction instead of having to rely on notes taken during observations. Moreover, since interaction consists largely of people taking turns talking, most of it is preserved in the conversation itself.

In order to preserve the texture of the talk in conversations,

* The discussion here is greatly oversimplified; I suggest that the student who is seriously interested in conversational analysis read the work by Sacks (1972) cited in Additional Reading Suggestions.

various transcription conventions are used. These conventions are like punctuation in written language, in that they indicate pauses, emphasis, and other elements that can be heard in conversations but not easily seen when normal grammatical punctuation is used. There is no universal set of conventions; the ones described here are only a partial list, developed by the writer.

Talk Turn	Refers to the turn the speaker has while (an)other(s) in a conversation listen(s) or interrupt(s)
/1–2 . . . n/	Indicates the number of seconds between the preceding and present turns or silences in one speaker's talk; n is any positive integer
/#/	Indicates very short interval, less than one second
/ /	Indicates the point at which the next speaker overlaps the person speaking. (Two speaking at once)
/	Indicates the point at which the following speaker interrupts and stops speaker
[ ]	Encloses the portion of an utterance that overlaps with the previous line
/j/	Indicates overlap; that is, there is no separation between speaker turns
but	Indicates emphasis
BUT	Indicates heavy emphasis

Example:

1. A   Hiya Joe. Whatja doin?
2. B /#/   Aww nutin much./1–2–3/ Why don't ja sit down//
3.   and hava bite/.
4. A /j/   [I gotta go over to th] library before it closes.
5. B /#/   Well uh /#/ it won't close for uh uh bout an
6.   hour. LOOK there's Pete! HEY PETE COMERE!

Once the conversation has been transcribed from a tape recording, the analyst has, as far as possible at least, a record of the conversation as it sounded on the tape in writing that can be analyzed.

The sequential structure of conversations can be analyzed by considering the whole conversation as it sequentially progresses from openers, to topics, to closings; or a conversation can be analyzed in terms of smaller sequences. However, the importance of such sequential structures is that, once the sequence has been initiated, only certain forms of responses can follow. That is, the structure of conversations is a causal factor of what occurs in conversations.

For example, the *question-answer sequence* (Q-A) is simply the sequence of an answer following a question (Schegloff, 1968). In the reading by Sanders (Chapter 12), the author shows how such a sequence was used in police interrogations. The interrogator would ask a question that conversationally obliged the person being interrogated to supply an answer. The interest for conversational analysis is not whether an answer to a question is correct, truthful, or even informative; rather, it is that, following a question, the next talk is in the *form* of an answer.

The *greeting sequence* is one in which a conversation is initiated when one member of the talk-group utters a greeting form and the other member(s) respond(s). These are usually a simple "Hi" followed by a "Hi" from the other, but more elaborate greeting sequences can also be found.

Finally, the *summons-reply sequence* (S-R) is one in which one person calls out to another and the other replies. For example, a boss may call his employee, "Hey, Jim," and the employee may respond with, "Yeah, whaddaya want?" These sequences can be found in all kinds of conversations, even though the content of the talk varies.

The two readings in this section represent the two forms of content analysis discussed. Chapter 11, by Jacobs shows how different general forms of accounts for suicides were discovered in analyzing suicide notes. The last reading is a conversation analysis incorporating the Q-A sequence to show how the police use conversational structure to get suspects to talk.

REFERENCES

CICOUREL, AARON. 1964. *Method and Measurement in Sociology*. New York: The Free Press.

SACKS, HARVEY. 1972. "An Initial Investigation of the Usability of Conversational Data for Doing Sociology." In David Sudnow (ed.), *Studies in Social Interaction*, pp. 31–74. New York: The Free Press.

SCHEGLOFF. E. A. 1968. "Sequencing in Conversational Openings," *American Anthropologist*, 70, pp. 1075–95.

SIMON, J. L. 1969. *Basic Research Methods in Social Science*. New York: Random House.

WARWICK, D. P., and S. OSHERSON (EDS.). 1973. *Comparative Research Methods*. Englewood Cliffs, N.J.: Prentice-Hall.

11. Written Document Analysis

A PHENOMENOLOGICAL STUDY OF SUICIDE NOTES
—Jerry Jacobs

ACCORDING TO DURKHEIM, THE PROSPECT OF FINDING A COMMON denominator in the personal situations of suicides is minimal.

. . . the circumstances are almost infinite in number which are supposed to cause suicide because they rather frequently accompany it.

In defining the range and effect of personal circumstances on the individual, Durkheim tells us:

> . . . some men resist horrible misfortune, while others kill themselves after slight troubles. Moreover, we have shown that those who suffer most are not those who kill themselves most. . . . At least, if it really sometimes occurs that the victim's personal situation is the effective cause of his resolve, such cases are very rare indeed. . . .

Given the above assumptions, it is not surprising to find that,

> Accordingly, even those who have ascribed most influence to individual conditions have sought these conditions less in such external incidents than in the intrinsic nature of the person, that is, his biological constitution and the physical concomitants on which it depends.[1]

[1] Emile Durkheim, *Suicide: A Study in Sociology*, New York: The Free Press, 1951, pp. 297–298.

From *Social Problems*, Vol. 15, No. 1 (1967), pp. 60–72. Reprinted by permission of the author and The Society for the Study of Social Problems.

What is most interesting, of course, is that Durkheim abandoned the search for a common denominator to suicide before beginning it. Never having studied a specific case of suicide in detail, indeed at all, so far as I know, how could he know that "some resist horrible misfortune, while others kill themselves after slight troubles," or that "those who suffer most are not those who kill themselves most," or that the victim's personal situation is very rarely the cause of suicide? The author feels that such common-sense assumptions are unwarranted.

There is no need to intuit, as Durkheim has done above, the effects of one's personal situation on suicide. We have available, after all, the best possible authority on the subject—the suicide himself.

> I claim that any man who commits suicide of necessity suffers more than any who continues to live. I don't want to die. I cannot make any outsider realize by anything I can write how I have tried to avoid this step. I have tried every subterfuge to fool myself, to kid myself along that life wasn't so bad after all.[2]

The above statement is much more consistent with the position of suicidal persons as related in suicide notes, letters, and diaries than the contentions of Durkheim given above. It is, of course, opposed to what Durkheim believed, since persons do not appear to be killing themselves over arbitrary "personal problems" or "impulsively" as in the case of insane suicides. Everyone is forced to kill themselves for the same reason, i.e., they suffer more "than any who continues to live" and are unable, notwithstanding their every effort, to resolve the suffering. In brief, those who suffer most are those who kill themselves most.

The last sentence of Durkheim's concluding statement warrants particular attention as it relates to those who "ascribe most influence to individual conditions" in seeking an explanation of suicide. Such persons rely primarily upon case history accounts, suicide notes, or interviews with suicidal persons as sources of data. However, even they ". . . sought these conditions less in such external incidents than in the intrinsic nature of the person. . . ."

[2] "A Youth Who Was Prematurely Tired," in Ruth Cavan, *Suicide*, Chicago: University of Chicago Press, 1928, p. 242.

This has been the general approach of psychiatrists, psychologists, and of some less positivistic sociologists. The reason for this has been that even among those dealing with the individual's personal situation through the study of case histories or suicide notes, they found no common denominator for suicide. The inability of previous investigators to explain suicide as resulting from a conscious rational process has led them to conclude the necessity of in some way inferring the "real" meaning of the suicide's story, either by superimposing upon the data an unconscious irrational explanation or some other such synthetic system.

> They (suicide notes) strongly suggest the possibility of viewing them as projective devices (in much the same way as MAPS tests or TAT protocols are projective products) from which information may be *inferred* about the subject (emphasis added).[3]

Psychiatrists also tend to interpret the accounts of their patients from this general perspective. Here the emphasis is on the unconscious, irrational elements, the apparent rational aspects notwithstanding.

> . . . suicide is not preeminently a rational act pursued to achieve rational ends, even when it is effected by persons who appear to be eminently rational. Rather, it is a magical act, actuated to achieve irrational, delusional, and illusory ends.[4]

The dilemma confronting those proceeding on the above assumption is well put by C. Wright Mills.

> The quest for "real motives" set over against "mere rationalization" is often informed by a metaphysical view that the "real" motives are in some way biological. Accompanying such quests for something more real and back of rationalization is the view held by many sociologists that language is an external manifestation or concomitant of something prior, more genuine, and

---

[3] Edwin S. Shneidman and Norman L. Farberow, "Appendix: Genuine and Simulated Suicide Notes," in *Clues to Suicide*, New York: McGraw-Hill, 1957, p. 197.

[4] Charles William Wahl, "Suicide as a Magical Act," in Edwin S. Shneidman and Norman L. Farberow, editors, *Clues to Suicide*, New York: McGraw-Hill, 1957, p. 23.

"deep" in the individual. "Real attitudes" versus "mere verbaliza-tion" or "opinion" implies that at best we only infer from his language what "really" is the individual's attitude or motive.

Now what *could* we *possibly* so infer? Of precisely *what is* verbalization symptomatic? We cannot infer physiological pro-cesses from lingual phenomena. All we can infer and empirically check is another verbalization of the agent's which we believe was orienting and controlling behavior at the time the act was performed. The only social items that can "lie deeper" are other lingual forms. The "Real Attitude or Motive" is not something different in kind from the verbalization of the "opinion." They turn out to be only relatively and temporally different.[5]

The author feels that in order to overcome this telling criticism it is necessary to offer an explanation of suicide which is both derived from and validated by some empirical referent. I feel the life situations of suicides as related by them in suicide notes offer such a potential. I will seek to establish the common de-nominator of suicide in the formal aspects of a process, rather than in some independent event such as a childhood trauma or a later "precipitating cause."

Suicide notes offer an invaluable source of data for gaining some insight into what it was that brought the individual to adopt this form of behavior. Their importance is based upon the assumption made by this and other authors that they contain an unsolicited account of the victim's thoughts and emotions re-garding his intended act and, often, what he felt was responsible for it.[6] A study of suicide in Philadelphia by Tuckman, Kleiner, and Lavell reveals that of the 742 suicides which occurred be-tween 1951 and 1955, 24 percent left suicide notes.[7] Shneidman and Farberow note that in each year of a ten year period between 1945 and 1954, from 12 to 15 percent of those committing suicide in Los Angeles County left suicide notes.[8]

There seems to be no significant difference in the social, men-

---

[5] C. Wright Mills, "Situated Actions and Vocabularies of Motive," *American Sociological Review*, 5 (December, 1940), p. 909.

[6] Jacob Tuckman, Robert J. Kleiner and Martha Lavell, "Emotional Con-tent of Suicide Notes," *American Journal of Psychiatry*, (July, 1959), p. 59.

[7] *Ibid.*

[8] Shneidman and Farberow, *op. cit.*, p. 198.

tal, or physical condition of persons leaving notes and those who do not.[9] With few exceptions, suicide notes are coherent.[10] Tuckman *et al.* further acknowledge: "In this study, the writers were impressed with the possibility that in a number of cases, the suicide could have resulted from a conscious 'rational' decision . . . although, to a lesser extent, unconscious factors may have been operating."[11] Having analyzed 112 notes of persons successful in suicide in the Los Angeles area, I was also taken with their rational and coherent character. The conscious rational factors were after all obvious in the notes themselves, whereas the unconscious factors to a lesser extent "may have been operating."

Most theories of suicide make some provision for both psychic and environmental factors. Whereas environmental factors are often cited and categorized by those analyzing suicide notes, none has offered an explanation of psychic factors which can be verified by the notes themselves. The psychic formulations of psychiatrists and psychologists are always of an inferred nature.

The author believes that an explanation of suicide can be empirically derived from the notes themselves without the necessity of referring to a synthetic outside system. There is no need to proceed in the traditional fashion of either imputing meaning to the notes or, since there are essentially an infinite number of categorical distinctions to be made, categorizing them on whatever common sense grounds strike the analyst as being either potentially "fruitful" or expedient, e.g., demographic, environmental, physical, or psychological categories. A description of suicidal motivation and the experiences and thought processes involved in acquiring it are not likely to be arrived at without some broader theoretical perspective which in turn is given to some empirical validation by the notes themselves. The author intends to offer such a formulation after first briefly considering some existing sociological theories of suicide.

FORMER SOCIOLOGICAL THEORIES OF SUICIDE

I do not wish to get involved in a critique of previous sociological theories of suicide within the limits of this paper. However,

---

[9] Tuckman *et al.*, *op. cit.*, p. 59; and Shneidman and Farberow, *op. cit.*, p. 48.

[10] Tuckman *et al.*, *op. cit.*, p. 60.

[11] *Ibid.*, p. 62.

by way of giving some general indication of how this formulation differs from others, it may be noted that Durkheim,[12] Gibbs and Martin,[13] Henry and Short,[14] and Powell[15] all have in common the fact that their theories rest basically on an analysis of official suicide rates. The theories consist essentially of an explanation of these official rates by imputing meaning to the correlations which are found to exist between the rates and certain social conditions. They are not based on actual cases of suicidal persons, their beliefs or writings.

Some of the above, while using the common base of statistical analysis of official suicide rates, incorporate psychological and psychoanalytical notions as well. Durkheim was also aware that, ultimately, if social norms were to act as a constraint, they must be internalized. Having acknowledged this, he did not involve himself in how this was to be accomplished. The author's formulation not only recognizes that norms must be internalized if they are to constrain the individual (or inversely, that the constraints of internalized norms must be overcome if one is to act contrary to them), but undertakes to set forth the process whereby this is accomplished. It also views suicide as a social fact which has its antecedents in previous social facts. It differs from Durkheim's formulation, however, in that it undertakes to establish these previous social facts through analysis of suicide notes.

BASIS OF THE FORMULATION

The data and insights upon which this formulation is based come from two main sources: 112 suicide notes of adults and adolescents who succeeded in suicide in the Los Angeles area, and insights gained by the author through his participation in a study of adolescent suicide attempters for 2½ years.[16]

[12] Emile Durkheim, *op. cit.*

[13] Jack P. Gibbs and Walter T. Martin, *Status Integration and Suicide*, Eugene, Ore.: University of Oregon Press, 1964.

[14] Andrew F. Henry and James F. Short, *Suicide and Homicide*, Glencoe, Ill.: The Free Press, 1954.

[15] Elwin H. Powell, "Occupational Status and Suicide: Toward a Redefinition of Anomie," *American Sociological Review*, 23 (April, 1950), pp. 131–139.

[16] Adolescent Attempted Suicide Study, supported by the National Institute of Mental Health and conducted at the Los Angeles County General Hospital under the direction of Joseph D. Teicher, M.D., Professor of Psychiatry, University of Southern California School of Medicine, and Jerry Jacobs, Ph.D., Research Associate, University of Southern California School of Medicine.

Whereas participation in this study has provided me with many valuable insights used in the formulation, the data on which it is based are taken from the 112 suicide notes previously mentioned. The paper will offer a sampling of notes from the various categories identified by the author. These will be analyzed and discussed within the framework of a theoretical perspective which is designed to account for the conscious deliberations that take place before the individual is able to consider and executive the act of suicide. This is seen within the broader context of what the individual must experience in order to become capable of these verbalizations. The notes provide the basis for the formulation and, at the same time, offer the reader a means of verifying it. It is the author's belief that such verification is not contingent upon these notes in particular, but that any set of notes collected from within the same cultural environment would do as well.

The key to this formulation, i.e., the concept of trust violation, and how the individual accomplishes it while remaining convinced that he is a trusted person, is taken from Donald Cressey's work on embezzlement, *Other People's Money*.[17] The final form of the envolved hypothesis reads:

> Trusted persons become trust violators when they conceive of themselves as having a financial problem which is non-shareable, are aware that this problem can be secretly resolved by violation of the position of financial trust, and are able to apply to their own conduct in that situation verbalizations which enable them to adjust their conceptions of themselves as users of the entrusted funds or property.[18]

This conception of trust violation is extended to the act of suicide, i.e., the individual's violation of the sacred trust of life, and to the verbalizations he must entertain in order to reconcile the image of himself as a trusted person with his act of trust violation—suicide. It followed from these considerations that an excellent source of data for this undertaking would be the transcribed accounts of these verbalizations found in suicide notes. Here the similarity with Cressey's work ends, since the method of the author in studying the above is not one of analytic induction.

[17] Donald R. Cressey, *Other People's Money*, Glencoe, Ill.: The Free Press, 1951.
[18] *Ibid.*, p. 30.

Both suicides and suicide attempters are considered in this paper. The events and processes leading them to these acts are held to be equatable within the following definitions of these terms, i.e., the suicide attempt is considered as a suicide attempt only if death was intended but did not result. Persons "attempting suicide" with the intent of not dying but only of using the "attempt" as an "attention-getting device," a "manipulative technique," etc., were not considered by the author as suicide attempters within the limits of this paper. The intentions of persons "attempting suicide" as an attention-getting device may miscarry and result in death. Persons actually attempting suicide may, through some misinformation or fortuitous circumstance, continue to live. This in no way alters their intent or the experiences which led them to entertain the verbalizations necessary for establishing this intent. It is in this sense that suicide and suicide attempts are considered by the author to be synonymous.

These three categories of persons were distinguished from one another in the following way. The authors of the 112 notes to be discussed in this paper were all considered to be suicides based upon a designation assigned to them by the Los Angeles County Coroner's Office upon investigating the circumstances of their death. The distinction between suicide attempters and "attention-getters" was based upon the adolescent's account of his intentions at the time of his act. All adolescent suicide attempters in the above-mentioned study were seen within 48 hours of the attempt. Their intentions were related to three separate persons during their voluntary commitment at the hospital—to the attending physician who treated them in the emergency room, to the psychiatrist during a psychiatric interview, and to the author or his assistant in an interview which lasted about two hours. The designation by the author of suicide attempter was based upon a comparison and assessment of these three accounts. The three adolescent suicide attempters referred to later in this paper in a section dealing with the "next world" all intended at the time of the attempt to take their own lives.

INTRODUCTION TO THE FORMULATION

Nearly all of the suicide notes studied were found to fall within one of six general categories, i.e., "first form notes," "sorry illness notes," "not sorry illness notes," "direct accusation notes," "will and testament notes" and "notes of instruction." The sum total of all six categories of suicide notes and the explanations given for the notes taking the form they do, constitute "The Formulation"—a systematic explanation for all but ten notes, i.e., 102 out of 112 notes studied by the author. The exceptions are noted later. The ten point process to be discussed is characteristic of "first form notes." Thirty-five of the 112 notes took this form. In addition, "sorry illness notes" also contained all or most of the characteristics found in "first form notes," depending upon their length. The reader is cautioned not to view the other four forms of notes as exceptions which tend to negate the process associated with "first form" and "sorry illness notes." These four forms and the explanations accompanying them are not exceptions but qualified additions that supplement the scope of the original ten points.

By way of analogy, consider the statement "light travels in a straight line," except when it encounters an opaque object, except in the case of refraction, except in the case of diffraction, etc. One does not say of these "exceptions" that they tend to negate the Principle of the Rectilinear Propagation of Light. They simply work to narrow its scope and set its limits. (The recognition and discussion of the four categories of notes cited above serve the same purpose.) To the extent that one is able to explain the "exceptions" in such a way that the explanations are consistent with the evidence, the sum total of these explanations constitutes a more detailed and inclusive understanding of light, or, in the case of the author's formulation, of suicide. The author also believes that the formulation will provide an explanation of suicide, within this culture, that is both empirically derived and more consistent with the evidence than any he has thus far encountered.

THE FORMULATION

Trusted persons appear to become trust violators when they conceive of themselves as having a problem, the nature of which is a view of the past plagued by troubles, a troubled present, and the expectation of future troubles erupting unpredictably in the course of their lives. Paradoxically, these unpredictable troubles occur with absolute predictability in that it is held that they are sure to come—as sure as they are here now, unexpectedly, as sure as they arose unexpectedly in the past, and as sure as one's future existence to arise unexpectedly in the future. The problem is thus seen to be as absolute as life and must be resolved by something no less absolute than death. Since it is impossible to dispose of the problem of change, where change is viewed as unanticipated, inevitable, and inevitably for the worse, and since one sees it necessary to resolve this problem in order to live, i.e., to fulfill one's trust, and since the absolute nature of the problem makes it amenable only to absolute solutions, and since there is only one absolute solution, one finds it necessary to resolve the problem of living by dying, or—to put it another way—one appears to betray one's most sacred public trust by the private act of suicide.

Implicit or explicit in most of the suicide notes is the notion that "they didn't want it this way . . . but. . . ." From this perspective, they are now in a position to view themselves as blameless, i.e., trusted persons, while at the same time knowing that you will view them as trust violators because you have not experienced what they have and therefore cannot see the moral and reasonable nature of the act. With this in mind, they beg your indulgence and ask your forgiveness, for, in short, they know what they're doing, but they also know that you cannot know.

Life's problems, which one is morally obligated to resolve by way of not violating the sacred trust to live, can only be resolved by death, a not-too-pretty paradox, but from the perspective of the potential suicide, a necessary and consequently reasonable and moral view. From the absence of choice, i.e., no freedom, emerges the greatest freedom—"the recognition of necessity"—stemming from the apparent lack of choice. Thus it is that the suicidal person sees in the act of suicide at long last the potential for the freedom he has sought in life. This can be seen in the notes themselves. The note writers are rarely "depressed" or "hostile." The notes are by and large very even, as though at the time of writing the suffering no longer existed and a resolution to the problem had been reached. Tuckman states that 51 percent of the notes he studied expressed "postive affect without hostility" and another 25 percent expressed "neutral affect."[19] This is further supported by the finding of Farberow et al. that the period of highest risk was not during the depression or "illness" but just after it, when the patient seemed much improved.[20]

First Form Notes. The outline presented below describes the formal aspects of a process that the individual must first experience in order to be able to seriously entertain suicide and then actually attempt it. The extent to which this process is operative will be illustrated through an analysis of "first form" notes. The extent to which the other five forms of notes deviate from the characteristics found in "first form notes" will be discussed in the explanations accompanying each of the five remaining forms. The sum total of all six forms of notes and their accompanying explanations constitute "The Formulation," i.e., a systematic rational explanation of suicide based upon the suicide's own accounts at the time of the act.

Durkheim went to great lengths to show that private acts contrary to the public trust are irrational and/or immoral and constrained by public sanctions from ever occurring. In order to overcome these constraints and appear to others as a trust violator, the private individual must 1) be faced with an unexpected, intolerable, and unsolvable problem; 2) view this not as an isolated unpleasant incident, but within the context of a long biography of such troubled situations, and the expectation of future ones; 3) believe that death is the only absolute answer to this apparent absolute dilemma of life; 4) come to this point of view (a) by way of an increasing social isolation whereby he is unable to share his problem with the person or persons who must share it if it is to be resolved, or (b) being isolated from the cure of some incurable illness which in turn isolates him from health and the community, thereby doubly insuring the insolubility of the problem; 5) overcome the social constraints, i.e., the social norms he had internalized whereby he views suicide as irrational and/or immoral; 6) succeed in this because he feels himself less an integral part of the society than the others and therefore is held

---

[19] Tuckman et al., op. cit., p. 61.

[20] Norman L. Farberow, Edwin S. Shneidman and Robert E. Litman, "The Suicidal Patient and the Physician," *Mind*, 1:69 (March, 1963).

less firmly by its bonds; 7) succeed in accomplishing step 6 by applying to his intended suicide a verbalization which enables him to adjust his conception of himself as a trusted person with his conception of himself as a trust violator; 8) succeed in doing this by defining the situation such that the problem is (a) not of his own making (b) unresolved, but not from any lack of personal effort, and (c) not given to any resolution known to him except death (he doesn't want it this way, but . . . it's "the only way out"); 9) in short, define death as necessary by the above process and in so doing remove all choice and with it sin and immorality; and finally, 10) make some provision for insuring against the recurrence of these problems in the afterlife.

Thirty-five out of 112 notes were "first form notes" and expressed all or most of the above aspects, depending on their length. All "first form" notes are characterized by the author's begging of forgiveness or request for indulgence. The following will serve to illustrate the general tenor.

It is hard to say why you don't want to live. I have only one real reason. The three people I have in the world which I love don't want me.

Tom, I love you so dearly but you have told me you don't want me and don't love me. I never thought you would let me go this far, but I am now at the end which is the best thing for you. You have so many problems and I am sorry I added to them.

Daddy, I hurt you so much and I guess I really hurt myself. You only wanted the very best for me and you must believe this is it.

Mommy, you tried so hard to make me happy and to make things right for all of us. I love you too so very much. You did not fail, I did.

I had no place to go so I am back where I always seem to find peace. I have failed in everything I have done and I hope I do not fail in this.

I love you all dearly and am sorry this is the way I have to say goodbye.

Please forgive me and be happy.

Your wife and your daughter.

First, the problem is not of their own making. At first glance the suicide seems to be saying just the opposite. "You did not fail, I did," "I have failed in everything." However, having acknowledged this, she states: "Tom, I love you so dearly but you have told me you don't want me and don't love me. *I never thought you would let me go this far.*" Then, of course, she loves them. It is they who do not love her, and this is "the problem."

Second, a long-standing history of problems. "Mommy, you tried so hard to make me happy and to make things right for all of us. I love you too so very much. You did not fail, I did," or "Tom . . . you have so many problems and I am sorry I added to them," etc. It seems from this that she has created a long-standing history of problems. She was, nevertheless, subject to them as well. "Daddy, I hurt you so much and I guess I *really hurt myself.*"

Third, the escalation of problems of late beyond human endurance. "It is hard to say why you don't want to live. I have only one real reason. The three people I have in the world which I love don't want me," or "Tom, I love you so dearly but you have told me you don't want me and don't love me."

These particular problems are clearly of recent origin and of greater magnitude than any she had previously experienced. By her own account, had she experienced problems of this order before, she would have taken her life before, since they led to her losing what had previously constituted sufficient reason for her to go on living.

Fourth, death must be seen as necessary. "It is hard to say why you don't want to live. I have only one real reason. The three people I have in the world which I love don't want me," or ". . . but now I'm at the end . . . ," and finally, "I love you all dearly and am sorry this is the way *I have to* say goodbye."

Fifth, beg your indulgence. "I love you all dearly and am sorry this is the way I have to say goodbye."

Sixth, they know what they're doing but know you cannot know "Daddy . . . You only wanted the very best for me and *you must believe this is it.*"

It is the author's opinion that the suicide's message in point (3) is the same as that given by nearly all the others who attempt or succeed in suicide, insofar as this is a particular case of the general condition of "a progressive social isolation from meaningful relationships." Ellen West, whose case history is perhaps the most famous, wrote in her diary less than a year before taking her life:

> . . . by this fearful illness I am withdrawing more and more from people. I feel myself excluded from all real life. I am quite isolated. I sit in a glass ball. I see people through a glass wall, their voices come to me muffled. I have an unutterable longing to get to them, I scream, but they do not hear me. I stretch out my arms toward them; but my hands merely beat against the walls of my glass ball.[21]

All of the remaining "first form" notes have all or most of the above characteristics in common. *All of the notes in this class, without exception, beg forgiveness or indulgence on the part of the survivors.*

Illness Notes. Requests for forgiveness or indulgence may be omitted when the writer feels that the public may have made exceptions to its general indignation at suicide, exceptions which should be known to all, e.g., in the case of persons suffering from an incurable disease, suffering great pain, etc. In such cases, the suicide may feel that no apologies are necessary, and requests for forgiveness may be included or excluded, due to the ambiguity surrounding the degree of public acceptance of the above view.

Thirty-four notes were included in the "illness" category. Twenty-two of these omitted requests for forgiveness; twelve included them. This category of notes has most of the same general characteristics as those of the "first form." How many conditions of the "first form" notes are met by those of the "illness" category depends primarily on their length. The two formal distinguishing features of these two sets of notes are that the "illness" set may or may not beg forgiveness for the reasons stated above, and, secondly, the source of the problem is generally better defined and restricted to the area of illness, pain, etc., and its social and personal implications to the individual. Some examples of illness notes follow.

[21] Ludwig Brinswanger, "The Case of Ellen West," in Rollo May et al., editors, *Existence*, New York: Basic Books, 1958, p. 256.

Sorry Illness Notes:

Dearly Beloved Children: For the last three weeks I have lost my blood circulation in my feet and in my hands. I can hardly hold a spoon in my hand. Before I get a stroke on top of my other troubles of my legs I decided that this would be the easier for me. I have always loved you all dearly. Think of me kindly sometimes. Please forgive me. I cannot endure any more pains. Lovingly, mother.

Not Sorry Illness Notes:

If you receive this letter you will know that I have emptied my bottle of sleeping pills.

And a second note by the same author addressed to the same person included the line: *"Surely there must be a justifiable mercy death."*
Another reads:

Dear Jane: You are ruining your health and your life just for me, and I cannot let you do it. The pains in my face seem worse every day and there is a limit to what a man can take. I love you dear.

Bill

Notes of Direct Accusation.   None of the notes in this class beg forgiveness or offer an apology. The suicide feels that not only is the problem not of his making, but he knows who is responsible for his having to commit suicide. As a result, he feels righteously indignant and omits requests for indulgence, especially when the note is directed to the guilty party. "Direct accusation notes" are generally very brief, rarely more than a few lines long. Ten of the 112 notes studied were of the "direct accusation" type. For example:

You Bob and Jane caused this—this all.

Goodbye Jane. I couldn't take no more from you. Bob.

Mary, I hope you're satisfied. Bill.

If you had read page 150 of Red Ribbons this wouldn't have happened.

Last Will and Testaments and Notes of Instructions. None of these notes contained requests for forgiveness or indulgence either. This omission, as in the above case, results from the form of the notes themselves. These notes usually concern themselves exclusively with the manner in which the suicide's property is to be apportioned. They give no mention of the circumstances of the suicide and, as a result, there is no need for the notewriter to admit of guilt or request forgiveness. None of them do so.

Last Will and Testaments:

I hereby bequeath all my worldly good and holdings to Bill Smith. $1 to Chris Baker, $1 to Ann Barnes. Signed in sober consideration.

Mary Smith

Notes of Instructions. The following are some examples of notes of instructions. They are almost always very brief and the above comments regarding "last will and testaments" apply here as well.

Call Jane. S Street, Apt. 2. Thank Officer No. 10.

I have gone down to the ocean. Pick out the cheapest coffin Jones Bros. has. I don't remember the cost. I'll put my purse in the trunk of the car.

Precautions Taken to Exclude This World's Problems from the Next World. To guard against the eventuality of a similar set of troubles erupting in the afterlife, the very thing one is dying to overcome, one of six possible courses of action are formulated and internalized. These forms first came to the attention of the author while studying suicidal adolescents; the suicide notes tend to bear them out.

(1) The potential suicide who was in the past quite religious and a diligent church-goer rather abruptly stops attending church and starts considering himself a non-religious person. He thereby disposes of heaven and hell, makes death absolute, and secures for himself all the benefits of the nonbeliever with respect to the act of suicide.

(2) The person who attended church irregularly but had enough religious training to make him ambivalent about an afterlife, suddenly begins to make inquiries of very religious persons as to whether "God forgives suicides" or "Will God forgive anything?" And those to whom the question is put, believing that He does, or pleased that it was asked, or anxious for the convert, or for whatever reason, say "Yes, of course, if you really believe, God will forgive anything," at which point the suicidal person suddenly "gets religion" and tries very hard to "believe," thus securing a place in heaven free from future troubles.

The following is an abstract of a note written by a 16-year-old female suicide attempter. Both the adolescent and her mother reported that the girl's preoccupation with religion began unexpectedly within the last few months. The note is illustrative of the adolescent's attempt to resolve the anticipated problems of the hereafter through the process described in (2) above.

> Please forgive me, God. . . . In my heart I know there is a Christ everywhere in the world that is being with everyone. Every second of every day and he represents God in every way. I know that in my brain (mind) I think evil things about different situations and sometimes I think that Christ never existed. But my heart always is strong and that when I think that Christ never lived I know that in my heart He did. . . . Mother thinks that there is no hell and no heaven (I guess) and I know there is a hell and heaven. I don't want to go to the devil, God, so please forgive me to what I have just done. John L. said that if I believe in and accept Jesus that I would go to heaven. Some people say that if you ask forgiveness to God for things you do to yourself or others, that he would forgive you (if you believe in Jesus and love him) . . .
>
> . . . Heaven is so peaceful and the earth is very troublesome and terrifying.

(3) The religious person, believing that suicide is an absolute, irreversible, and damnable sin, will make an attempt to resolve this by asking a mother or some other authority, "Will God forgive anything?," knowing full well that suicide is the exception, and will be answered, "If you believe." The Pope's pronouncement to the contrary notwithstanding, the suicidal person will accept this and act as though it were true.

(4) The religious person, believing that he is unable to secure a place in heaven or insure an absolute death, or any other resolution to his present problem, will fly in the face of God, e.g., "Even if I go to hell, at least I won't have those headaches and worry about the baby and that will be one thing anyway." At least you don't have to violate a trust in hell, for no one on earth has ever told you how to act in hell, and you are left to your own resources without the problem of becoming a trust violator. Its very ambiguity allows for a happy ending, or beginning.

Parts of a lengthy note written by a man to his wife and family serve to illustrate the uncertainty of the hereafter.

> My Dearest Ones:
> When you get this it will all be over for me on earth but just the beginning of my punishment for what I have done to you all. . . . I have given what I am about to do lots of thought and each time I have thought about it there seems no other way . . . I don't know what's on the other side perhaps it will be worse than here.

It is interesting to see that the author of the note begins by stating that his punishment in the hereafter is just beginning. It is a very positive statement; the punishment seems a certainty. However, the letter ends on this note: "I don't know what's on the other side *perhaps* it will be worse than here." The "perhaps" nature of this statement provides for the possibility that "perhaps" it will be better. In the hope of tipping the scales in the right direction, the suicide concludes his note with . . .

> I love you all May God help me and forgive for what I am about to do.
> Again good-bye.
>
> Jack and Daddy

(5) Another group concerned with the prospect of hell will request in a suicide note that others "pray for my soul" or "God forgive me" and—having taken this precaution—hope for the best.

(6) Reincarnation is the last form of possible salvation: "Maybe it will be better the next time around; it couldn't be worse." This resolution to life's problems and the hope of preventing

future ones was discovered through interviews with adolescent suicide attempters. One 15-year-old Jewish boy, who until a year ago when the family moved from New York had been attending the synagogue regularly, suddenly stopped attending services and recently became preoccupied with the prospect of reincarnation. A 14-year-old Negro Baptist girl, who until about a year ago had been a steady churchgoer, also stopped attending church and became interested in reincarnation. It is perhaps unnecessary to point out how peculiar it is for a Jew and a Baptist to undergo a conversion to the expectations of reincarnation, especially since there seemed to be no external indoctrinating influence. Both adolescents also recognized its peculiarity to the outsider and although they mentioned its existence, refused to discuss it in detail.

In brief, religious convictions do not appear to be ultimately binding upon the individual as a constraint against suicide, since one tends to interpret religious dogma as one has a need to interpret it.

It is true that Durkheim dealt at length with this notion by establishing the degree of social integration within various religions as the constraining factor against suicide, rather than the religious dogma per se. However, what has not been discussed is the way in which religious dogma, specifically intended to prevent suicide, can, with the proper "rationalization," serve to encourage suicide. The preceding discussion dealt with why and how this is actually accomplished by the potential suicide.

The author acknowledges that some exceptions occurred within the above categories. But among the 112 suicide notes studied, the paucity of cases falling into a "residual category" is heartening. There were ten of these in all, four of which contained the only elements of humor found in all of the notes. For example

> Please do not disturb. Someone sleeping. (Hung on the dashboard of his car.)

CONCLUSIONS

If it is true as Hume believed that ". . . such is our natural horror of death, that small motives will never be able to reconcile us to it . . ."[22] it is also true that the horror of life is no small motive. I believe that most people prefer the uncertainties of life to the uncertainties of death, because in life they have defined for themselves the possibility of certain sets of events occurring and live in the expectation that "anything can happen," i.e., "life is full of ups and downs." If one's view of life excludes uncertainty, i.e., life is not full of ups and downs—only downs, and anything can't happen—things can only get worse, then one might better try the uncertainties of death for its very ambiguity allows for either. By accepting death one provides the possibility of resolving life's problems, while at the same time insuring against future problems (or at least providing the possibility of resolving future problems when they arise).

I believe it is necessary to take seriously what the suicide writes in attempting to explain to the survivors, as a reasonable person, why he is committing suicide, and suggest that the reader will be aided in this task by applying the formulation presented by the author. I am further convinced that a fuller understanding of suicide will emerge only if one's procedures for "transcending the data" do not end by ignoring it, and that the "data" transcended ought to have some direct relation to the real life phenomenon under study, i.e., suicide.

---

[22] David Hume, "Of Suicide," in Alasdair MacIntyre, editor, *Hume's Ethical Writings*, New York: Collier Books, 1965, p. 305.

EXERCISES   This set of exercises deals with two of the many ways in which written documents can be analyzed. We will be using examples of popular media analysis since such documents are most readily available to students. Written documents can be used as a source of information that has little to do with the type or form of the documents themselves as the subject of analysis. For instance, the vital statistics in newspapers can be used to analyze various trends in a community, or, if viewed over time, they can be used as indicators of social change. On the other hand, the form and distribution of the media can be the subject of analysis rather than a direct source of information. The first exercise deals with using popular media as a direct source of information, and the other three exercises deal with analysis of the form and distribution of media.

Exercise 1

In this exercise, the medium to be employed is the daily newspaper, and the information to be analyzed is the number of applications for marriage licenses. Under "Vital Statistics," "The Daily Record," or some similar title, newspapers provide information dealing with civil, criminal, and governmental records. Included in this information are the names and ages of couples applying for marriage licenses. For this exercise, record the ages of the men and women who have taken out a marriage license and compute the mean, median, and mode for the ages of the men and women. Use a sample of a year in case one age group is overrepresented in certain months. This will necessitate your going to the library and looking up the information from the old newspapers kept there. If your library has microfilms of very old newspapers, compare the average ages of marriage over the years to see whether the marriage age has gone up or down. If it has, this will indicate that some form of social change has occurred.

Exercise 2

This exercise will involve a little detective work.

One indicator of a society's values and interests is the media the population reads or views. The more popular a certain theme, the more this theme can be taken as a characteristic interest of the society. To find these interests, locate the subscription rates of the forty most popular magazines and the viewer ratings of the forty most popular television programs. Analyze the magazines and the television programs in terms of themes or contents and compile a list. For instance, you may find that the most popular television programs are comedies, or that magazines dealing with domestic matters (i.e., household management) have the greatest circulation. The detective work will involve finding these subscription rates and television ratings.

Exercise 3

The purpose of this exercise is to compare two popular magazines, *Playboy* and *Reader's Digest*, to find what themes predominate in each. In this way, you will be able to see two very different trends in American society, one traditional and conservative, the other modern and liberal. The fact that both have very high subscription rates attests to their popularity, and the fact that they are very different in their treatment of values points to a pluralistic society.

To carry out this exercise, a group approach would be the most expedient, since the contents of several issues will have to be examined. Since both magazines are issued monthly, twelve copies of each would give a year's sample, and this should be sufficient. Each student will be given one copy of each to analyze in terms of the subjects discussed, the general themes of the contents, and whether the treatment of each issue represents a conservative or liberal viewpoint. Also, a list of key issues, such as race relations, women's liberation, pollution and the environment, and any other topical issue should be examined to see how each publication treats these issues. If one or the other magazine ignores an issue that the other has several articles or stories about, this, too, should be noted.

After each student has examined and analyzed his copies, this information should be pooled with that from others who analyzed other issues. Finally, the results of the two groups should be compared to find what two very different lines of interest dominate American society.

EXERCISE 4

This exercise deals with the content of a communication medium. Even though the form of the medium is different, the same techniques will be employed. The problem is to find whether there is any relation between the form and content of television commercials and the type of program sponsored by the advertiser.

To make this analysis, take a random sample of television programs, using a television program directory as the source of the sample. Then record on an "analysis form" (see below) the type of program; the program topic; the audience that would be assumed to view such a program; the sponsor's service, product, or message; the form of propaganda used; and whether the commercial appealed to reason.

Below is a list of types of propaganda typically employed by advertisers.

Band Wagon:	Appeals to join everyone else and become popular
Testimonial:	A well-known person of high status recommends product, service, or cause
Slogan:	A phrase is repeated over and over so that viewers will remember the commercial
Demonstration:	The virtues of the advertiser's wares or service are demonstrated
Entertainment:	The commercial is entertaining but says little about the product, except to associate it with the entertainment
Straight Claim:	The advertiser simply claims his service is the best. (Differs from testimonial in that no celebrity is used.)
Favor:	The commercial tries to present the advertiser as doing a favor for the consumer

Once you have collected your data, see whether certain kinds of propaganda are used (1) with one type of audience more than others, (2) with one type of product, service, or cause more than others, and (3) with one type of program more than others. This will give insight into not only types of propaganda in relation to what the advertiser is selling but also how the sponsor views the audience, what the society sees as valuable, and some of the reasons you may be purchasing one thing over another.

Analysis Form

Time and day of program

Name of program

    Program format:
      a. Movie
      b. Regular series
      c. News
      d. Special (specify)
      e. Cartoon
      f. Other (specify)
    Program topic:
      a. Variety
        1. Musical
        2. Comedy
        3. General
      b. Law
      c. Medicine
      d. Police or private detectives
      e. Western
      f. Situation comedy
      g. Nature
      h. Travel
      i. Soap opera
      j. Drama
      k. Comedy
      l. Adventure
      m. Other (specify)
    Audience (estimate audience):
      a. General
      b. Adult
      c. Children

Sponsor's service, product, or message:*
   a. Product
   b. Service
   c. Message
Form of Propaganda:†
   a. Band Wagon
   b. Testimonial
   c. Slogan
   d. Demonstration
   e. Entertainment
   f. Straight claim
   g. Favor
   h. Other (specify)
Appeal to reason?
   a. Yes
   b. No

* If more than one sponsor use separate forms.
† Sponsor may use more than single form.

The analysis form should be typed on duplication masters, and enough forms should be made so that there is a form for each commercial. Because of the amount of television viewing necessary, it is suggested that this be done as a group project.

ADDITIONAL READING SUGGESTIONS

ALBRECHT, M. C. 1956. "Does Literature Reflect Common Values?" *American Sociological Review*, 21, pp. 722–729. Discusses the extent to which the content analysis of literature can be used as a cultural indicator. This is an especially good article if one plans a historical or comparative analysis using literature as a data resource.

BERELSON, BERNARD. 1952. *Content Analysis*. New York: The Free Press. A valuable resource on how content analysis can be employed in dealing with sociological problems. Also explains how the analysis is executed.

NIXON, R. C. 1924. "Attention and Interest in Advertising," *Archives of Psychology*, 11, pp. 1–68. A useful analytic tool for the content analysis of propaganda in commercial advertising. You might want to consult this article for Exercise 4 of Chapter 11.

ZITO, GEORGE V. 1975. *Methodology and Meanings.* New York: Praeger Publishers. Chapter 2 provides an excellent discussion of content analysis as a quantitative method. Several examples of how to use content analysis.

12. Conversation Analysis

PUMPS AND PAUSES:
STRATEGIC USE OF
CONVERSATIONAL
STRUCTURE IN
INTERROGATIONS
—William B. Sanders

INTRODUCTION

MY PURPOSE HERE IS TO SHOW how the sequential structure of conversations is strategically employed by police in their interrogations. On the one hand, the sequential structure of conversations suggests that certain strategies are more efficient than others in getting a suspect to talk. On the other hand, if certain strategies are found in police interrogations, their usage will reveal various sequential structures of the conversation. Thus, it will be necessary first to show what strategies are suggested by the conversational structure and how they operate as strategies, and secondly to show how these strategies, to the end of forcing a suspect to talk, reveal certain conversational structures. The latter task is the more important in that it points to the consequences of the sequential structure of conversations in general and can be applied to forms of conversation other than interrogations.

INTERROGATIONS AS Q-A SEQUENCES

To begin this analysis, I will take Schegloff's (1968) question-answer (Q-A) sequence as the prototype of an interrogation. Basically, the interrogator asks the questions, and the suspect answers them. It should be noted that, in police manuals on interrogation, the interrogator is cautioned to control the talk, and his control

This selection was prepared especially for this volume.

can be summed up by the euphemism often heard in police dramas, "I'll ask the questions" (Kidd, 1940:73).

Not "just any talk" in an interrogation is sufficient for the interrogator. He attempts to keep the suspect on the right track, and the questions he asks can be taken to be efforts to direct the talk to salient issues. However interesting this might be, the issue of relevance per se will be ignored, here; our focus will be, rather, on questions as mechanisms for keeping the talk going. Likewise, answers given by suspects can be viewed as evasive or straightforward, truthful or false, excuses, justifications, boasts, admissions, or any other type of response; but our interest here is not in the content of responses. Rather, the replies will be examined in structural juxtaposition to questions.

In addition to showing that questions structurally demand replies and are therefore useful strategies for "forcing talk," I want to show that, once a question has been asked and the suspect begins to talk, the interrogator "pumps" the talk with nonquestion talk and grunts, which function to leave the "talk-turn" with the suspect. Secondly, pauses or gaps will be shown to be strategies that force the suspect to keep talking. That is, if the suspect ceases to talk before the interrogator is ready for him to stop or before he decides to ask another question, the lack of response by the interrogator leaves the suspect with an awkward silence which he is obliged to fill with talk.

In order to show this clearly, I will impress transcription conventions that should highlight the matters of interest while ignoring other transcription conventions. The first convention is the "numbered pause," illustrated by parenthetically numbering the pauses from "1" to "n" (the number of seconds in the pause). For example, an eight-second pause would look like this: (1-2-3-4-5-6-7-8). For briefer pauses, one second or less, standard conventions will be used; for example, /#/ denoting an interval of less than one second, and /*/ denoting an interval of approximately one second.

A second convention employed indicates difference between what I have referred to as a "pump" and what is normally taken to be a turn. Turns will be indicated by placing a "Q" (interrogator) or an "A" (suspect) in the left-hand margin on the line where either speaker's turn begins. "Pumps," or utterances designed to keep the speaker's talk going, will be indicated by equal signs (=) placed before and after the pump and by underlining the pump at the place in the speaker's turn where it occurs. For example, the pump in the following segment is done by Q in A's turn.

> . . . for a shotgun, which ah everybody in the shop knows about it. = <u>Uh huh</u>= And then ah /*/ they already. . . .

The Q-A sequence, taken as an utterance pair (Schegloff, 1972: 77) in conversational organization, poses the following proposition: If the first half of the pair is observed in the conversation, the second half will follow. That is, if a question is asked, the next talk in the sequence will be an "answer." Schegloff has pointed out the expectation that, if the next talk is not formulated as an answer to the question, the question will be asked again. A nonanswer—i.e., talk that is something other than answer or silence —is to be taken as an event. One form of nonanswer talk after a question has been discussed by Schegloff (1972) as an "insertion sequence," which seems to be taken as an "answer in the process of development" by the questioner. Even though the talk following the question is not an answer, it points to one in the sense that it can readily be seen as leading up to an answer.

The focus of this paper is not on the appropriateness of the response but, rather, on the fact that a question has the property of *action selection* (i.e., a question selects the next action in the conversation, an answer) and of *speaker selection* (i.e., the question directed to a particular person selects that person to speak next). Whether or not the suspect is evasive and the question has to be repeated is only tangentially interesting. The fact of response to a question and recognition of the obligation to fill in awkward silences, indicated by who speaks after a long pause, are the main events of interest in this analysis.

Another relevant feature of the Q-A sequence is that a question and only a question can *assign* silences. As soon as a question is asked, the silence "belongs" to the next speaker and not to— never to—the questioner. On the other hand, an answer that does not include a question, as insertion sequences do, can never leave the next speaker—in this case, the questioner—with the silence. Any silence after one question is asked and before another question is asked will be the nonquestioner's silence, whether or not he has given what he takes to be an answer, since an answer can always be construed to be incomplete (Garfinkel, 1967:40). In this way, the questioner can force the other to talk. In interrogation situations, where the questioner is the interrogator, the silences always belong to the suspect; he is always obliged to talk, and the interrogator never is.

The silence in the pauses will be shown to belong to the suspect, in that he does the talking before and after the pauses. Similarly, the pumps can be seen to be done by the interrogator but in the suspect's talk-turn. This can be seen, in that the pumps do not alter the suspect's talk, except by keeping him talking. The following transcript segment of an interrogation illustrates this feature.

The first transcript begins after incidental procedural matters have been discussed with the suspect. I will take it to be the "beginning" of the talk concerning the incident for which the suspect was arrested.

TRANSCRIPT 1

```
 1        Q. Do you want to tell me about the weapon? Where
 2           you got it? When you got it?
 3 /#/   A. Ah (1-2-3-4-5-6-7) it was just about two weeks
 4           =Uh huh= (1-2-3) before Christmas (1-2-3-4) and
 5           I bought it from this at the gun shop /#/ ah,
 6           (1-2-3) Whewww six, six-hundred block I can't
 7           remember the exact address. Six (1-2-3-4) six
 8           something ah (1-2-3-4) Parksburg.
 9 /#/   Q. Six-hundred block Parksburg?
10 /#/   A. I think that's it.
11 /#/   Q. Do you know the name of the shop?
12 /#/   A. Ah (1-2-3) something about I think it's Crafts.
13           He doesn't have a sign up there or anything /#/
14           ah (1-2) but it's Crafts Gun Shop I believe
               =Uh huh=
15           Bennings is the man's name.
16        Q. Bennings?
17        A. (1-2) No, Bekins =Bekins=
18        Q. (1-2) And you bought the gun there?
19 /#/   A. Yeah.
20        Q. About two weeks before Christmas?
21        A. (1-2-3-4) And ah he held it for five days and then
```

In the transcript segment, the first point to be noticed is that there is some talk after every question. Secondly, of the 38 seconds of silences in the talk, all but two seconds belong to the suspect (A). Both of these observations support the contention that questions force the talk and the silences on the recipient of the question. Between lines 3 and 8, some 25 seconds of silences take place, all followed by A's talk. Moreover, the pauses on lines 4 and 6 appear to be at points of possible utterance completion, suggesting that, even if A attempted to give the turn to Q, he could not do so, since, as I have argued, the silences belong to the recipient of the question, and it is up to the questioner to decide when *his* question has been answered. Until then, he can leave the silences with the recipient of the question.

The pump that occurs in the first response by A is in a position that does not appear to be a possible utterance completion. Because it does not occur at a possible completion point, it strengthens the argument that such "minimal responses" may be something other than talk-turns, as I am attempting to show. It appears to be there in relation to the first pause, which lasted a full seven seconds, and it appears to be in A's turn. The first pause, in other words, prompted the interrogator to pump A's turn as soon as A started talking instead of waiting for a possible completion point, which would seem to be after the word "Christmas" in line 4. At the first point of possible completion, A stops; but, since there is an awkward silence, he tacks on ". . . and I bought it from this at the gun shop."

Another interesting feature of the transcript segment occurs on line 17. It appears that the interrogator wanted the suspect to keep on talking, but what was meant to be a pump turned out to give the interrogator the silence; thus, the "pump" functioned as a "stopper." (Stoppers will be discussed later.) He realized this quickly, however (two seconds of silence), but, perceiving that he had to say something, ended up asking the suspect what he had just been told. The interesting feature is that he *did* say something in order to keep the suspect talking, and what he used was a question. A's response in line 19 did not go anywhere, so Q quickly followed with another question, which gave the silence and the turn back to A, resulting in a lengthy account of how he came to get the gun. (Only part of the reply is in the transcript segment.)

The point, however, was not to elicit new information, since the interrogator had just been told when the suspect had bought the gun. This gave the silence to the suspect (four seconds), and he did begin talking.

The next segment is near the end of the interrogation. The interrogator's question is of a procedural nature, so that no inference can be made that the suspect was intoxicated during the interrogation. (The suspect said he had had two beers before the interrogation.) It appears that the interrogator is attempting to end the interview, but he nevertheless gets a lengthy reply from the suspect. The pumps here do not seem to be intended as pumps, but, structurally, they function that way. There are several pauses where the interrogator could have taken a turn as possible utterance completion points, but for some reason he let the suspect keep on going.

TRANSCRIPT 2

```
 1       Q. Do you think the alcohol is affecting you in any way?
 2 /#/  A. No this /#/ whole /#/ deal is a like I said I never
 3         realized ah I jus (1-2-3) be put in this position
 4         jus fer =Yeah= cause I was (1-2) ah (1-2) course
 5         I did lie when he asked me if I'd been convicted
 6         of a felony. I told him no /*/ but ah (1-2) I mean
 7         ah /*/ I didn't buy it from jus anybody ej ah y'know.
 8         =Yeah= I did buy it from a gun shop =Yeah=
           and like
 9         I said eh juh this is all easily be checked out I
10         tell ya eh juh ah /#/ the gun for a shotgun which
11         ah everybody in the shop knows about it =Uh huh=
12         and then ah /*/ they already gave it back to me
13         because the way it didn't shoot straight and like
14         I said duh eh the guy that I bought it from ah (1-2)
15         he'll verify that I brought it back and complained
16         about it not shootin' good too and ah /*/ well every-
17         thing I said y'know. I know heh huh =Yeah= heh
           /*/
18         I got eh /*/ it all ah (1-2-3-4) wheww like I said
19         I didn't know ah I didn't realize I could be (1-2)
20         took to jail for a felony fer (1-2-3-4-5-6) the way
```

```
21          the way ah (1-2) christ // I would huv never bought
22          the thing to start with the ah = Yeah =
23 / j / Q. [Have you ever]* Have you ever seen me before?
```

This last interchange does not seem to be an attempt by the interrogator to get the suspect to talk. Talk does occur, however, and in relation to the same structural features as in Transcript 1. Following the question, the suspect talked, filled in silences, and was pumped by the interrogator, even though the interrogator may not have intended his "= Yeah =" to be a pump.

The significance of this transcript is that after the question, in the context of the entire interrogation, the interrogator *immediately* gets the information answering his question when A responds with "No. . . ." The rest of the suspect's talk is largely irrelevant to the question. Thus, it can be inferred that the interrogator did not attempt to make or trick the suspect into talking. Rather, the suspect's talk was encouraged structurally. The sequential structure of the Q-A sequence not only forces the obligation to talk, but the speaker in the answer half of the Q-A sequence can talk in the response to the question for as long as he wants, and the questioner is conversationally obliged to listen.† Hence, not only does a question force talk from a recalcitrant conversationalist, it also gives the floor to a talkative speaker, which may prove difficult to regain. This difficulty can be seen in line 21, where Q has to overlap A then repeat his next question in line 23 after A finally stops in line 22.

There are six pumps that appear to keep the talk going, with the exception of the last one, at the very end of A's talk. It might seem that this last pump is not a pump at all, and this brings into question the notion of a pump as opposed to the notion of a turn. (Any utterance can be treated as a turn.) However, it should be pointed out that the last pump occurs after an overlap, where the interrogator attempted to introduce a new question. Secondly,

* The brackets indicate that this portion of the conversation overlapped at the point indicated by double slashes (//).

† The difficulty of regaining the floor after having asked a question has been experienced by sociological interviewers. Most of the emphasis in teaching interviewing techniques is in how to get the subject to answer questions, but very little has been done to explain how to stop subjects once they have started.

there is no gap between Q's final "=Yeah=" and his next question. It can be seen either as a preface to his question, and therefore misplaced in the transcript, or as a verbal period on A's talk. It does not appear to be a preface, since on the tape it sounds similar to the other pumps, and there is a marked difference in the tone of the question compared to Q's final "=Yeah=." It appears, rather, that Q's turn begins with "Have," and A's turn ends with =Yeah=."

Since I have argued that pumps function to keep the speaker's talk going, and since, from examining the transcripts, the other pumps appear to do so, this last one is troublesome. On the one hand, it is clearly not the beginning of Q's turn; on the other hand, it clearly stops A's turn as a speaker at a place that does not appear to be a point of possible utterance completion. Moreover, it does not do what a pump is supposed to do; thus, it must be something else. The "something else" will be called a "stopper," since it functions to stop the other's talk and gives the listener a chance to slip in and take his turn. It is only coincidental that the "same" word is used as a stopper as is used for a pump. The real importance is not what word is used as a pump or stopper but how they are used in the sequential structure of the conversation. (In Transcript 1, the repeating of the speaker's last word functioned as a stopper in line 17.) Stoppers are devices to stop the other's talk, so that the listener may take his turn as a speaker; they are not the initiators of the listener's turn, or "starters."

SUMMARY AND CONCLUSION

At the beginning, we proposed that the sequential structure of conversations can be employed strategically by police in their interrogations. We noted the strategies that are suggested by the conversational structure, how they operate as strategies, and, more important, how they reveal the structure of conversations. First, it was shown that questions force the talk-turn on the recipient of the question by leaving him with the obligation to fill in any silences following the questions. This structural feature suggests the Q-A sequence as a strategic device in interrogations, in that it obliges the suspect to talk. Moreover, it was shown that the questioner could "pump" the respondent, obliging him to answer the question without taking the turn and the obligation to talk away from him. In turn, the successful use of the Q-A strategy revealed how the sequential structure of the Q-A sequence operates in conversations. Thus, one could expect to find the same structural forms in any conversation in which the Q-A sequence is used. Radio and television talk-show hosts, guests at cocktail parties, teachers attempting to stimulate class discussion, and other conversation situations in which the actors feel compelled to keep the talk going employ the Q-A sequence to the end of avoiding interactional silence and directing the obligation of talking to another party.

REFERENCES

GARFINKEL, HAROLD. 1967. *Studies in Ethnomethodology.* Englewood Cliffs, N.J.: Prentice-Hall.

KIDD, LT. W. R. 1940. *Police Interrogation.* New York: Basuino.

SCHEGLOFF, EMANUEL A. 1968. "Sequencing in Conversational Openings." *American Anthropologist,* 70, pp. 1075–95.

———. 1972. "Notes on a Conversational Practice: Formulating Place." In David Sudnow (ed.), *Studies in Social Interaction,* pp. 74–119. New York: The Free Press.

EXERCISES   The purpose of this set of exercises is to give the student rudimentary experience in taping conversations, transcribing the tapes, and analyzing the transcriptions. The importance of conversation analysis lies not so much in the taping or transcription of the tapes as in the search for the social structure of conversations and their effect on what is said and how it is said. This type of analysis is quite complex and requires extensive training. However, the first step is to get the conversation down on tape and then transcribe the tapes to reflect the texture of the conversation. The following exercises are meant to introduce this new and promising area of research in sociology.

Exercise 1

First, tape a segment of a television talk show on which there is a lively exchange of talk between the host and one or more guests. Next, tape a segment of a movie or another television program that involves actors delivering lines from a script. Now take segments of the two tapes that have ongoing discussions between two or more participants. The segments should be no more than five minutes long, for even this small amount of talk will reveal aspects of interest and will require a good deal of transcription.

Once the transcriptions are completed, using the transcription conventions presented in the introduction, determine which conversation contains the most overlaps, interruptions, and pauses. In normal conversations and unrehearsed discussions, there should be more interruptions and overlaps, and unequal amounts of time in the pauses between speakers' turns. Whereas the actors have their conversations laid out in advance, conversationalists create theirs as an ongoing process. The differences between actual conversations and dramatized ones can be clearly seen in terms of these aspects.

Exercise 2

In the study of police interrogations, it was seen that interrogators could employ the sequential structure of conversations to force a talk-turn on the suspect. Talk-show hosts can use the same strategy in getting their guests to speak. Whenever the talk starts to lag on a talk show, you should find the host asking a question.

This can be seen by analyzing the transcription of the television talk show in terms of the Q-A sequence.

EXERCISE 3

A class discussion will be used as the source of data for this exercise, to analyze the points at which speakers change in a conversation.

Choose a class in which discussions are common. Ask the instructor if you may tape some class discussions and, when you set up your tape recorder, explain what you are doing to the class. Have the tape recorder present and running for several sessions, so that students and instructor have a chance to get used to it and overcome any inhibitions they might have about speaking "for the record." Then, once you feel that the discussions are the same as before you introduced the recorder, transcribe a segment of the tape.

The analysis here involves finding where one speaker stops talking and another begins. The points where speakers change should normally be "completion points," or those places in talk where a thought has been completed. You will notice that, in any talk, there are several possible completion points where another speaker could have taken a talk-turn, and these points can be located by first identifying the forms of completion points where speakers change. Similarly, overlaps can be used. Often where overlaps occur, the speaker who was overlapped will finish his thought even though another has begun to talk. Generally, however, you should find that one speaker's thought has been completed, and then, without a gap or overlap, another speaker will take over.

ADDITIONAL READING SUGGESTIONS

SACKS, HARVEY. 1972. "An Initial Investigation of the Usability of Conversational Data for Doing Sociology." In David Sudnow (ed.), *Studies in Social Interaction.* New York. The Free Press. Examines how transcriptions from conversations can be used for sociological research. Provides an analytic framework and underlying logic for conversational analysis.

SCHEGLOFF, EMANUEL A. 1968. "Sequencing in Conversational Openings," *American Anthropologist,* 70, pp 1075–95. A very good discussion of the structure of the question-answer sequence in conversational openings. It should be consulted when completing the exercises using Q-A sequence analysis.

Index